ANTI - POVERTY
PROGRAMS

T & A

ANTI - POVERTY PROGRAMS

ROBINSON O. EVERETT

Editor

OCEANA PUBLICATIONS, INC.

Dobbs Ferry, New York

1966

Originally published in Winter 1966

by

LAW AND CONTEMPORARY PROBLEMS

DUKE UNIVERSITY SCHOOL OF LAW

CONTENTS

iii

Titles Published in
The Library of Law and Contemporary Problems

POPULATION CONTROL, The Imminent World Crisis
MELVIN G. SHIMM, *Editor*, (and others)

EUROPEAN REGIONAL COMMUNITIES,
A New Era on the Old Continent
MELVIN G. SCHIMM, *Editor*, (and others)

AFRICAN LAW, New Law for New Nations
HANS W. BAADE, *Editor*, (and others)

ACADEMIC FREEDOM, The Scholar's Place
in Modern Society
HANS W. BAADE, *Editor*, (and others)

THE SOVIET IMPACT ON INTERNATIONAL LAW
HANS W. BAADE, *Editor*, (and others)

URBAN PROBLEMS AND PROSPECTS
ROBINSON O. EVERETT, RICHARD H. LEACH, *Editors*, (and others)

ANTI-POVERTY PROGRAMS
ROBINSON O. EVERETT, *Editor*, (and others)

FOREWORD

Will we have the poor always with us?[1] Many answer "Yes" with Malthusian resignation to the inevitable; indeed, some traditional welfare programs appear to assume this inevitability. A few persons go even further in their reply and glorify the role of poverty as an incentive to achievement; they suggest that without a vivid threat of poverty mankind would degenerate into sloth.[2]

In recent years, however, the view has gained increasing acceptance that substantial inroads against indigency can, and should, be made. Several years ago the Ford Foundation with its "gray areas" program helped evolve the concept of community action as a means for breaking the cycle of poverty.[3] Private and public agencies gave increasing recognition to the importance of education and of vocational training and retraining for this purpose. Then came the Economic Opportunity Act in which new federal forces and funds were committed to the war on poverty—and victory in this war became an important objective of the Johnson Administration.[4] This act purported to require greater coordination of existing federal efforts against poverty,[5] but at the same time it authorized imaginative new programs. Furthermore, it created a new partnership between local communities and the federal government. The recent burst of congressional activity also included legislation relevant to the war on poverty in such fields as education[6] and civil rights,[7] and an Appalachian program under which, largely through new public works, federal assistance would be furnished to an entire indigent region.[8]

---

[1] *John* 12:8; *Mark* 14:7; *Matthew* 26:11.

[2] Max Weber suggested that the protestant ethic and doctrines of salvation by grace were related to the rise of capitalism in that business success became partially equated with spiritual salvation. See MAX WEBER, THE PROTESTANT ETHIC AND THE SPIRIT OF CAPITALISM (Parsons trans., 1956 ed.) Many persons today consider that poverty is the result of indolence and vice; and that one who is hardworking and virtuous can attain affluence. At the other extreme, there is substantial opinion that "love of money is the root of all evil" and that poverty may even be a goal to be sought, as by entering a monastery.

[3] One of the most successful of these "gray area" programs was initiated in New Haven, Conn. Establishment of The North Carolina Fund represented an effort to apply a similar approach on a broader, statewide basis.

[4] There have been reports that prior to his death President Kennedy, impressed in part by Michael Harrington's *The Other America*, had also made plans to launch a war on poverty.

[5] While coordination among federal agencies is vital, there also must be achieved coordination of federal and local antipoverty efforts, coordination of federal programs with state activities, and coordination of local public and private efforts to combat poverty. The problems in achieving the desired cooperation include: interagency jealousies, professional biases, and difficulties in communicating to the participants the broad goals being sought.

[6] Elementary and Secondary Education Act of 1965, 79 Stat. 27 (codified in scattered sections of 20 U.S.C.A. (Supp. 1965)).

[7] Civil Rights Act of 1964, 78 Stat. 241, 42 U.S.C. §§ 1971, 1975a-d, 2009h-6 (1964).

[8] Appalachian Regional Development Act of 1965, 79 Stat. 5, 40 U.S.C.A. App. A (Supp. 1965).

Enough information is now available to permit a realistic appraisal of current antipoverty programs. And the urgency of the need for this appraisal is heightened by the circumstance that the demands of the Viet Nam conflict may require selective curtailment of domestic federal programs. Moreover, the expanding defense effort may even be changing some of the dimensions of poverty; for instance, it probably mitigates poverty attributable to unemployment but, by inducing inflation, pushes into poverty people, such as the aged and the disabled, who are dependent upon fixed incomes.

In appraising antipoverty programs, a significant threshold inquiry concerns the premise on which aid is extended to the indigent. Does society have an obligation or duty to the indigent to extricate him from the morass of poverty? Does he have a correlative "right" to receive a certain minimal income? Certainly the existence of such a right would be inconsistent with imposing numerous conditions and limitations upon the indigent's receipt of assistance. Under such a view, he could not be required to relinquish or waive fundamental rights, such as that of privacy, in order to obtain public assistance.[9] And procedural safeguards, such as an opportunity for a fair and impartial hearing, might be necessary in order to preserve the indigent's "right" to assistance, such as welfare payments or the opportunity to reside in public housing.[10]

Some critics of the present antipoverty programs complain that the Office of Economic Opportunity has often encouraged rigidity, rather than local innovation. However, without substantial intervention from Washington, chiefly through refusal to fund,[11] local programs might have deviated from norms which apparently were accepted by Congress—for example, maximum feasible participation of the poor and nondiscriminatory representation of minority groups. Without some federal control "local autonomy" might become a euphemism for the use of antipoverty funds to achieve the objectives of local political machines. On the other hand, excessive federal control breeds resentment and lethargy which paralyze community action.

Several students of antipoverty programs have been disturbed by failure to involve the States more intimately.[12] In other federally-assisted programs, such as urban

---

[9] The question has been raised of the extent to which the recipient of public assistance should be subject to "midnight raids" or to inspections made at the whim of public officials. See Reich, *Midnight Welfare Searches and the Social Security Act*, 72 YALE L.J. 1347 (1963); Sparer, *Social Welfare Law Testing*. The Practical Lawyer, April 1966, p. 13. Furthermore, should the dispensers of public assistance make efforts to assure that this assistance is being used only for "necessaries" such as food and clothing, and not for "luxuries" like a television set or an automobile.

[10] The case of Housing Authority of the City of Durham v. Thorpe (Sup. Ct. No. 769), decided by the North Carolina Supreme Court on May 25, 1966, raises the issue whether an occupant of public housing is entitled to procedural protections, such as notice, confrontation, and a hearing, before being expelled from the housing project.

[11] Title six of the Civil Rights Act affords a precedent for refusal to fund local programs that are discriminatory. 78 Stat. 252, 42 U.S.C. §§ 2000d-d4 (1964). Some complaints have been voiced that the Office of Economic Opportunity in refusing to fund certain projects had invoked standards which exceeded the authority delegated to it by the Congress.

[12] See Sanford, *Poverty's Challenge to the States*, *infra*, pp. 77-89. Of course, the governor's veto over

renewal, public housing, and development of airports, state activity has often consisted of the enactment of an enabling act. Perhaps this limited role mirrored the interests and attitudes of state legislators prior to the reapportionment cases. However, the antipoverty programs must now be appraised in terms of the goal of a dynamic federalism, wherein the States are more than vestigial organs.

What about the role of private groups? Private organizations helped stimulate the war on poverty in the first place, and clearly to attain any breakthrough in this war will require their continued support. Participation by industry and labor organizations in developing new training programs for indigents is only one example. Moreover, some of the skilled personnel needed to administer antipoverty programs must be furnished by private groups.

In many government programs significant activities have been contracted out to nonprofit organizations; for example, several defense agencies have utilized nonprofit corporations for research and evaluation functions.[13] Similarly the nonprofit corporation has been frequently used in implementing community action in connection with antipoverty programs. By this means some new personnel and ideas have been introduced into the war on poverty; and several restrictions applicable only to government agencies have been bypassed. However, a comprehensive appraisal of antipoverty programs should include consideration of the extent to which some of the policies applicable to governmental agencies should be applied to nonprofit corporations which are coordinating community action with the aid of public funds. For example, to what degree should community action programs be subjected to statutory and policy restrictions concerning the appointment, compensation, and activities of government employees or the expenditure and use of public funds—restrictions such as those imposed by civil service and merit system legislation, the Hatch Act,[14] or advertised bid requirements. Moreover, in using the nonprofit corporation in antipoverty programs, how can excessive diffusion of responsibility and the establishment of conflicting power structures best be avoided?

In combating poverty, mere paternalism is clearly inadequate—and perhaps even self-defeating. Unless the indigent themselves participate in the war on poverty, they may retain feelings of anonymity, frustration, hostility, and despair—feelings manifested occasionally by senseless rioting. With this in mind, the Office of Economic Opportunity has insisted on broadening the boards of directors of community action programs to include substantial representation of the indigents—which, in many instances, has been equated to one-third membership on a board. Sometimes

---

community action programs—a veto which has recently been restricted—does not assure affirmative participation by the state in formulating these programs.

[13] For example, the Rand Corporation has performed some vital research and evaluation tasks for defense agencies. For an interesting symposium on the whole problem of contracting out governmental activities and functions to private organizations, see Symposium—*Administration by Contract: An Examination of Governmental Contracting-Out*, 31 GEO. WASH. L. REV. 685-783 (1963).

[14] 53 Stat. 1139 (1939), 54 Stat. 767 (1940), 5 U.S.C. §§ 118i, 118k-n (1964).

the poverty-stricken have participated in elaborate elections to choose their representatives on the board. "Community organizers" have been provided to mobilize the indigent—occasionally with resulting criticism of the political implications of their organizational activity. Emphasis has been placed on hiring indigents whenever possible to perform tasks with antipoverty programs.

Even with all these measures, has sufficient participation by the poor been obtained? Some who have studied the "politics of the poor" give a negative answer to this query; and they may suggest that it is unrealistic to expect that local politicians and officials will relinquish to the indigent any significant control over the expenditure of antipoverty funds. Other observers consider that participation by the poor has been only a slogan employed by cynical persons seeking to use the poor as an instrument to attain or retain political power.

Examining the participation of the poor in antipoverty programs leads readily to consideration of the relationship to these programs of the civil rights movement. There is a disproportionate incidence of poverty among minority groups; indeed, some view the federal war on poverty as an answer to demands by these groups. On the other hand, federal civil rights legislation may help lessen conditions of poverty by destroying barriers to economic opportunity. And at the same time some of the assistance available through antipoverty programs may place members of minority groups in a better position to utilize opportunities newly afforded by civil rights legislation.

Antipoverty programs have their own bureaucracy; and the success of the programs hinges on the effectiveness of that bureaucracy. Difficulties in obtaining qualified personnel have often impaired this effectiveness; and a necessity is now being recognized to develop new professions and subprofessions in order properly to staff antipoverty programs. Moreover, since indigents are often especially helpless and vulnerable in their dealings with any bureaucracy, a need exists for developing better methods to prevent or remedy arbitrary action on the part of the public officials with whom they must deal.[15]

Since this symposium appears in a legal periodical, it is not amiss to emphasize that the legal profession is one of the greatest potential allies of indigents in implementing effective nondiscriminatory antipoverty programs. Of course, the Bar may itself require some restructuring and some reexamination of its own standards. For example, canons of ethics designed to prevent solicitation of clients should not be applied to curtail the availability of legal services to the genuinely indigent.[16] However, we trust that once again the legal profession will meet the challenge posed by

[15] To a considerable extent the congressional committee has performed functions in connection with antipoverty programs that might have been performed by an ombudsman or a citizens' advice bureau under other systems. See Rosenblum, *Controlling the Bureaucracy of the Antipoverty Program, infra*, pp. 187-210; and Leach, *The Federal Role in the War on Poverty Program, infra*, pp. 18-38.

[16] The American Bar Association is apparently aware of the need for efforts along these lines and has undertaken reexamination of the Canons.

its acknowledged and time-honored duty to assist the underprivileged and down-trodden. And, in performing this responsibility, lawyers and judges may find reawakened their interest in helping society evolve through law to meet changing conditions and needs and to solve contemporary problems.[17]

ROBINSON O. EVERETT.

---

[17] The increased responsibilities recently placed upon the Bar in representing indigent defendants in criminal cases have apparently rekindled the legal profession's interest in the administration of criminal justice and may ultimately produce some much-needed changes. The recently installed law school courses and seminars concerning law and poverty may similarly help induce overdue changes in our legal system.

THE WAR ON POVERTY

Hubert H. Humphrey[*]

I

The Problem

In today's America there is a paradox in the midst of plenty.

On the one hand we have the highest standard of living the world has ever known. Our standard of living keeps going up; income per capita keeps climbing. According to the Council of Economic Advisers the gross national product for 1964 was 628.7 billion dollars. The President's Economic Report for 1966 states that the gross national product increased by $47 billion in 1965. The value of the nation's output of goods and services rose more than one-third from 1960 through 1965. The rate of unemployment dropped from 6.6 per cent in December 1960 to 4.1 per cent in December 1965 and is now below 4.0 per cent. During this last year corporate profits, after taxes, were twenty per cent above the 1964 level. 2.2 million people moved above the poverty line in 1965.

But there also exists what Michael Harrington has called "the other America"[1]— an America in which one-fifth of our nation lives—an America in which 32,000,000 of our citizens live without adequate education, housing, or medical care.

Nearly fifteen million of those living in abject poverty are children. It is an America in which some of these children cannot go to school because they have neither clothes nor shoes; some, when they arrive in school, are crippled in performance by hunger, illness, or physical affliction, social deprivation, or racial discrimination.

It is an America of bewilderment, suspicion, depression, and despair.

For the first time in our history we have the ability to rid our society of this other America. In his State of the Union message in 1964 President Johnson stated, ". . . we have the power to strike away the barriers to full participation in our society. Having the power we have the duty . . . ."

Because of the enormous productive capacity and current explosion of knowledge and research statistics, we have the resources to wage an all out war on poverty.

America has continually made attempts to improve the lot of its poor. In the recent past we have had the "New Deal" and the "Fair Deal." In nearly every generation we have had social reform legislation working to mitigate the harshness of poverty. Edgar May states in his book *The Wasted Americans*[2] that prior to the

---

[*] Vice President of the United States.
[1] MICHAEL HARRINGTON, THE OTHER AMERICA (1962).
[2] EDGAR MAY, THE WASTED AMERICANS (1964).

war on poverty the welfare programs of the past were basically outgrowths of two opposing views on poverty:[3]

The first one, "Go to the ant, thou sluggard, consider her ways and be wise." (*Proverbs* 6:6)

The second, "And if thy brother be waxen poor and fallen in decay with thee, then thou shalt relieve him. Yea, though he be a stranger or a sojourner, that he may live with thee." (*Leviticus* 25:35)

In America it has been the philosophy of the former rather than the latter that most often prevailed.

While Jeremy Bentham would have been comfortable in our own time, with his views on the necessity of houses of industry, insurance, education and health care, it was the ideas of the severe English Poor Laws which were imported and generally upheld by the colonists. The American Puritans regarded poverty as a sin, a sign of moral bankruptcy. Debtors' prisons and punitive workhouses reflected this philosophy of the causation of poverty.

But by the nineteenth century a growing number of people needed substantial and long term help. Factors were being injected into the equation of poverty which seriously limited an individual's control over his own destiny.

The concept of free agency—that is, freedom, within limits, to make those essential choices which will shape one's own life—has been basic to the American philosophy.

But by the Civil War, the factory was appearing throughout some sections of the country. This was to alter radically the degree to which many workers controlled their own destiny. In postwar years the factory system moved from textiles and consumer goods to heavy industry. With this came not only the unparalleled prosperity of our own time, but more immediately, the development of a large laboring class that lived so close to destitution that the slightest drop in employment brought mass suffering. For this growing industrial proletariat, life at best was marginal. And the impersonal nature of the forces that determined employment and wage levels seemed to inject a deterministic element into the workers' lives that robbed them of substantial control over their very existence.

These conditions motivated social reformers to instigate private charities and local and state welfare programs of uneven value. The "go to the ant" theory of the social Darwinists represented the opposite reaction to the same stimulus.

While social Darwinism is deservedly discredited today, in that we see poverty as a condition which might overwhelm anyone due to forces beyond his control, the national portrait of the poor is still that of the 1930s—middle class individuals lacking money.

But the poverty which we are combating today is not merely the lack of material goods. Poverty today is a culture, an institution, a way of life.

---

[3] *Id.* at 2.

The impoverished man is the unskilled worker—the man whose job opportunities are shrinking. In the last four years, our economy has created over three times as many jobs for people in the field of education as it has for factory hands.

He is the skilled worker replaced by automation and cybernation.

He is the sick, the disabled, the aged.

He is the school dropout, the illiterate. While our statistics on housing and health have not shown conclusive correlation with poverty causation, the most basic and most substantiated factor is known. That is education. The factor most common to almost all the unemployed and under-employed is lack of basic education.[4]

He is the small farm owner, the tenant farmer, the farm worker, the migrant worker.

He is the victim of race prejudice.

He is the man who for reasons beyond his control cannot help himself.

He is the man engulfed by poverty, a vicious cycle out of which it is incredibly difficult for him, his children, and his grandchildren to escape.

A decent standard of living cannot be had without money; money is gained through employment; a job requires education; and education takes money. Lack of education means no employment; unemployment means lack of funds for education of the children of the unemployed. It also means living in conditions of social as well as physical deprivation, which too often result in children entering school with such crushing handicaps that their eventual failure is assured.

Hence poverty is passed on from generation to generation with almost genetic certainty.

But as the forces of government and private philanthropy try to break this cycle of tragedy, the elimination of one of the component parts seems to demand as a prerequisite the elimination of another.

The impoverished man is all too often one who for reasons beyond his control cannot help himself.

II

APPROACHES

A balanced attack on poverty must provide at least four somewhat distinct remedies: job creation, job preparation, transfer payments, and equal employment opportunity.

First, aggregate demand must be maintained at a high level. A downturn in our economic growth rate would undo all the other programs which might be conducted. Educating and training men for jobs that do not exist is futile.

Since passage of the Employment Act of 1946,[5] it has been recognized explicitly

---

[4] See Cohen, *A National Program for the Improvement of Welfare Services and the Reduction of Welfare Dependency*, in POVERTY IN AMERICA 279-80 (Gordon ed. 1965).

[5] 60 Stat. 23, as amended, 15 U.S.C. §§ 1021-24 (1964).

that the federal government has a primary responsibility for maintaining aggregate demand. This act not only made mandatory the annual Economic Report of the President and created the powerful Council of Economic Advisers and the Joint Economic Committee of Congress, but also vested in the federal government specific responsibility for maintaining employment, production, and purchasing power. In the following discussion, it is a prerequisite that the economic growth rate remain at an acceptable level.

But economic growth, though essential, is not enough. It is no help to someone not in the labor market to have a booming economy; or if new jobs being created are of a technical nature for which one is not equipped; or if one is in a group which society would rather not have work (e.g., the aged, or women with small children); or if one is sick or disabled; or if by reason of race or color one is denied a job for which he is qualified. Other basic approaches are needed to meet these types of problems.

The second approach in combating poverty focuses not upon the creation of jobs but upon the education and training of men for jobs. Such programs as the Job Corps,[6] the Neighborhood Youth Corps,[7] the Manpower Development and Training Act of 1962 (MDTA),[8] and the Vocational Education Act of 1963[9] are examples of this approach.

The third approach relies upon transfer payments to persons in need. Some groups will be out of work temporarily in the most healthy of economies; others will be unemployed for long periods; other groups society prefers to remain outside the labor force; others must have the effects of poverty ameliorated. Hence there exist transfer payments, e.g., aid to the unemployed with children, hospital and doctor care for the aged, Social Security, and rent supplements.

Finally, even though a job may exist for one who is qualified, he might be forced into the ranks of the unemployed or made to hold a job beneath his qualifications or ability by discrimination on the basis of his race, color, religion, sex, or national origin. The Council of Economic Advisers reported in 1965 that if Negroes had received the same average pay as whites having the same education, the personal income of Negroes and of the nation would be $12.8 billion higher. If Negroes had the same educational attainments as white workers, and earned the same pay and experienced the same unemployment as whites, their personal income—and that of the nation—would be $20.6 billion higher. Finally, if Negroes were afforded the same educational benefits as whites and job discrimination ceased, the total gross national product would rise by an estimated $23 billion.

---

[6] Provided for by the Economic Opportunity Act of 1964, tit. 1, pt. A., 78 Stat. 508, 42 U.S.C. §§ 2711-20 (1964).
[7] 78 Stat. 512, 42 U.S.C. §§ 2731-36 (1964).
[8] 76 Stat. 23, as amended, 42 U.S.C. §§ 2571-2620 (1964).
[9] 77 Stat. 411, as amended, 20 U.S.C. §§ 15aa, bb, aaa, 35-35n (1964).

In moral terms, discrimination is indefensible. In economic terms, its terrible cost hurts the entire nation.

We have then, the issues of job creation, job preparation, transfer payments, and job discrimination. Within these guidelines, some of the recent antipoverty programs should be reviewed before analyzing in more detail the Economic Opportunity Act of 1964.[10]

Due in part to the massive dislocation caused by the depression of the 1930s, efforts of the past centered primarily upon the device of transfer payments. And today these are essential to meet the needs of many groups within our society. But Social Security, unemployment compensation, public assistance, old age and medical benefits, while necessary, do not eliminate the root causes of poverty.

It should be observed parenthetically, however, that one measure of the past, the Servicemen's Readjustment Act of 1944[11]—the "G.I. Bill"—by paying veterans to go to school, provides an interesting model for future programs aimed at other groups in our population.

The Area Redevelopment Act[12] in 1961 marked a turning point in our approach to poverty, since it focused upon the elimination of poverty rather than the amelioration of some of its effects. In this act, structural unemployment was attacked in a novel way. Loans, grants, and technical aid were extended to communities classified as depressed.

Two recent programs are patterned on this general idea. The Appalachian Regional Development Act of 1965[13] is based on the notion that the states and the federal government should join as partners to encourage private industry to invest in an area of the country that has historically lagged behind the rest of the nation in economic development. The administration of the program is housed in a Commission which is composed of representatives of the governors of the eleven states that comprise the regional and federal representatives. While the federal government has a fifty-one per cent majority vote in the Commission, no program can be commenced in a state without the state's prior approval.

The aims of the program are to build nearly 3,500 miles of highway in Appalachia to promote mobility and commercial access, to establish health facilities, and to develop conservation of land, water, and timber resources. The Commission is also authorized to build community educational and health facilities which will then be operated with funds from the Office of Economic Opportunity.

The Manpower Development and Training Act of 1962 was again aimed at structural unemployment, but this time the focus was not upon job creation but job preparation. Here the impact of automation and other forces in the job market

---

[10] 78 Stat. 508, 42 U.S.C. § 2701-981 (1964).

[11] Ch. 268, 58 Stat. 284 (now 38 U.S.C. §§ 1801-25 (1964)).

[12] 75 Stat. 47 (1961), as amended, 42 U.S.C. §§ 2501-25 (1964).

[13] 79 Stat. 5, 40 U.S.C.A. App. A (Supp. 1965).

on young people and displaced older workers was ameliorated by vocational training and retraining.

The Vocational Education Act of 1963 is of a similar nature. Though not aimed at precisely the same group, it is designed to attack the problem of structural unemployment by providing vocational training for young people.

The Elementary and Secondary Education Act of 1965[14] and the Higher Education Act of 1965[15] are of great significance, not only because of the groups they immediately affect, but also in terms of the precedent set for federal aid to, and responsibility for, education. Under the former, the federal government is authorized to make grants to states which have school districts with large numbers of children from low-income families. Subject to the approval of state and federal educational agencies, grants may be used in any way the school district feels proper.

The Higher Education Act of 1965 authorizes federal scholarships for college students, federally guaranteed low interest loans, aid to small colleges and other community service programs, and special grants for college libraries.

In keeping with the dominant direction of recent antipoverty legislation, most attention has been paid those acts relating to job creation and job preparation rather than transfer payments. But one vitally needed form of transfer payment passed last year. Known popularly as medicare, this program is aimed at the rapidly increasing percentage of our population over sixty-five. Administered by the Social Security Administration, the act allows the federal government to cover most hospital and nursing home costs, diagnostic studies, and home health-care visits for those over sixty-five.

Special mention should be made of two laws not usually associated with poverty but which have a direct bearing upon the problem. The Civil Rights Act of 1964[16] and the Voting Rights Act of 1965[17] help to assure that all levels of government will be responsive to the needs of all groups in our society, and that there will be equal opportunity for jobs on the basis of merit rather than race, color, religion, sex, or national origin. Since the incidence of poverty falls with undeserved severity upon various minority groups, especially the Negro American, the discrimination in employment and lack of power over government which has caused this disparity in job opportunity must be ended. The Civil Rights Act of 1964 and the Voting Rights Act of 1965 do not guarantee this result but do establish these objectives as national policy and establish the framework of law whereby they can be realized.

III

THE ECONOMIC OPPORTUNITY ACT OF 1964

The legislation which most clearly reflects the philosophical trend of present

[14] 79 Stat. 27 (codified in scattered sections of 20 U.S.C.A. (Supp. 1965)).
[15] 79 Stat. 1219, 20 U.S.C.A. §§ 1001-144 (Supp. 1965).
[16] 78 Stat. 241, 42 U.S.C. §§ 1971, 1975a-d, 2000a to h-6 (1964).
[17] 79 Stat. 437, 42 U.S.C.A. §§ 1971, 1973-73p (Supp. 1965).

thinking—*i.e.*, achieving the proper balance between job preparation, job creation, and transfer payments—is the Economic Opportunity Act of 1964.[18] Here, the older dominance of transfer payments is modified by an increased emphasis upon job preparation and, to a lesser extent, job creation.

The objective of the Economic Opportunity Act of 1964 is to further the policy of this country in eliminating "the paradox of poverty in the midst of plenty . . . by opening to everyone the opportunity for education and training, the opportunity to work, and the opportunity to live in decency and dignity."[19]

While the budget given the Office of Economic Opportunity in fiscal 1966 only amounts to a little over $1.5 billion, as opposed to the many billions of dollars spent on poverty in other federal programs, the Economic Opportunity Act charges the Director of the Office of Economic Opportunity with overall responsibility for advising the President on the total war on poverty. As a result, the impact of the institutions created by the Economic Opportunity Act upon the philosophy of the total war on poverty will be greater than its budget, when compared with budgets of the 200-odd other federal programs, would indicate. To aid in this coordination, the act also created the Economic Opportunity Council.

An Information Center to help in the effective coordination of the various anti-poverty programs has been established. The Center collects, analyzes, correlates, and makes available in one place to public officials and interested private institutions current information on the program.

To eliminate poverty, quite obviously something more than a bigger relief check is needed. A far-sighted remedial approach to exterminate the conditions which cause poverty is required if its deadly cycle is to be broken.

A basic cause of poverty is lack of proper education.

A student who leaves school before receiving a high school diploma will be in serious trouble in obtaining and keeping adequate employment. Several reasons result in a student's leaving school. One important reason is that our school program has all too often failed to prepare our young people in the primary grades with those tools necessary to continue in school at secondary and college levels.

Due in part to our increased knowledge of intelligence and intelligence testing, we now know that the intelligence quotient is not the completely static thing we once thought, but is at least somewhat elastic and can be especially affected by proper stimulation before a child is six. Children who come from culturally deprived families often have no familiarity with pencils, crayons, writing paper, books, or complete sentences. These children are in serious trouble before they enter the first grade. The chance to provide that vital stimulation which may be necessary to ensure their eventual graduation from high schools may be irrevocably lost before the student ever reaches school, the way our educational system is now established.

---

[18] 78 Stat. 508, 42 U.S.C. §§ 2701-981 (1964).

[19] Economic Opportunity Act of 1964. § 2, 78 Stat. 508, 42 U.S.C. § 2701 (1964).

To help correct this deficiency, Operation Head Start was launched last summer by the Office of Economic Opportunity. Special programs were developed to provide enough background for pre-school children from culturally deprived homes to permit them to enter first grade at least on a closer level of equality with their classmates than would have been the case without the program. Head Start will now operate year round, and will involve the parents of the participating children so that all the growth of the children will not be negated by poor home environment.

During fiscal years 1965 and 1966, there were 371 Head Start programs involving 149,028 children at a cost to OEO of $61,135,185.

Many youngsters have not been able to stay in school for financial reasons. With a lack of education and lack of job skills these youngsters soon become a statistic in the unemployment figures. To help these young people between the ages of sixteen and twenty-two the Economic Opportunity Act of 1964 established the Job Corps.

There are three types of Job Corps centers. First, the conservation centers, which are located in our national parks and forests. These Corpsmen divide their time between conservation work and basic academic instruction. They also receive counseling in work attitudes and general, psychological guidance.

Second, the men's urban centers, varying in size from 1,000 to nearly 3,000 students. Here Corpsmen receive academic instruction and vocational training. At Camp Kilmer, New Jersey, for example, courses are offered in such fields as retail merchandising and health services. At Camp Parks, in California, Corpsmen are receiving instruction in such diverse fields as welding, electronics, office management, culinary arts, and television production.

Third, the women's centers, accommodating about three hundred young women each are located in urban areas. The women receive academic and vocational training along with instruction in home management skills and child care.

As of January 1966 there were 17,190 youths in eighty-four Job Corps centers.

To help young people between the ages of sixteen and twenty-two who remain at home, the Economic Opportunity Act of 1964 established the Neighborhood Youth Corps, administered by the Department of Labor. Those enrollees who are in school spend a maximum of fifteen hours per week in the program. Those that have dropped out of school or who have finished school spend as much as thirty-two hours per week in the program and are limited to an enrollment period of six months. If they return to school, however, they may continue in the Corps. Enrollees receive specialized academic instruction, vocational guidance and counselling in an effort to help them understand the need for proper work attitudes.

In fiscal year 1965, 642 projects were approved for 278,426 participants; in fiscal 1966, 798 projects were approved for 238,805 participants at a cost of $153,502,759.

For those high school students who show promise of an ability to do advanced work, but do not have the necessary achievement level or skills to gain admission to college, the Office of Economic Opportunity developed and administers Upward Bound as part of the Community Action Program (CAP).

There are two programs for those who are in college or are working toward graduate degrees. One, the Work Study program, established by the Economic Opportunity Act of 1964, provides job opportunities for those college students who need a source of income in order to continue their education. The Higher Education Act of 1965, mentioned previously, is a second source of assistance for college students.

Other approaches to the elimination of poverty have been instituted by the Economic Opportunity Act of 1964.

Under this act, rural families may obtain loans which enable them to refinance their farms and improve their homesites. In fiscal 1965, 11,104 loans were made to individuals totalling $18,733,800. To date, fiscal 1966 has seen 6,537 loans totalling $11,057,747.

To assist the very small businessman, the act established a Small Business Loan program, aimed generally at those businessmen whose operations are too small or whose credit is not sufficient to meet the demands of the usual small business loan. Not only is the businessman aided by the loan, but it is hoped that it will enable him to expand and create new jobs for the community's unemployed. In fiscal 1965 through January 1966, 832 loans totalling $10,174,269 have been made.

For heads of families who are out of work the act established the Work Experience program. Although this does not give the high level of technical training that is offered by the MDTA program, it does enable participants to qualify for income-producing jobs. From this point the individual may wish to enter the MDTA program for advanced training. In fiscal year 1965 through January 1966, 218 projects had been approved for 107,162 participants, at a cost of $150,705,612.

The Economic Opportunity Act of 1964 also created VISTA, a domestic Peace Corps, to help communities combat poverty. There are now 2,073 volunteers working at sixty urban and 153 rural projects, including work with migrants, Indians, the mentally retarded, and the Job Corps, in Appalachia and in urban areas.

Finally, the act created the Community Action Program, funded and directed by the Office of Economic Opportunity. This program represents a departure from previous methods of coping with the problem. It is the so-called "umbrella approach," in which all antipoverty social welfare programs (hopefully, both state and federal) are administered on a community-wide basis by a single agency. This agency is composed of all elements to be formed within the community—the social welfare agencies, the elected officials, the business leaders, and most important of all, the members of the target groups.

The typical community action program might include a vocational education program, Head Start for pre-school children, literacy training, social work, a Foster Grandparents project, and part-time work for needy college students. There are 872 grantees, including 623 community action agencies, 130 state and 119 university community action organizations. Some grantees have a contract which provides for only one service, such as Head Start, or perhaps a literacy program with an Indian tribe. Others include a battery of operations under the community action umbrella.

Over the last two years, the 872 grantees have received 1,703 grants totalling $313,568,566—$152,110,309 in fiscal 1965, and $161,458,257 in fiscal 1966. These figures include grants to twenty-seven institutions for administration of Upward Bound projects at a cost of $3,236,634 to OEO. It also includes twenty projects to provide legal services to the poor at a cost of $1,481,436; twenty-two Foster Grandparents projects funded at a cost of $2,800,000; and the operating cost of Head Start, quoted above.

The impoverished, as stated in the Economic Opportunity Act of 1964,[20] must have as large a voice in the program as is feasible. The statutory requirement of participation by the poor has been criticized at both extremes.

On the one hand, critics have said that the poor would not respond, would not participate. The most recent facts belie this. A recent analysis of the New York, Washington, Atlanta, Chicago, Austin, Kansas City, and San Francisco boards, representing sixty-two per cent of all grantees, indicates that 27.5 per cent of board members are poor.

On the other hand, conservative critics have feared that participation of the poor was an invitation to anarchy. This too has been disproved by time, with harmonious relations generally existing between all elements on the various boards.

The poor get into board positions in a wide variety of ways, demonstrating the flexibility and range of choice OEO wisely leaves to the local community action agencies. Of course some get there by ordinary, routine appointment processes. But for others the road to a share in community power is more interesting.

For example, in Philadelphia, the first step for a poor person to become one of the twelve on the thirty-one-member Philadelphia Anti-Poverty Action Committee (PAAC) is to run for office in his neighborhood, just as he would if he were running for political office. Twelve poverty neighborhoods each elect twelve-member community action councils, with all residents eligible to vote. One of the twelve elected leaders of each council is then named to the PAAC Board.

In Detroit, each of the four poverty areas has an advisory council which elects four persons to the city's governing board. The sixteen so chosen join with twenty-three representatives of private and public agencies (including the mayor), religious organizations, minority groups, business and unions to run the community action agency.

In Louisiana, the thirteen representatives of the poor on the twenty-seven-member board of the six-parish Acadiana Neuf, Inc., are elected at "town meetings" in the poverty pockets.

---

[20] Sec. 202(a)(3), 78 Stat. 516, 42 U.S.C. § 2782(a)(3) (1964).

In Taney County, Missouri, poor persons on the board were elected by mailed ballots.

These examples show the local imagination and creativity which OEO deliberately encourages. As more and more of the expected total of 2,000 community action agencies come into being, there is likely to be more and more experimentation. The administrators of OEO want it to continue because they believe that neither their experts nor the leaders of any local community have found (or can find) the one best way to give power to the poor which will be best for all communities.

The administration's "war on poverty" has had its critics. Some of the criticism is justified. We have learned much by wide-ranging programs, some of which were frankly experimental. Mistakes have been made. We must now benefit by those mistakes and heed those critics whose criticism has been constructive.

However, much of the criticism has not been of this variety. Some would abolish the "war on poverty" because a simple solution to the problem has not been found in the year following passage of the Economic Opportunity Act of 1964. It would be as logical, and as constructive, to propose that all research on cancer be discontinued since a complete cure or preventive has not yet been found, in spite of the millions of dollars spent on research.

Industry, labor, the universities, and all levels of government must push on in our attempt to fashion new weapons to destroy an old adversary.

A generation ago, the American author Thomas Wolfe expressed the goal for which we work: "To every man his chance, to every man regardless of his birth, his shining golden opportunity—to every man the right to live, to work, to be himself and to become whatever thing his manhood and his vision can combine to make him—this . . . is the promise of America."

For that part of our population which needs direct aid—the aged, mothers who head families, the sick, the unemployed—increased transfer payments adequate to permit them to carry on decent lives for themselves and their families.

For children, adequate preparation that will permit them to participate in school with their classmates on the basis of equality.

For young people who have dropped out of school and too often out of society, basic education and vocational training coupled with personal guidance to bring them back.

For everyone, an education limited only by one's ability to learn.

For the worker automated out of a job, retraining and possible relocation.

For the rural poor, regional development to provide jobs and training to permit their realization.

For all minority groups, the right to an education which will permit them to compete for jobs on an equal basis with anyone; the right to participate in all levels of government to ensure that its powers will be fairly used; the right to be able to spend one's income on adequate housing of his choice; the right to fulfillment rather than the right only to opportunity made unreachable by factors beyond an individual's control.

For all the people, a relationship between government and private industry which ensures a vibrantly growing economy which can provide not only the goods and services, but also the jobs necessary to permit all to share in the abundance of this land.

These are the goals of the "war on poverty."

THE FEDERAL ROLE IN THE WAR ON POVERTY PROGRAM

RICHARD H. LEACH*

I

For most of American history, the federal government was content to leave the relief of the distress caused by poverty to state and local units of governments or to private welfare organizations. It did not see for itself any more positive a role. Nor did the public expect the federal government to do anything more. Obsessed with the conviction that opportunity beckoned everywhere, and with the idea that poverty was an unavoidable part of civilization and, as taught by those who preached the Gospel of Wealth, the result of individual weakness, the American people were not particularly concerned with the larger problem of poverty. As a result, they did not envision a role for the federal government in combating it. The Depression began to bring about a change in viewpoint, and the administration of Franklin D. Roosevelt proclaimed the national interest in the economic well-being and security of all Americans as a part of its "New Deal." Under that banner, the government cooperated with the states in guaranteeing minimal assistance to impoverished Americans and inaugurated a series of programs providing Americans with a wide range of welfare services. It might well have moved on from concern for the alleviation of distress to concern for removal of the causes of distress if World War II had not so quickly intervened. The war removed the urgency from the problem of poverty, however, and post-war administrations, faced as they were with great problems of adjustment to the post-war world, both at home and abroad, and finding the nation generally prosperous, were not required to make any change in the federal role. The social legislation of the thirties was continued, and in some cases expanded, but there was no pressure for the government to do more. It was not until the administration of John F. Kennedy that a general climate favorable to more positive action by government on a broader front was established, and it remained for President Lyndon Johnson to zero in on poverty. President Johnson set the achievement of a "Great Society" as the goal of the American nation and as the first step toward such a society demanded an attack on poverty. Indeed, Johnson saw in a "war on poverty" an opportunity to do something both intrinsically worthwhile and symbolically important to the Great Society he postulated. Thus by 1964 the way was

* A.B. 1944, Colorado College; A.M. 1949, Ph.D. 1951, Princeton University. Professor of Political Science, Duke University. Author, [with Alpheus T. Mason] IN QUEST OF FREEDOM: AMERICAN POLITICAL THOUGHT AND PRACTICE (1959); [with Redding S. Sugg, Jr.] THE ADMINISTRATION OF INTERSTATE COMPACTS (1959); [with Robert H. Connery] THE FEDERAL GOVERNMENT AND METRO-POLITAN AREAS (1960). Contributor to periodicals of articles chiefly in the field of American national and state government.

prepared for the development of an antipoverty program and so finally for a role for the federal government in that endeavor.

It is the purpose of this paper to see how that role was visualized by the President and Congress and how it has developed at the hands of the Office of Economic Opportunity (OEO) since the war on poverty was actually launched. It will be the thesis of the remarks that follow that the federal role was not clearly defined at the outset and that as of Spring 1966 it still remains obscure. Some of the circumstances which may explain that obscurity will be discussed, and a few comments made as to the possible future development of that role. It is obviously too early to expect a final judgment to be made; but if, as it seems likely, a virtual revolution in federal role is in the making, it is important to initiate inquiry and to begin to maintain a careful watch. For more than a drive to eliminate poverty is at stake here; the delicate balance of the federal system may be involved as well.

II

The President did not declare war on poverty on the spur of the moment. For some while there had been a rising volume of protest at the human and economic waste produced by poverty in the United States and of suggestions as to how to attack and overcome it. Michael Harrington led those who protested from the outside,[1] and the Council of Economic Advisers led the protests within the government. A large portion of the 1964 report of the Council was devoted to the problem of poverty. The Council concluded its discussion by calling for a "new federally led effort" to get at the problem, which effort, the Council declared, should "marshal already developed resources, focus already expressed concerns" and coordinate the "diverse attacks" on poverty being made by individual communities, state and local governments, private organizations, and federal agencies carrying on programs in such fields as education, health, housing, welfare, and agriculture.[2] The nation's attack on poverty, the report concluded, "must be based on a change in national attitude. . . . It is time . . . to allow Government to assume its responsibility for action and leadership in promoting the general welfare."[3]

Just what the Council visualized as the exact role the federal government ought to play as it assumed that responsibility, it did not say. Nor were others any more helpful. Thus Senator Hubert Humphrey, soon to be Vice President and to be entrusted with overall supervision of the government's poverty effort, believed that "Government alone cannot solve the problem. Political leaders can stimulate goals, make speeches, write books, and introduce legislation, but in the final analysis it is the union of government, private industry, and free labor which gets the job done."[4] Indeed, Senator Humphrey asserted, "federal domination" of such an

[1] MICHAEL HARRINGTON, THE OTHER AMERICA (1962).
[2] COUNCIL OF ECONOMIC ADVISERS, ANNUAL REPORT 77 (1965).
[3] Id. at 78.
[4] HUBERT H. HUMPHREY, WAR ON POVERTY 15 (1964).

effort was to be avoided and "joint-venture planning" utilized instead. As his model for the war on poverty, Humphrey used the World Bank, where "politics are kept to an absolute minimum."[5] "The Bank," Humphrey pointed out,[6]

> does not initiate projects and keeps hands off local policy. Although the Bank may advise and consult as to desirable projects, and even engage in some promotional activity, all projects and applications are originated locally. The Bank reviews them to make certain that they will make a substantial contribution to local living standards and that they are economically feasible

and it grants funds to those of which it approves. But that is all it does. The federal government could do no better than to follow that pattern, Humphrey seemed to say, in the war on poverty. The federal government would be only a partner,[7] albeit the moneyed partner, with responsibilities perhaps for planning and coordination but little more. In the last analysis, the program had to be a cooperative one.

Even John Kenneth Galbraith, on whom Democratic policy-makers had leaned for advice and counsel for many years, and whose views President Johnson might as likely have solicited as those of Senator Humphrey, did not offer a much clearer idea of the role he expected the federal government to play in the action on poverty he recommended. As Galbraith saw the problem, it was "the problem of people who for reasons of location, education, health, environment in youth, mental deficiency, or race, are not able to participate effectively—or at all—in the economic life of the nation."[8] These people must be rescued, Galbraith declared, and in their rescue both "a steady expansion in economic output" and a "broad and equitable distribution of services" would be required. But though he went on to speak of "public effort and public funds" being necessarily involved, and called for assumption of such an effort as one of the "needed tasks of government,"[9] he did not spell his ideas out any further.

Whether President Johnson in fact did consult either Humphrey or Galbraith is not important. What is important is that they added nothing in their public expressions at least to what the Council of Economic Advisers had had to say about how to wage an effective war on poverty. And no one else seems to have addressed themselves to the question at all. Thus the President does not seem to have had the kind of assistance in formulating his proposals one would ordinarily expect him to have had. At least in his special message to Congress in which he amplified the brief declaration of war on poverty he had made in his State of the Union speech, he did not bring the federal role in the proposed poverty program any more sharply into focus than the others had done.

---

[5] Id. at 36.
[6] Id. at 37.
[7] Id. ch. 11.
[8] Galbraith, Let Us Begin: An Invitation to Action on Poverty, Harper's Magazine, March 1964, p. 16.
[9] Id. at 16, 18.

In his message, the President spoke of "men and women throughout the country" preparing plans to attack poverty in their own local communities, and he emphasized that no plans would be "prepared in Washington and imposed upon hundreds of different situations." All plans would instead be "local plans." He went on to declare, however, that he had no intention of letting the war on poverty become "a series of uncoordinated and unrelated efforts," and that, to prevent such an eventuality from occurring, he was establishing in the Executive Office of the President an Office of Economic Opportunity (OEO). He did not go on to say how he expected the Office to work with the hundreds of local communities he visualized making plans, nor did he say anything else which served to give a clue as to what the actual federal role in the war on poverty might be.

It is very probable, of course, that no precise description of the federal role in the projected war on poverty could have been made at that point. The President had, after all, already entrusted the conduct of the war to Sargent Shriver, whom he had designated as Director of the new Office of Economic Opportunity. In developing the Peace Corps, Shriver had been given relatively free rein by the President and Congress; and, despite his obvious disdain for orderly procedures and standard methods of organization,[10] he had been outstandingly successful. President Johnson would have been very unlikely to have asked Shriver to handle the war on poverty any differently. Nor is there any indication that he did so. Thus the President must have known that by entrusting the antipoverty effort to Shriver, he was to a large extent giving the determination of the federal role in that war over to Shriver as well. From the outset, the federal role in the war on poverty was, in other words, necessarily to be a factor of Shriver's personality and unique methods of operation. To the extent that not every aspect of either his personality or his methods of operation was known, to that extent the federal role in the war on poverty could not be known either.

But if the President had already designated Shriver to head up the antipoverty program and had created the Office of Economic Opportunity to back him up, neither the President nor Shriver probably expected the whole responsibility for defining the federal role to devolve on Shriver. The President had already indicated his own personal interest in the whole program and had evinced a determination to keep his hand in, and he was certainly aware of the role other federal agencies would necessarily have to play in conducting the broad scale attack on poverty he intended to wage. For his part, Shriver had consulted with a wide variety of people in education and civic groups, in business, labor and agriculture, and in state and local government in the process of heading up the task force on poverty for the President; and, in his own words the first day of the hearings on the Economic

[10] See Loftus, *Aid to Aged Poor Reported Lagging*, N.Y. Times, Dec. 22, 1965, p. 15, col. 6, where he speaks of "Shriver's administrative theory of setting up countervailing forces," and Haddad, *Mr. Shriver and the Savage Politics of Poverty*, Harper's Magazine, Dec. 1965, p. 43, at 45.

Opportunity Act of 1964, he had found "that the leaders of business as well as the leaders of labor and the leaders of voluntary organizations as well as the leaders of local government . . . [were] ready to enlist in [the] war against poverty."[11] He had found, in other words, a firm determination on the part of those groups to keep the poverty program from becoming completely centralized in Washington. In advising the President, he must have relayed his findings.

In any case, the draft bill authorizing the war on poverty was unique, Shriver was to tell Congress, "in the extent of its reliance on local leadership and initiative." The program being recommended, he went on, "creates a partnership between the Federal Government and the communities of this Nation. It also creates a partnership with business and labor, farm groups, and private institutions."[12] However, just as the President had not given any details of how such a cooperative endeavor might be made to function, neither did the draft legislation. This declared it to be "the policy of the United States to eliminate the paradox of poverty in the midst of plenty" and made it the purpose of the legislation to "strengthen, supplement, and coordinate efforts in furtherance of that policy."[13] But nothing further was said to relieve the ambiguity of that original declaration. Indeed, the body of the bill only further confused the picture. Thus, the Job Corps and VISTA (titles one and six) were offered as wholly federal programs. The Community Action Program (part A of title two), admittedly the heart of the proposal, was, on the other hand, proposed as partly local and partly federal, while the Adult Basic Education program (part B of title two) was to be based on state plans and to be administered by state educational agencies. Still other aspects of the program involved direct aid to individuals (titles three and four). And even with regard to those parts of the program involving the federal government, the proposed act did not vest the development of the federal role in the Office of Economic Opportunity alone. Rather, it assigned a variety of roles to a variety of federal officers and agencies. Thus the Job Corps and VISTA were left pretty much up to the Director of OEO to develop and administer, as was the development of the guidelines for federal funding of community action programs. But a number of other federal units were also given responsibilities:

—the U.S. Civil Service Commission was charged by section 107 with enforcing the ban on political discrimination placed on Job Corps enrollees
—the Secretary of Agriculture was empowered to activate part D of title three (indemnity payments to dairy farmers)
—the definitions set by the Farmers Home Administration were to be adhered to in the program of grants to farmers

[11] *Hearings on H.R. 10440 Before the Subcommittee on the War on Poverty of the House Committee on Education and Labor,* 88th Cong., 2d Sess., pt. 1, at 20 (1964).
[12] *Id.* at 21.
[13] S. 2642, 88th Cong., 2d Sess. (1964). The administration bill was subsequently incorporated into the statute. Economic Opportunity Act of 1964, § 2, 78 Stat. 508, 42 U.S.C. § 2701 (1964).

—the Small Business Administration was entrusted with operating title four of the act

—the Secretary of the Treasury was obligated to set the rate of interest to be charged on loans under part A of title three and section 404

—the Secretary of Health, Education and Welfare was charged with executing the agreements with the states in the Adult Basic Education Program and with conducting the Work Experience Program under title five.

—the President was authorized not only to appoint the Director of OEO and his chief assistants but to fix their salaries, move the OEO itself out of the Executive Office of the President, appoint members to the National Advisory Council, and direct other federal agencies to cooperate with OEO.

Last, but far from least, Congress itself was given a part to play in the program. Not only was it placed in the position of imposing conditions upon several of the programs and limiting the power of the Director in a number of ways; in one area it was even given the chance to make it clear what the federal role was *not* to be. In both sections 205 and 614, the proposed legislation provided that no grant or contract authorized under the terms of the act might provide for general aid to elementary or secondary education in any school or school system. But beyond that, the draft legislation was not descriptive of the actual role to be played by the federal government in the war against poverty.

Thus, when Congress began to hold hearings on the proposed legislation in March 1964, it had an unusual opportunity to clarify matters. Unfortunately, it did not seize that opportunity. Although special subcommittees of both the House Committee on Education and Labor and the Senate Committee on Labor and Public Welfare held hearings (those in the House at considerably more length than those in the Senate), and as a result of those hearings, a good many changes were made in the administration bill, the matter of federal role was not raised by the majority of the witnesses and was given virtually no attention in the majority reports. Thus, for example, Senate Report No. 1218 merely repeated the same kind of language already used to describe operations under the act: "Each of the . . . programs authorized by this bill," it declared, "will contribute to and reinforce *the efforts of the community* to strike at poverty at its source." It was to be the "special function" of the Director of the Office of Economic Opportunity "to coordinate the programs authorized under this bill, to see that these programs, and other Federal programs related to the war on poverty augment and reinforce *the efforts of the individual communities* in the war on poverty."[14] Only a few minority members questioned the legislation in terms of federal role. Representative Peter Frelinghuysen (R., N.J.) pointed out that the bill[15]

charts a new and unjustified course for governmental responsibility in general and for the Federal role in particular. It proposes a Federal bureaucracy whose in-

[14] S. Rep. No. 1218, 88th Cong., 2d Sess. 7 (1964). (Emphasis added.)
[15] *Id.* at 81.

fluence would permeate every nook and cranny of civic responsibility—public and private.

I cannot conceive of such intervention being in the best interest of liberal democratic institutions.

On the Senate side, Senators Goldwater and Tower observed that "the administration has determined, apparently, that Federal intrusion into State and local matters must be complete and untrammelled where the political and sociological imperatives of the war on poverty are involved."[16] How much better, thought Senator Javits, it would have been if the federal government had declared a joint war "with the States and local governments" instead of a federal war alone.[17] In committee and in floor debate, the Republican and Southern Democratic opposition to the bill hit over and over again at the problem the legislation posed for traditional federalism and specifically for state and local autonomy and at the danger of having the program's legitimate goals frustrated by the bureaucratic confusion and overlapping which was built into the proposal before them. In the end, however, the bill was passed pretty much as it was submitted. The only change bearing on the federal role which the minority was able to introduce successfully was the provision for a gubernatorial veto of the location of Job Corps centers and the stationing of VISTA volunteers within the confines of a state. For the rest the blurred picture of the federal role was not much improved. The House Committee on Education and Labor, indeed, emphasized in its report that the legislation did not originate or pass as a wholly federal program; rather, it noted that "As a nation, we clearly have the capacity to achieve . . . victory [over poverty]; what we need now is a commitment on the part of the people, the communities, private organizations, and all levels of government."[18] Passage of the bill constituted such a commitment and made possible a plan of action in which "the Federal Government will work cooperatively with the local and State governments so that the treasured local-State-Federal partnership may be maintained."[19] Particularly with regard to the community action part of the program was the cooperative nature of the antipoverty enterprise stressed. Community action programs were based, the Committee declared, "on the belief that local citizens know and understand their communities best and that they will be the ones to seize the initiative and provide sustained, vigorous leadership." They are based, too, the Committee went on,[20]

on the conviction that communities will commit their ideas and resources and assume responsibility for developing and carrying out local action programs. Thus, the role of the Federal Government will be to give counsel and help, *when requested*, and to make available substantial assistance in meeting the costs of those programs.

[16] *Id.* at 83.
[17] *Id.* at 87.
[18] H.R. REP. No. 1458, 88th Cong., 2d Sess. 1 (1964).
[19] *Id.* at 3.
[20] *Id.* at 10. (Emphasis in original.)

Thus, as matters stood when the Economic Opportunity Act of 1964 was passed, a vast program had been authorized and hundreds of millions of dollars appropriated to get it started, but no clear picture of the role the federal government was to play in its development and operation had been drawn. It was obviously an action program and a cooperative one, one in which there were at least three partners—the federal, state, and local governments—if not more than that, if the references in all the discussion leading up to the passage of the act to labor, business, agriculture and private organizations meant anything at all. Funding by the terms of the act was to be up to ninety per cent provided by the federal government, and the Office of Economic Opportunity was given a great deal of discretion with regard to making grants. But it appeared that, in essence, the federal role was at most a complementary one to the primary efforts of states, and particularly of local governments, to wage war on poverty at home and that in fact it was neither a departure from existing roles nor a very large one at that.

III

Before turning to an examination of how the federal role in the poverty program has evolved since the program has been in operation, a few comments are in order. Although it will probably never be known precisely why the federal role in the antipoverty program was left so poorly defined, it may be that there are one or more general explanations for the fact. In a way the war on poverty was the product of a particular moment of time. It marked the end of the Johnson administration as a caretaker of the Kennedy program and provided the bridge to the development of a peculiarly Johnson program. As such, it was important to get it into early and dramatic operation. Something else might have been chosen for the occasion, but the fact is that nothing else was. Thus the war on poverty was in a sense in the position of an actor who is thrust onto the stage before he has learned his part or even found out who else is in the play. Only a little more time might have served both the actor and the poverty program in good stead.

It may also be that very little thought was given to the role the federal government should play in the program. Certainly there is evidence in other respects that the program was advanced hurriedly and without the careful planning which might have been expended on it. The entire program, Robert Theobald observed, reflected a dire "lack of research." "We don't know enough; we have not done enough research; we are flying blind," he complained[21]—a conclusion with which a number of other observers agreed.[22] Had the program awaited the conduct of further research, some of it might have gone into the question of federal role.

[21] Theobald, *Johnson's War on Poverty*, New Politics, Fall 1964, p. 14, at 23-24.
[22] See, *e.g.*, Hechinger, *Head Start to Where?*, Saturday Rev., Dec. 18, 1965, p. 59, with regard to Project Head Start; Cope, *It's What's Happening, Baby*, 19 NATIONAL REV. 930-32 (1965) with regard to the Job Corps.

There is probably some substance in the suggestion, too, that the poverty program was launched as an article of faith. As a recent *Time* essay commented, it reflected "the uniquely American belief . . . that evangelism, money and organization can lick just about anything, including conditions that the world has always considered inevitable."[23] The whole program, Paul Jacobs concluded, was based on "an almost mystical belief in the infinite potentials of American society. Poverty, like polio, will be defeated when the right vaccine is found."[24] In such a rarified atmosphere as this, consideration of such a thing as the role of the federal government seems unnecessary, if not actually somehow subversive.

Moreover, it should not be overlooked that the war on poverty was declared in 1964, an election year, and despite the broad support for it in every quarter, the fact of its timing inevitably had political overtones. The whole question was dealt with along political lines in Congress, and both political parties and candidates in the presidential election were glad to get whatever mileage they could out of it. In political debates there is often a great deal of smoke, but just as often too little heat to succeed in refining the metal.

Or the failure to enunciate clearly the federal role in the poverty program may have resulted from the belief of those responsible for its development that there was little to be gained by stating the obvious. Through a number of welfare programs, some of them thirty years old already, the federal government had already begun to play a role in the nation's fight against poverty. To the extent that the expanded war on poverty has built upon and utilized these older programs, it may have seemed that no new role at all was involved, but merely an extension of an existing—and by 1964 presumably a familiar—one. Thus no detailed analysis seemed to be necessary then.

Finally, it should be noted that it is always and in every case futile to expect the federal role in any area of activity to emerge in sharp and perfectly clear focus. The very nature of the American system of government prevents it. Not only is the federal role always determined to some extent by the nature of each separate program's leadership (thus the poverty program, as noted above, was foreordained to be a product of Shriver's ability and enthusiasm), by the nature of the times and the climate of opinion which prevails when it is undertaken (the economic boom was the largest thing in sight in mid-1964 and the war in Viet Nam had not begun to escalate), but that role is also and always divided, even as the American system of government itself is divided, between several units in the two houses of Congress, between Congress and the executive branch, and between a number of units in the executive branch, as well as in many cases between the federal government and the states and their subordinate units. In every program every year, there is always concern to see that that program is visualized the same way in both houses of

---

[23] *The Poor Amidst Prosperity*, Time, Oct. 1, 1965, p. 34.
[24] Jacobs, *America's Schizophrenic View of the Poor*, 201 NATION 191, 196 (1965).

Congress, that the executive unit charged with its administration carries it out the way Congress intended, and that there is the desirable degree of coordination of effort between the several units in the executive branch concerned with its execution. And it should never be forgotten that the federal role in many programs is a direct product of the strength and vigor of state and local governments. In areas where the latter are strong and active, as they are in education, for example, the federal role is usually less. Where state and local governments on the other hand are weak or have acted irresponsibly or not at all, or are divided among themselves, the federal role can be expected to be much larger. Certainly a case can be made for the fact that the states had not distinguished themselves in the poverty area prior to 1964.

IV

It is of course idle to speculate on which, if any, of the factors just discussed were operative when the poverty program came into being. In any case, it is not necessary because the program has been in operation long enough now to give some idea of what the federal role is in fact, even if what it was intended to be remains obscure. Even so, however, it is still probably not possible to see that role as it may finally turn out to be. For one thing, twenty months is far too short a period of time to permit anything like final judgment to be rendered; for another, there is some evidence that so far the public has only been allowed to see what OEO press agents have wanted it to see;[25] and finally it is always true that a role at the outset of an enterprise may very likely change as the program settles down into routine.

This latter point may be particularly pertinent with regard to the poverty program, if the judgment of two careful observers is correct. It was their considered opinion that at least by September 1965 only "verbal solutions" had been reached to the problems of poverty "at the federal level" and that it was by then "quite apparent that the ease of conceptualizing anti-poverty programs at the federal level had just about been matched by the difficulty of translating these into meaningful operative actions at the local level."[26] The full impact of the antipoverty program has as of this writing thus yet to be felt, and as a result no last word can be written about the federal role therein.

Certainly the chief conclusion which can be drawn from the evidence on the poverty program so far available is that it is having a profound effect on local government in the United States. That effect is not so evident in connection with the

---

[25] See Hechinger, *supra* note 22, at 58, who is convinced that the war on poverty has been the object of an "official oversell" from the beginning; see also Haddad, *supra* note 10, at 45, who recognizes the fact that Shriver "uses the levers of power with one eye on the press."

[26] Bensman & Tobier, *Anti-Poverty Programming: A Proposal*, Urban Affairs Quarterly, Sept. 1965, pp. 54-55. Their conclusion was supported a little later by a writer for the Associated Press, who wrote on Nov. 28, 1965, that the poverty program was only then "beginning to emerge from the planning stage." Price, *War Against Poverty Is Now a Light Skirmish*, Durham Morning Herald, Nov. 28, 1965, § D, p. 1.

Job Corps and VISTA, or any of the other programs under the several titles of the act, as it is in connection with the community action programs. There OEO in general and the Director, Sargent Shriver, in particular, have asserted themselves positively and in so doing have begun the development of a role for the federal government which was not only not specifically called for by the Economic Opportunity Act but one which in the long run may be the most significant aspect of the poverty program. At Shriver's original suggestion, while he was serving as head of the task force developing plans to recommend to the President for the war on poverty, the act requires the "maximum feasible participation of the residents of the areas and the members of the groups served"[26a] by the community action programs—that is, the poor themselves. The act, however, did not go on to define what was meant by the phrase, with the result that in practice it has been defined by the OEO and especially by Shriver. As so defined, it has cast the federal government in a role it has never before played so directly, for, in effect, enforcing that requirement of the act, as interpreted by OEO, has involved the federal government in nothing less than reshaping American local government. As Richard Cloward put it, "the involvement of the poor is precisely [a question] of power and its redistribution."[27] Where resistance to that involvement by local politicians has been encountered—and it has been quite frequently—the role of the OEO and thus of the federal government has been one of forcing local political organizations to alter their traditional patterns of operation and admit representatives of the poor to their poverty councils. As Shriver himself put it,[28]

> Before we grant one cent, we require the involvement of the whole community in the planning and operation of the program. We specify representation of the poor. In effect, we are asking those who hold power in the community to "move over" and share that power with those who are to be helped. We insist that this can't be just a token involvement. It must be a real one.

Not only are the poor to be involved, but Negroes and other minority groups as well. Shriver has made it clear that OEO regards it as part of the federal function in the community action part of the war on poverty to force integration on local community action groups. Indeed, he declared, no community action program would be funded unless it contributed to "undermining the barriers of discrimination."[29] And in several instances, OEO has declined to fund until integrated community councils were evolved.

"The war on poverty," Shriver told the House Committee on Education and Labor in April 1965, "is not just aimed at individuals. . . . It is an attempt to change institutions as well as people." It is concerned with "hostile or uncaring or ex-

[26a] Sec. 202(a)(3), 78 Stat. 516, 42 U.S.C. § 2782(a)(3) (1964).
[27] Cloward, *The War on Poverty—Are the Poor Left Out?*, 201 NATION 55, 58 (1965).
[28] Shriver, *How Goes the War on Poverty?*, Look, July 27, 1965, p. 33.
[29] *Id.* at 34.

ploitive institutions," whether they are governmental or private,[30] and especially with the traditional institutions of local government, which for many years had ignored "the views of the poor themselves or of representative community groups."[31] In the place of such institutions, Shriver once commented, he hoped to see "a forward-looking mayor, interested in serving all the people, responsive to the needs of the electorate . . . [providing] democratic leadership" to the whole community.[32] The community action program, Shriver concluded, was the special tool of the federal government to bring such changes about. The community action program, he observed, is a program[33]

> where an entire city, or neighborhood, or county, or State enters into a binding agreement to pull itself up by its bootstraps. *In effect, it means that communities are applying to us for a new type of corporate charter.* They are incorporating themselves as a new enterprise—a new business—the business of creating opportunity for the very poor.

When a community applies to OEO for funding, and OEO makes a grant, the charter of which Shriver speaks is issued. Through the conditions OEO sets as a requirement for funding, in other words, it achieves its objectives at the local level.

> Again and again, communities throughout the country have been denied funds until they clearly established their willingness to give representation to the poor and minorities. Sometimes, the action was widely publicized; other times, it was not. . . . If the politicians frustrate local efforts for poverty planning, we will withhold or withdraw federal funds. We have followed this hard line from the first days of the program, and have no intention of abandoning it now.[34]

Funding can also be used positively to accomplish the same objectives. Thus, in at least one instance OEO awarded money to a local effort to educate and arouse the poor so as to be better able to participate effectively in local antipoverty councils. Part of the grant to the Community Action Training Center at Syracuse University was to be expended on training the poor to organize to achieve power in the community. The professional organizer, Saul Alinsky, was employed for a while by the Center as a consultant and lecturer in the program. As Shriver wrote to Representative Adam Clayton Powell (D., N.Y.) on May 12, 1965, OEO "can condition the funding of a particular application or of future programs upon the more effective utilization of resources, upon the inclusion of programs not applied for, or upon the use of agencies whose proffers of service have not been accepted."[35] For

---

[30] *Hearings on Examination of the War on Poverty Program Before the Subcommittee on the War on Poverty Program of the House Committee on Education and Labor*, 89th Cong., 1st Sess. 16-17 (1965) (opening statement of Sargent Shriver).
[31] I OFFICE OF ECONOMIC OPPORTUNITY, CONGRESSIONAL PRESENTATION 83 (1965).
[32] Shriver, *supra* note 28, at 33.
[33] *Hearings, supra* note 30, at 17 (opening statement of Sargent Shriver). (Emphasis added.)
[34] Shriver, *supra* note 28, at 33-34.
[35] Letter from Sargent Shriver to Adam Clayton Powell, in *Hearings, supra* note 30, at 78.

what the community action program is all about is social change. As Senator Winston Prouty (R., Vt.) has pointed out, the poverty program "involve[s] a mobilization of local people and a restructuring of socio-economic patterns, which must necessarily put a certain amount of strain on the social fabric."[36] If the war on poverty is to succeed, Shriver has determined that OEO can do little else but use its power to fund so as to produce the changes it deems to be required. Even if doing so involves OEO—"the federal government"—in "a ruthless struggle for power" with officials of local government, so be it. For experience has already taught OEO that it "cannot aristocratically rise above politics and hope for the best. It must [instead] enter the struggle and win the battle."[37]

It could be—and it has often been the case—that OEO decides the battle can be won in a particular community only by avoiding the local government unit altogether. The act permits the Director to pick whatever agency or agencies, public or private, seem to him most appropriate to accomplish the program's objectives in each community. The choice is essentially an *ad hoc* one, made on the basis of the peculiar circumstances of each community. "We are trying to create at the local level," Shriver told the House Subcommittee on the war on poverty program, "to the extent that we can, a . . . unit which will bring all the resources of the community to bear on poverty . . . ."[38] Public officials "are not the only representatives who have an interest in combatting poverty," Shriver has declared. Other groups may quite as legitimately be entrusted with the conduct of the local antipoverty effort if they have a more "intelligent program" to offer.[39] In a number of cases, in recognition of this possibility, OEO has awarded grants to such a group over the competing claims of the traditional unit of local government. It has not done so without objection,[40] but it "has used [its authority] . . . sparingly and reluctantly in the absence of more forceful guidance from Congress" on the matter.[41] To the extent that such nongovernmental agencies are chosen, important questions of responsibility and accountability are raised for answer.

One other impact of OEO on local government might be mentioned, although it seems to be more a potential than a realized fact. It would appear that in its ability to choose which agencies shall carry on community action programs OEO has an opportunity to bring about real change in the governmental structure of the nation's metropolitan areas. Shriver has declared repeatedly that OEO's general policy is to permit "maximum flexibility to local community action organizations"

<hr>

[36] III CONG. REC. 20101 (daily ed. Aug. 18, 1965).

[37] Haddad, *supra* note 10, at 50.

[38] *Hearings, supra* note 30, at 41.

[39] *Id.* at 54.

[40] See the complaint of Representative Albert Quie (R., Minn.), one of the most outspoken critics of the war on poverty, to his colleagues in the House that a citizens committee might be selected to run a poverty program in his district instead of the county commissioners. III CONG. REC. 16955 (daily ed. July 21, 1965).

[41] N.Y. Times, Aug. 20, 1965, p. 1, col. 4.

and that under that policy it will permit agencies to establish a program "for a city, *an entire metropolitan area, a number of cities plus adjoining rural areas, and a variety of other political and geographic configurations.*" In no instance has OEO yet required "an amalgamation of geographic or political areas into one community action program." But it will not hesitate to do so, Shriver assured Representative Powell, in "those cases where there is a clear showing that the local plan is unwise, uneconomic, or unfairly discriminates against adjacent areas or communities."[42] Thus, it may be possible for OEO to launch an attack on the governmental fragmentation which has been the greatest stumbling block in the way of progress in solving the nation's metropolitan area problems. If it begins to exert pressure to force community action programs to embrace entire areas, it might not take long for the other functions of government at the local level to begin to follow suit. The long term impact of this kind of pressure might thus be the most important contribution the war on poverty could make to American life. For it is widely held that the nation's urban problems will continue to defy solution until those problems are dealt with on a unified basis. If OEO were to lead the way, it would reach into the very center of American local government.

It is not only through making grants originally, however, that OEO exerts influence on local government and so brings the federal government into a new relationship therewith. Both in monitoring the operation of local programs and in considering applications for the renewal of grants when they begin to run out, OEO will have additional opportunities to make the presence of the federal government felt in local affairs. Although it is too early yet for renewal applications to have begun to come in in any quantity, OEO has already started to supervise program operations to assure that the program as projected in the original application is in fact being carried out. Funds to both HARYOU-ACT, the controversial antipoverty program in Harlem, and the antipoverty program in Boston were cut off in 1965 while OEO made an investigation of charges of mismanagement. To handle such investigations, OEO has created an Inspections Office, composed, in Shriver's words, "of persons who are knowledgeable about poverty" and who give him directly "their independent evaluations of what . . . others are doing or saying they are doing, using our money. So we have had fairly good intelligence so far about the various community action programs . . . and whether we are getting our money's worth and whether somebody is trying to gyp us someplace or other."[43] In addition to suspension of funds, publicity can be used to bring erring local agencies back into line. While these tools are not unique to the poverty program, and indeed are available to most other federal agencies responsible for administering grant-in-aid programs, in combination with other powers OEO has over local governments they take on greater significance.

---

[42] *Hearings, supra* note 30, at 78. (Emphasis added.)
[43] *Id.* at 69.

Despite the undeniable power OEO possesses to induce change at the local level of government, it ought in all fairness to be noted that the OEO guidelines for the community action programs were not drawn up arbitrarily and imposed by fiat. On the contrary, the community action program guidelines were drawn up with the advice of local representatives called especially to attend at least two meetings to discuss them. Moreover, the exercise of OEO discretion in applying the guidelines can only take place after a local agency has submitted an application. Like a court, OEO cannot act until someone else brings a case before it. It lacks altogether the power to initiate action on its own.[44] Finally, despite a number of instances of alleged—and probably actual—interference with local program operations, the published records of OEO give no indication that interference has been general or that it has become the standard practice of the Office in relation to local antipoverty efforts. Quite the contrary. Community action programs, once established, are not regarded as parts or adjuncts of OEO. The record shows that OEO has extended wide latitude both in original program design and in program operation to local agencies and has not unduly overridden local authority. Indeed, that the federal hand has not yet been overly oppressive is suggested by William Haddad, who noted that "Though the War on Poverty can chalk up many victories in the cities and the more industrialized areas, it is stalemated in some rural counties of the South—notably in Appalachia, where the local politicians could teach big-city bosses a trick or two." Unless OEO "can somehow change this pattern," of absolute boss control over local affairs, there is no real possibility that those areas can benefit from the poverty program—or indeed that a larger federal role will actually develop there—at all.[45]

The impact of the federal government on local government is without doubt the most important effect the antipoverty program has had in operation. It should be noted, however, that the program may be having a negative impact on the states as well. For although a gubernatorial veto was inserted into the act at the last moment, and though OEO has granted some funds to states for their own use in coordinating local antipoverty programs, by and large the whole war on poverty ignores the states and establishes the most direct and powerful connections between Washington and the thousands of city halls and county courthouses in the nation that have ever been developed. The implications of such connections are hard to describe at this stage, but the very vigor with which the states have insisted on some sort of a role in the antipoverty effort attests to their concern about the matter.

V

Although the potentiality of an alteration in the federal system seems to be the

---

[44] The act does permit (Economic Opportunity Act of 1964, § 207, 78 Stat. 518, 42 U.S.C. § 2787 (1964)) the Office of Economic Opportunity to make demonstration grants, and in the development of these grants the Office may be active from the beginning.

[45] Haddad, *supra* note 10, at 48.

most obvious lesson to be learned from a year or more of operation under the poverty program, other developments have taken place which may be significant as well. Most of the remarks in the preceding sections have spoken of the federal role as if it were one. In fact, as noted above, it began divided; and in operation it has, if anything, become even more so. The Director has, as predicted, emerged as the dominant figure in the war on poverty—so much so that in journalese he was dubbed the "poverty czar" and that appellation has stuck. There is not an aspect of the entire program that has not felt his influence; and presumably now that he is free to devote full time to conducting the war on poverty, it will be cast even more closely in his image. Even so, the Director and OEO are not synonymous. The Community Action Program is under the immediate supervision of T. M. Berry, a Negro, with whom Shriver has been reportedly at increasing odds. Once having been appointed, however, he cannot now for obvious reasons be easily removed. Moreover, pressures from Congress and constituents, as well as from state and local leaders, forced the decentralization of OEO before it had been functioning very long. There are now regional offices in New York, the District of Columbia, Atlanta, Chicago, Kansas City, Missouri, Austin, and San Francisco, which serve to dilute both the Director's power and the unity of OEO still further. And outside of OEO, Vice President Humphrey has evidently played a role of some importance in the antipoverty effort which has not always coincided with Shriver's own wishes. Designated by President Johnson to oversee the administration's entire antipoverty program, it was Humphrey who brought an end to "interagency squabbling" in the early days of the program,[46] and even as late as early December 1965, newspaper reports cast Humphrey in the role of chastiser of Shriver in behalf of the President, who was reported to be anxious both to keep peace in his political family and retain the services of Shriver in the war on poverty.[47] The President himself has retained his interest in the program, as evidenced most recently by his State of the Union address. If he has not personally become involved in its operation, he has evidently made use of the Budget Bureau as his staff arm to do so. At least, in the fall of 1965, widely circulated reports had it that the Bureau had "allegedly 'suggested' that Mr. Shriver stop emphasizing the participation of the poor in policy-making."[48] As the editors of *America* remarked, "Just what did happen remains obscure,"[49] but there is no reason to suppose that the Budget Bureau has less power over programs administered by the OEO than it does over those entrusted to other federal agencies—which power is enough to make it a force to be reckoned with in OEO operations. Finally, a number of other federal agencies than those originally involved in the poverty effort have come to have a role to play, thus further fractionalizing the

[46] Life, March 26, 1965, p. 42.
[47] See, *e.g.*, Evans & Novak, *Tensions in Anti-Poverty War Show Up*, Durham Morning Herald, Dec. 3, 1965, § A, p. 4.
[48] 113 AMERICA 741 (1965); see also N.Y. Times, Nov. 5, 1965, p. 1, col. 5.
[49] 113 AMERICA 741 (1965).

over-all federal role. The Department of Interior through the loan of departmental officers to run Job Corps centers, the U.S. Employment Service through its role in selecting Job Corpsmen, and the National Institute of Mental Health and the Public Health Service with regard to community action program grants involving community health centers and environmental health projects, have all been added to the roster.

Congress has continued to claim part of the role as well. The chairman of the House Committee on Education and Labor and the Chairman of that Committee's subcommittee on the war on poverty program sent out task forces to investigate alleged problems in OEO administration in late March and held a series of hearings in April 1965; the Senate Appropriations Committee, under the prodding of Senator John Stennis (D., Miss.), looked into Project Head Start;[50] and the Senate Committee on Labor and Public Welfare looked into "a number of problems involved in administration of the act by the Office of Economic Opportunity" on its own.[51] The upshot of the several investigations was basic approval of OEO's conduct of the war. No fundamental changes were made in the program, and the amount authorized to be expended on it in fiscal 1966 was nearly doubled. Even though Congress was thus demonstrably satisfied with the over-all program, it acted in several ways to tighten up the administration of the community action part of the program. In so doing, it went a little way toward clarifying in law the role it visualized for the federal government in the program. Thus, it noted the criticism that information about the poverty program had not been easily available and through the report of the Senate Committee on Labor and Public Welfare declared its expectation that OEO would "undertake, pursuant to its coordinating obligation under section 611 of the act, to establish a procedure for assembling such information so that public information may be complete and readily available."[52] Further to that end, the act itself was amended to require OEO to provide "reasonable opportunity" for public hearings to be held on proposed programs.[53] In response to requests from state officials, the act was amended so as to provide for continuing consultation with state agencies in the development, conduct, and administration of community action programs[54] and to require the Director to notify governors of the receipt of an application for a community action program from a private agency in a community where a public agency is carrying on a program.[55] On the other hand, the use of the gubernatorial veto was weakened by an amendment giving the Director

[50] N.Y. Times, Nov. 2, 1965, p. 19, col. 1.

[51] S. Rep. No. 599, 89th Cong., 1st Sess. 6 (1965).

[52] Id. at 7.

[53] Economic Opportunity Amendments of 1965, § 11, 79 Stat. 975, 42 U.S.C.A. § 2782 (Supp. 1965).

[54] Economic Opportunity Amendments of 1965, § 15, 79 Stat. 976, 42 U.S.C.A. § 2789(a) (Supp. 1965).

[55] Economic Opportunity Amendments of 1965, § 17, 79 Stat. 976, 42 U.S.C.A. § 2789(d) (Supp. 1965).

power to override a veto if he finds a proposed program after all to be "fully consistent with the provisions and in furtherance of the purposes" of the law.[56]

Thus, if the federal role as it may be exercised by the Director is strengthened, the whole picture was further confused by the apparently more intimate involvement of the states. The probability is, however, that concessions to gubernatorial complaints were politic and that appearances may well turn out to be deceiving, the federal role being left indeed stronger and more dominant than it was before. However, Congress did not change the basic idea of local initiative in the community action part of the program, so that the federal-local axis is still there. Congress can be counted on to continue to watch as that axis is used in the months and years ahead and may find it necessary to make corrections in behalf of local governments, even as it already has in behalf of the states. In any case, Congress gives no indication of considering the matter closed.

Nor does the Republican Party. The whole question of the federal role in the poverty program remains very much a political issue and promises to continue so for some time. The Democratic Party has made the elimination of poverty an article of faith and has pledged its efforts toward making sure that the federal government does whatever is necessary to win the war against it. While the Republicans can hardly—and, indeed, have not—come out against the objective of the war, they have been increasingly astringent in their remarks about how the war is being waged. The Republican Party platform of 1964 contained a plank condemning the antipoverty program as overlapping with and contradictory to "the 42 existing Federal poverty programs" and charging that the program would "dangerously centralize Federal controls. . . ." A number of Republican members of Congress have continued to keep a sharp eye on the program in operation, as the hearings on the Economic Opportunity Amendments of 1965 attest. By early 1966, it had become obvious that the issue of federal role would be a major one in the 1966 congressional elections. Already the Republicans are planning to make a demand for increased involvement of the poor in community action programs in an attempt to embarrass the Democrats in the traditionally Democratic big cities, where the Republican Party has not fared well recently. On the first day of the second session of the Eighty-ninth Congress, Representative Charles Goodell (R., N.Y.) made a statement on behalf of himself and Representative Albert Quie (R., Minn.), the ranking minority member of the House *ad hoc* subcommittee on the war on poverty program, in which they proposed that Congress strip OEO of all its responsibilities except that for community action programs and that it immediately require one-third of the members of the board of every local community action agency to be from the poor themselves. "This will place them on an equal level with local [read Democratic] officials and social welfare agencies who now dominate the poverty program to the

---

[56] Economic Opportunity Amendments of 1965, § 16, 79 Stat. 976, 42 U.S.C.A. § 2789(c) (Supp. 1965).

point of suffocation. . . . [This would] offer hope that the poor can get some of the money now siphoned off into political [read Democratic] machines." Moreover, the two Republicans added, "A properly representative community action board can exercise truly local control of community action programs without constant intrusions by administrators from Washington."[57] The Goodell-Quie proposal challenges the Republicans to exploit the potential of this approach, and it would appear to be a challenge the Democrats cannot fail to meet, especially in the light of President Johnson's pledge to support the war on poverty as it now operates—a pledge renewed both in his State of the Union address and in the remarks he made a few days later when relieving Sargent Shriver of his Peace Corps assignment so that he could devote full time to the antipoverty effort.

Whatever the outcome of the political battle over the conduct of the war on poverty, it would seem to be a necessary conclusion from even a cursory study of the problem it is attacking that, if the war is finally to be won, the federal role in both its planning and its execution can only grow larger and more powerful in the years ahead. For it has become obvious that the successful termination of the war will require the federal government to take an increasingly active role in the national economy and the nation's social arrangements. Thus, part of the program is job training; it will ultimately be necessary to develop the economy so that jobs are available for those who have been trained. While much of the burden in this connection must be borne by the private sector of the economy, the federal government cannot avoid a major share of the responsibility, both because of its own dominant position in the economy and because of its duty under the terms of the Employment Act of 1946 and subsequent legislation. Moreover, as Bem Price has pointed out, "the poor must acquire a social and economic mobility they do not now possess."[58]

Part of the responsibility for making that acquisition possible must be accepted by individuals and groups, quite apart from governmental action and coercion. However, to the extent that acquiring such mobility depends on education, it need not be emphasized here to what a large degree the federal government is already involved in the funding of education or how much more federal aid will be necessary for an expanded educational program. The same thing can be said with regard to those parts of the antipoverty effort aimed at improving health, housing, and family life. In all of these a deep federal involvement is required. Moreover, as Mark R. Arnold wrote recently in *The National Observer*, the poverty program's concern with removing

> poverty's causes . . . raises serious questions about the role of Government in ending it. Americans traditionally have viewed the poor as victims of forces beyond the control of society. . . . But increasingly it is being argued that, in a

[57] 112 Cong. Rec. 34 (daily ed. Jan. 10, 1966).
[58] Price, *supra* note 26.

sense, the poor are maintained in a position of subservience by society itself. Discrimination in housing and employment keeps minority groups in the slums and out of good jobs.

Thus, it is argued, it is not enough to change the poor by teaching them new skills and improving their education. The poverty program must also work to change society—to [give the poor what is] needed to move up to the middle class.[59]

To do what is necessary to bring that about can hardly help but force the federal government to become a far more active participant in the antipoverty battle than it has been so far. As Arnold concludes, to raise "the expectations of the poor and not provid[e] the means of fulfilling them . . . [might] serve to provoke the very disruptions [the antipoverty effort] was intended to avert."[60] To provide those means, the federal government cannot rely solely on the "public relations approach," as Psychologist Kenneth Clark, who has played an instrumental role from the beginning in developing the war on poverty, has observed. What is needed, he declared, is a "tough-minded and independent . . . no damned foolishness approach."[61] Utilization of such an approach, needless to say, would considerably expand the traditional federal role vis-à-vis the solution of domestic problems and even add a new dimension to the newer federal role which has begun to develop under the Economic Opportunity Act of 1964. Success in this endeavor could well take a generation or more. The problem of identifying the federal role may, thus be a continuing one facing students and practitioners of American government.

Finally, it may be that the development of the federal role in the war on poverty will be hinged directly to the federal government's decision as to how to proceed in the crusade for civil rights. Certainly, the antipoverty drive and the drive to extend civil rights are closely intertwined, since a substantial portion of the thirty-five million Americans deemed to be poor are Negro. Civil rights leaders have already mounted a campaign against OEO to obtain faster and more adequate action against poverty, and if the pressure mounts and the administration continues to support the cause, OEO may find it hard to balance its long-term objectives with the short-term necessity of averting racial strife. In such a contest, it is obvious which alternative would have to be chosen; and what effect such a choice would have on the over-all poverty program can only be conjectured. In all probability, however, it would have a profound effect.

VI

The war on poverty is a going concern. Despite criticisms of details, there is growing recognition of its effectiveness. President Johnson has pledged that it will

[59] Arnold, *A Balance Sheet on Mr. Shriver and His Program: Why 1966 Will Be a Crucial Year in the War on Poverty*, The National Observer, Dec. 20, 1965, p. 7.
[60] *Ibid.*
[61] Quoted in Price, *supra* note 26.

continue to be supported to the maximum extent possible, Viet Nam notwithstanding. Thus it can be expected to become a semi-permanent feature of the American scene. As such, it will make demands on the federal government and, in turn, contribute to shaping the government's relations with the other units of government in the federal system and with the American people as well. As the initial plans for the war were developed and as the first skirmishes were fought, just what pattern the government was following in developing its role was not at all clear. Some of the possible explanations for that lack of clarity have been advanced above. Perhaps all of them are wrong. It may be that the genius of the American system of government lies in the fact that it is not dogmatic, that it does not require explicitness, that it permits a role to be changed and altered as time and circumstances demand. A good case in point would be the federal role in education, which for many years was as obscure as the federal role in the poverty program is today and which only now is assuming a definite and reasonably clear form. The poverty program is in many respects merely an extension of the federal government's concern for education,[62] so perhaps it is futile to expect its role to develop differently than that of its parent.

In any case, it will probably be a good while before a final description of the federal role in the poverty program can be formulated. What has been done so far in the war against poverty has been done on a "crash basis," as is usually the case in war, and with the same disregard for niceties that has marked government actions in other wars. As the war on poverty settles down from emphasis on "day-to-day action programs" and begins to undertake "comprehensive planning which resolves unmet needs" of the nation,[63] however, greater attention will probably be given to the formalities and to an explication of role. Whatever finally evolves, it will no doubt show that in some ways the poverty program has introduced the federal government to a new role. Under its aegis, money has begun to flow directly to local community agencies with no way-stops in between; and those agencies must consist, in part at least, of representatives of the recipients of the government's aid. Both these features serve to set the poverty program aside from other government programs, and both have implications for the federal role in other action areas which it is still too early even to suggest. One can be sure at least that the example of the poverty program will not be missed. Indeed, it may be that in the end, the war on poverty will be known more for the alterations it introduced in the pattern of American government than for any of the very real contributions to American society it seems likely to make.

[62] "The . . . attack on poverty under Mr. Shriver," the *New York Times* observed recently, "begins below kindergarten and goes all the way through the learning and earning years. About the only programs without a built-in education feature are those for the old and infirm." N.Y. Times, Jan. 12, 1966, p. 51, col. 3.

[63] Bensman & Tobier, *Anti-Poverty Programming: A Proposal*, Urban Affairs Quarterly, Sept. 1965, p. 54, at 55.

THE WAR IN VIET NAM AND THE "WAR" ON POVERTY

JOHN O. BLACKBURN*

Generations of students have learned from their professors of economics that productive resources are limited, and that, as a result, everything cannot be done at once. Producing more of any one good or service generally requires that less of some other(s) be produced; such is the venerable law of scarcity. Societies, unable to do everything, must somehow choose what things to do first; scarcity requires "economizing," or choosing the best use of limited resources.

A superficial reading of recent economic thought might appear to qualify this law. The presence of unemployed labor and capital makes it possible to increase outputs of some things without diminishing the outputs of anything else. Thus it might seem that under conditions prevailing in the 1930s or, to a lesser degree, in recent years, the law of scarcity fails to hold.

This is, as we have suggested, only a superficial view. A closer examination of the matter will reveal that the necessity for choice still stands. Under conditions of general unemployment of labor and capital, most present-day economists would prescribe monetary, fiscal, and other policy actions designed to raise the effective demand for goods and services, and thus put idle productive resources to work. Various monetary and tax devices, for example, might be (and recently in the United States have been) used to increase private business investment. Other types of tax reduction can stimulate consumer demand, while governments, particularly the federal government, may directly increase the demand for produced goods and services by raising government spending for collective consumption or investment.

In other words, there are many different ways to increase demand and put unemployed productive resources to work. Even though unemployment means that we have room to expand demand and thus get more of everything, we must still make a decision as to more of *what*; the necessity for choice is as urgent as ever. We may have more consumer goods, more capital goods or more public goods, but we must somehow choose how much of each. As usual, choosing more of one thing involves choosing less of another. Every selection of policies to increase demand and to reduce unemployment is also a choice as between various kinds of goods: public or private goods, consumer or investment goods. In summary, when the economy is at full employment, the traditional view of scarcity prevails; spending more on something (say defense) means spending less on something else (say poverty

* A.B. 1951, Duke University; Ph.D. 1959, University of Florida. Associate Professor of Economics, Duke University. Certified Public Accountant, Florida. Contributor to economic periodicals.

programs). With unemployment, the same necessity for choice is present, but it appears in the selection of policies to increase demand.

Viewing matters in this light, much of the recent public uproar over military spending for the war in Viet Nam versus spending for the "war on poverty" seems misleading in at least two ways. First, many writers seem to be saying that spending for poverty programs may have been all right when there was "slack" in the economy (or, as we would prefer to put it, when there were unemployed resources) but now that we are approaching full employment, we can no longer afford poverty programs. It would be much more accurate to say that the human and material resources put into antipoverty efforts could have been directed toward other ends all along. If we think that they are being misused now (in the sense of being directed toward less urgent ends), then they were probably being misused all along. Of course, the movement to a limited war footing may reorder priorities; in this sense it would be accurate to say that we can no longer afford any particular set of goods or services. Further, as we shall stress below, there is the possibility of a greatly expanded war effort; any decisions as to spending should take into account possibilities of rapid future shifts as well as present priorities.

A second misleading aspect of the present public discussion is the implication that poverty programs compete for resources only with military uses. No great intelligence is required to see otherwise; any one use of productive resources competes to some extent with all other possible uses. Military spending and poverty programs compete with private consumption and private investment, as well as all other objects of public expenditure.

The return of something like full employment does, of course, focus attention on the choices to be made. Indications seem clear that some types of spending, public or private, must be curtailed or we are likely to witness a considerable acceleration in the rate of price increases. We shall assume that, whatever the merits of the Viet Nam situation, military spending will take first priority. This does not necessarily mean that spending for poverty programs must be reduced, but it does certainly suggest that some spending for something must be reduced if inflation is to be avoided. What is indicated is that poverty programs and all other objects of public expenditure need to be carefully re-evaluated with respect to their costs and their benefits.

We may state, as a general principle, that any public programs for which benefits exceed costs should be retained, and paid for with higher taxes, if necessary. This is much easier to state as a general principle than to implement in any particular case. It does make clear, however, that the increase in military spending does not automatically require a cut in federal non-defense spending. If any programs are thought to be more useful than the expenditure on private goods of an equivalent sum, the principle of optimal resource use indicates raising taxes and continuing the programs. If government programs, poverty or otherwise, cannot meet this test, they should be dropped.

Resources employed in the poverty program, to repeat, have alternative uses. If they bring higher returns in their antipoverty uses than in producing other public or private goods and services, they should remain where they are. Further, there are frequently several different ways of accomplishing any given end, a truth of which our military establishment has been persuaded (with great effort) by Mr. McNamara. Businessmen would, and anyone should, naturally choose the least costly of several equally effective methods. These two considerations suggest what it is we need to know about the poverty programs, with more precision than has been yet offered.

First, what are the expected returns from the outlays? They are, of course, partly monetary and partly intangible. In the latter area we can proceed only by value judgments, but this need not preclude efforts to identify and estimate monetary returns to individuals, to the government, and to the economy. We must also bear in mind that costs of the programs include earnings foregone by participants in addition to direct government outlays. Quite possibly, some outlays might be justified by monetary returns alone, with all non-monetary benefits as clear gain to the economy. Or all outlays may so greatly exceed any conceivable monetary benefits that even over-generous allowances for intangible benefits could not justify the programs. How, for example, does the cost of retraining workers, on the average, compare with estimated additional earnings? With respect to the Job Corps, how much outlay per enrollee would be covered by estimated higher lifetime earnings? What percentage of success has been attained with the first classes, and which way does this percentage move with subsequent classes? At what percentage of success does the program "break even," given present costs and estimated higher earnings? One could readily design a full research agenda of similar questions for each phase of the program.

A second research agenda relates to alternative means of accomplishing desired ends. To some extent, rising demand and employment in themselves open exits from poverty income levels, even without special programs. In fact, widespread prosperity in some small measure works against some poverty program objectives by raising earnings of unskilled workers and encouraging marginal students to leave school. For each poverty program, what other means might accomplish each desired end? Could not more youths simply be taken into the armed forces even if mental and physical standards were relaxed somewhat? To the (possibly considerable) extent that inexperienced workers are "structurally" unemployable because of minimum wage legislation and other employment costs, might it not be profitable to erase such barriers and, if necessary, supplement low earnings in various other ways? What, in short, are other possible means of diminishing poverty, and what are their costs?

We must also keep in mind the possibility of a sudden acceleration in military spending and the resulting present need to maintain maximum flexibility in resource use. Further, the returns from antipoverty efforts may be far in the future; the appropriate rate for discounting them to the present may vary with the changing military situation.

We might pause at this point to consider in more detail questions of inflation and full employment. Full employment does not, of course, mean that measured unemployment is zero; there are always some people moving between jobs or temporarily unemployed (voluntarily) for other reasons. Such "frictional" unemployment is widely agreed to be unavoidable, even desirable, for a well-functioning market economy. There is much dispute, however, as to how much frictional unemployment our economy requires. Full employment, then, means measured unemployment of two per cent, four per cent, or whatever is the appropriate frictional level, with the further understanding that the number of jobs open and in the process of being filled is roughly equal to the number of unemployed persons in the process of moving between jobs.

In recent years there has been much discussion of "structural" unemployment, by which is usually meant that unemployed persons lack the skills or abilities to fill jobs that are open, or could be opened by an expansion of demand. To the extent that our remaining unemployment in the United States is frictional or structural, expanding demand by monetary or fiscal policy will largely raise prices without doing much to eliminate unemployment. Some of the poverty programs, incidentally, as well as earlier manpower training legislation, are aimed at reducing structural unemployment via education and training for persons now in low-income families.

There is some evidence from past experience that the level of unemployment—frictional, structural, and all other kinds—is inversely related to the rate at which wages and prices creep up. With a sufficiently vigorous demand for goods such as existed during World War II, virtually everyone can be employed, including those whom we would now regard as structurally unemployable. The penalty is, of course, rapidly rising wages and prices which serve, in part, to overcome minimum wage laws and other cost barriers to the employment of low-productivity workers. At the other extreme, there seems to be some level of unemployment at which wages do not rise at all so that rising labor productivity could result in gradually falling monetary labor costs and, possibly, falling prices of goods. Postwar data seem to indicate that unemployment of five per cent to six per cent is required for price stability (rising wages are absorbed by rising labor productivity) whereas an unemployment rate as low as three per cent is likely to be accompanied by price level increases of $3\frac{1}{2}$ per cent to $4\frac{1}{2}$ per cent per year.[1]

---

[1] For rough estimates of this nature, see Samuelson & Solow, *Analytical Aspects of Anti-inflation Policy*, 50 AM. ECON. REV. 177 (1960). Their estimates are based on data from the teens, twenties, and postwar period. Including the 1930s would greatly increase the estimate of unemployment consistent with price stability.

The enormous expansion in the output of goods and services during the period 1961-1964 was accomplished with virtual price stability. The broadest index of output prices that we have[2] advanced 1.3 per cent per year on the average, a figure well within the range of statistical errors or unrecorded quality improvements in output. However, unemployment remained above five per cent throughout the period. The rate of price increase rose in 1965 to 1.8 per cent while unemployment fell to 4.1 per cent at year-end. This recent behavior is quite consistent with the functional relationship between unemployment and the rate of inflation on which the above estimate of likely inflation at three per cent unemployment is based.

The President's Council of Economic Advisers is more optimistic (excessively so, one fears) about avoiding inflation. The Council's latest annual report[3] predicts unemployment of 3¾ per cent by December 1966, with an increase in the price level of 1.8 per cent to 1.9 per cent. The year-end prediction of unemployment has been revised downward to 3½ per cent by the Department of Labor, according to recent press reports, thus bringing the small size of the officially-expected price rise under further suspicion. The Council's expectation that low 1966 unemployment is consistent with less inflation than our past record would predict stems from five allegedly changed factors. First, it is argued that the composition of demand has been growing and will continue to do so in a "balanced" fashion, *i.e.*, without such drastic shifts in composition as have characterized some postwar inflationary periods. Second, labor productivity gains are expected to be larger and more widely distributed than in other post-war periods, thus permitting more union pressure on wages without cutting business profit margins. Third, the Council finds more responsible attitudes among business and labor leaders with respect to key price and wage decisions. Also cited are increased foreign competition and various manpower development policies which aim at reducing structural unemployment.

In evaluating the Council's position, one is tempted to skepticism. Specifically, it seems likely that increases in government spending are understated, as are expected increases in private fixed investment and inventories. One may also doubt whether spending for residential construction will remain at 1965 levels, though the rise in interest rates on mortgage credit will certainly contribute to this result. Total demand, therefore, may well rise more than the Council expects, and, to the extent that expectations of inflation spread, demand may rise by much more. This development would push unemployment rates lower and prices higher than the Council forecasts.

Skepticism is also in order as to the balanced nature of additional demand. The shift toward investment and military spending is reminiscent of the 1955-1957 experience, which period also marked the most rapid price level increase in the postwar period apart from the Korean build-up and the immediate post-war buying binge. Reliance on foreign competition, unfortunately, has ominous implications for our

[2] The implicit price deflator for gross national product.
[3] COUNCIL OF ECONOMIC ADVISERS, ANN. REP. (1966).

balance of payments. It may also be true that unions and businessmen might avoid price and wage increases in the face of mounting (and possibly understated) demands, but this remains to be seen. Our own experience to date has not been reassuring, and the experience of European countries with "income policies" is even less so. We must also face the possibility of a greatly expanded war effort without the idle resources of 1941 or (to a lesser extent) 1950. Any sudden rise in military spending beyond the levels now foreseen could rapidly touch off still other inflationary forces. Consumers and businessmen are sufficiently liquid to increase expenditures sharply for construction and inventories. A further consideration suggested by the present uncertainty is the need to avoid committing resources to long-range projects (such as construction) which cannot be quickly reversed.

It would appear, then, that our choice lies between a very likely rise in the price level of three per cent to four per cent (with the possibility of steeper rises following an expanded war effort), or some action to curtail demand.

A price level increase of, say, four per cent per year may seem like a modest enough figure; yet such a rate, if sustained, would double the price level in about eighteen years. The inequities of inflation are well known, but we should perhaps reiterate here some of the most important problems. The systematic provision for retirement in both public and private funds is a major activity in the United States, and eighteen or twenty years represents a rather short span in calculations which normally deal in forty to fifty year periods. It is difficult to imagine the destructive impact on our pension machinery of widely held expectations that prices might double every eighteen to twenty years, or increase four- to six-fold during the normal period of calculation for the accumulation and disposition of funds for retirement.

Worst of all, the burden of inflation falls in large measure on those who are already poor, or on those at income levels already close to the "poverty line." Poverty or near-poverty living involves a majority of the aged living on public or private pensions with fixed dollar incomes. This group is, incidentally, beyond the scope of the poverty programs, and stands to suffer most from inflation. To the extent that rising prices force down demand and thus help slow down the rate of inflation, the segment of society least able to afford lower real incomes (the aged poor) is called upon to make the largest sacrifice.

The question of poverty is indeed a complex one. Though we should all like to see poverty disappear, we may well disagree on measures to abolish it. The war in Viet Nam focuses attention on inflation as a problem which is more serious than at any time since 1957. There is the strong possibility that some element of aggregate demand will have to be restrained, so that spending for poverty programs, along with other types of public and private spending, becomes a target for potential restraint. We have suggested a cost-benefit test for all types of spending including the war on poverty; decisions as to where to reduce demand should be based on such tests. We should face realistically the threat of inflation and its impact on millions of the poor.

THE WAR OVER POVERTY*

CARL H. MADDEN†

The war *on* poverty is becoming a war *over* poverty. A struggle is being waged over the approach to alleviating poverty. The war over poverty could create a new social structure in our changing cities. Even more important, it could decide the fate of the developing revolution in our concepts of social welfare.

That revolution, not fully understood, would replace the relief dole as a major approach to treating poverty. It would substitute the positive policy goal of more human development, within a framework of rapid and stable economic growth, for the static or redistributional welfare concepts.

I

No one knows how many Americans are poor. It is most probably not two-fifths or even one-fifth of our population, as early writers in the current "war," such as Keyserling and Harrington, argued. Their numerical definition (Keyserling: family income under $4,000 per year; Harrington: family income under $3,000) of poverty was wrong. Their numbers were therefore wrong. And so, also, was the picture they created of America and American life. This is made clear by an authoritative interpretation of the 1960 census by the former director of the U.S. Census Bureau.[1]

Poverty, a harsh word, is defined as "the condition of being poor: *lack of what is needed*." This dictionary meaning is more accurate than any numerical definition. In terms of needs such as food, shelter, clothing, medical treatment, education, entertainment, and personal transportation, there is not as much poverty in the United States as has come to be believed.

This is made clear by Scammon's analysis of 1960 census data. Today few Americans suffer from lack of food because of deprivation. By 1960, only 6.8 per cent of American dwelling units were dilapidated. Even Michael Harrington

* The views expressed in this paper do not necessarily reflect the opinions of the Task Force on Economic Growth and Opportunity or the Chamber of Commerce of the United States.

† A.B. 1942, M.A. 1952, Ph.D. 1954, University of Virginia. Director of Research, Task Force on Economic Growth and Opportunity, Chamber of Commerce of the United States.

I should like to acknowledge the valuable assistance of Mr. Richard L. Breault, Associate Director of Research, Task Force on Economic Growth and Opportunity, in preparing this paper.

[1] For Keyserling and Harrington's definitions, see LEON H. KEYSERLING, POVERTY AND DEPRIVATION IN THE UNITED STATES—THE PLIGHT OF TWO-FIFTHS OF A NATION (1962); MICHAEL HARRINGTON, THE OTHER AMERICA (1962). For the refutation of their views, see BEN J. WATTENBERG & RICHARD M. SCAMMON, THIS U.S.A. 130-51 (1965). Keyserling's "under-$4,000 per year" for families and Harrington's "under-$3,000 per year" for families were both admittedly arbitrary; the point, however, is that, as Scammon, a former Director of the U.S. Bureau of the Census, writes, *no* numerical definition of poverty is correct.

acknowledged that the problem of lack of clothing is largely gone, in arguing that U.S. poverty is largely "invisible." Further, the 1960 census reports that almost three-quarters of families with incomes under $4,000 per year have washing machines to wash their clothes.

Medical treatment is potentially available to Americans of all income classes; and the poor for the most part share in public health and sanitation programs, in effect throughout the country. From 1961 to 1963, ninety-nine per cent of thirteen-year-olds were in school, as were ninety-seven per cent of fifteen-year-olds and ninety-one per cent of sixteen-year-olds. A census study of October 1960 showed that nineteen per cent of youth from families with less than $5,000 annual income got into college; this is about one in five, compared with a national rate for all incomes of thirty-one per cent or about one and one-half in five. As of May 1964, ninety-three per cent of American homes had television sets. By 1960, almost sixty per cent of families with less than $4,000 annual income had automobiles available. All these facts and others reported by the 1960 census, now five years old, are analyzed by Scammon.[2]

This does not mean that the problem of poverty in the United States should be underestimated or that its alleviation should not be a major policy goal. It does mean that the problem has in fact been exaggerated and distorted in many people's minds. The fact that the nation can undertake the major effort of minimizing poverty with such a high probability of success is itself a blessing unique in the history of great nations. Even so, as Scammon puts it:

> That poverty is not a major malignant disease, that the nation is not overrun by a huge, seething, hopeless invisible quintile of poor people—this, too, apparently needs public articulation. One of the reasons the "poor" are so "invisible," as Harrington states, is that there may be far fewer than have been written about.[3]

Harrington, associate editor of the socialist journal *Dissent*, was limited by lack of data in his interpretation. Poverty in the United States, as of now, is not measured accurately, and it could be measured much more accurately at low cost. This would require taking into account such variables as family composition, family size, age of family head, farm-nonfarm living, urban-suburban-rural living, size of city, and regional differences in living standards.[4] Approaches by Orshansky and Friedman,[5] admittedly still not adequate, are marked improvements over the faulty data that launched the war on poverty. Some government statisticians would suppress regional or other differences among families because they favor "national

---

[2] WATTENBERG & SCAMMON, *op. cit. supra* note 1, at 135-37.

[3] *Id.* at 138.

[4] TASK FORCE ON ECONOMIC GROWTH AND OPPORTUNITY, CHAMBER OF COMMERCE OF THE UNITED STATES, THE CONCEPT OF POVERTY 16-19 (1965) [hereinafter cited as THE CONCEPT OF POVERTY] recommends a more careful definition of poverty.

[5] Orshansky, *Counting the Poor: Another Look at the Poverty Profile*, Social Security Bull., Jan. 1965, p. 3; ROSE D. FRIEDMAN, POVERTY: DEFINITION AND PERSPECTIVE (1965).

norms," similar to social security and the minimum wage. If this position does not implicitly violate the basic methodology of science, it at least begs the question of measurement.

U.S. poverty is not a mass phenomenon, but a problem of specific individuals, families, and groups with "poverty-linked" characteristics. Far from being a single problem, poverty is linked with other difficult domestic issues, such as race, discrimination by sex, unemployment, education, sickness-disability-old age, agriculture, depressed areas, and regional differences.[6]

The United States was making much progress against poverty before the war on poverty began. It is still doing so, and the major source of that progress has been and is economic growth at high levels of employment. Smolensky has shown that, using a variable definition reflecting the changing national consensus, poverty declined by more than thirty-five per cent towards complete elimination in this century. Smolensky found further that high growth and employment rates led to a more rapid rise in the definitional level of poverty, but also that poverty declines faster as the definitional level rises faster.[7]

It is elementary that when everyone's income rises, the gain of the poor is most significant in human terms. Says Scammon:

> Much of our recent income revolution has involved precisely such [poor] families moving from the lower classes into the middle classes. . . . Thus, in 1947, 64 per cent of U.S. families lived on less than $5,000 per year. In 1963, that figure was reduced to 37 per cent (constant 1963 dollars).[8]

Because the well-off have gotten better off, the fact that the poor have gotten better off is obscured.

The shift since 1947 in people occupying the lowest end of the income distribution casts grave doubt on the Harrington thesis of a "culture of poverty." People in this quintile, according to Scammon, are more likely now to be old people, two-person families, and young individuals. Some of these people, such as young students, both single and married, are themselves moving through the lowest quintile, not without hope for the future. Further, these are people getting better off, not worse off, but only at a slower rate than others. Finally, they are people whose needs, by and large, are less than families with children, whose place they have taken in the lowest quintile.

Before the war on poverty, large sums were being spent to help the poor. Some sources have estimated that in 1964 Americans earmarked $31 billion for federal antipoverty programs alone.[9] When one adds funds spent by states, counties, cities,

---

[6] THE CONCEPT OF POVERTY 5-7. See also WATTENBERG & SCAMMON, op. cit. supra note 1, at 138-39.
[7] Smolensky, The Past and Present Poor, in THE CONCEPT OF POVERTY 33, 35-36.
[8] WATTENBERG & SCAMMON, op. cit. supra note 1, at 142.
[9] THE WAR ON POVERTY: A HANDBOOK 28 (National Catholic Coordinating Committee on Economic Opportunity, 1964).

and philanthropies, it may well be that Americans, before the war on poverty, were spending more to help the poor than on any other single national purpose except national defense. In December 1965 the Office of Economic Opportunity released a 414-page inventory of federal programs totalling $21 billion to help poor individuals and groups.

II

How can the poor be helped? First, it should be clear that the basic source of potential progress against poverty is an increase in per capita real output and income. This, in turn, means that output must grow faster than population; otherwise, no matter what measures are taken to help the poor, the real incomes of the society in general will not rise. Rising productivity in a society, therefore, is basic to its ability to reduce poverty.

Given rising productivity, national policy has available three basic ways to relieve poverty: income redistribution, area development, and human development.

To redistribute income is to transfer wealth or income from the nonpoor to the poor, however defined, for the purpose of providing living standards considered adequate by social norms. Income redistribution does not of itself increase the nation's total income; it reallocates what is available. An example is the Old-Age Assistance Program of the Social Security Act.[10]

Area development, as used against poverty, is an attempt to raise the income of poor people in a geographical area through raising total income in that area by investment in natural resources or physical capital goods without regard for market criteria. Area development rests on two assumptions which can be questioned. The first is that non-market investment in specific geographical areas will in fact be more productive in those areas than it would have been in market uses in other areas. The second assumption is that such investment in specific geographical areas will raise the incomes of poor people in those areas. An example of area development is the Appalachian Regional Development Act of 1965.[11]

Human development, as an antipoverty approach, tries to raise total income through investment in people, especially the poor, in order to increase their individual productivity. It rests on the assumption that investment in human beings will raise their income without reducing society's total income. An example is the Vocational Rehabilitation Act.[12]

A. Prevalence of Income Redistribution

By far oldest and most prevalent, income redistribution as the relief dole stems from our Anglo-Saxon heritage and goes back to the Elizabethan Poor Law. Its

---

[10] Section 202, 49 Stat. 623 (1935), as amended, 42 U.S.C. § 402 (1964).
[11] 79 Stat. 5, 40 U.S.C.A. App. A (Supp. 1965).
[12] 68 Stat. 652 (1954), as amended, 29 U.S.C. §§ 31-42 (1964).

motive was combined compassion and fear of disturbance,[13] not economic reasoning. Poverty was viewed as derived either from acts of God, personal weakness, or personal wickedness. If the poor are themselves to blame for their lot in life, or if God's will is at work, it is wasteful for society to invest in human development programs; it suffices to provide such people bare subsistence as a matter of conscience and to prevent disorder.

Dominance of the relief dole approach in this country well into the twentieth century rested on several factors. Among them were the English poor law concept, the Puritan ethic, the rags-to-riches epic of European immigrants, the strong optimism of people of enterprise in a secure and developing subcontinent, the prevalence of jobs calling for strong backs, and a social milieu of swift upward mobility for most.

B. Impact of the Great Depression

Millions of proud and self-respecting Americans, thrown into poverty through conditions beyond their control in the Great Depression, began to see poverty differently. Clearly the culprit was management of the economy, not personal weakness. The new national attitude, that poverty was remediable, took shape in New Deal measures such as public works employment, the Civilian Conservation Corps, and others to treat remediable poverty, and Social Security to make irremediable poverty less onerous. Today, the personal weakness concept of poverty has all but received the coup de grace. The Second World War showed that only a tiny handful of able-bodied people refuse to work when jobs they can fill are available. It also showed paradoxical progress against poverty despite the enormous waste of war, as real living standards rose with total output.

Yet New Deal measures were experimental, often mutually inconsistent, and stemmed more from strong conviction of a need to act than from purposeful and integrated movement of thought. A deeper conviction, not yet firmly articulated, is based not only on progress since the Great Depression but also on growing knowledge of the economy. This conviction holds that the motive force behind economic growth is application of science and technology to a market-based economy. It holds that scientific methods of analysis and standards of data-gathering and use can be extended to social organization. It holds that policy-making based upon reasoned and informed consensus within such a framework can resolve problems of poverty by combining rapid and stable economic growth in the market economy with intensive development of productive potentials of human beings, viewed not only as human economic resources but also as ends in themselves.

C. The Scientific Revolution and Progress Against Poverty

When Malthus wrote about population, he assumed that it would increase faster than the food supply. The pessimistic conclusion from his theory for social policy,

---

[13] See D. A. MacINTYRE, PUBLIC ASSISTANCE, TOO MUCH OR TOO LITTLE ch. 2 (N.Y. State School of Industrial and Labor Relations, Cornell University Bull. 53-1, 1964).

leading Carlyle to describe economics as "the dismal science," was that attempts to increase the welfare of the poor were self-defeating. The poor, given more than bare subsistence, would only multiply until, by an iron law, they fell back to bare subsistence once more. The only hope for Malthusians was for checks to population growth through moral restraint rather than the wars, famine, and disease that were the only grim alternative checks.

The history of technology in the Western world since the early nineteenth century, when Malthus wrote, dramatically refutes the inevitability of his theories. Thus, today, the scientist Berkner can write: "Man now sees—almost within his grasp—the promise of a society beyond the dreams of the sage and poet."[14]

In the past century, advances in science and technology have brought revolutionary changes in the living patterns and social institutions of the Western world. New discoveries have given means to solve or alleviate a vast array of human and social problems while they have given men unprecedented power over nature, life, and death. They have reduced hunger and disease, increased the span and numbers of lives on earth, lifted the burden of hard manual labor, ended the economic need or benefit of slavery; and they have given man *the chance* to reach the age-old ideal of a life freed from base want and scarcity.

This science- and technology-based revolution has been led by nations whose social organization stimulates the application of technology to meeting consumer demands. In the United States, a free market system within a governmental framework of diffused political power and ideals of freedom provides the needed economic organization. The basic principle of a free market system is that people are free to buy and consume what they wish and to produce and sell what they wish. People as consumers try to maximize the satisfaction from their limited incomes; the same people as producers try to maximize their income gained from using limited resources and capabilities. The efforts of these two groups interact to set prices of consumer goods and productive services so that the relation between any two prices measures their relative scarcity or abundance in satisfying wants.

This system has achieved high productivity in developing economic innovations. Such innovations are not inventions but successful application of invention to meet people's needs as they are expressed in markets. Innovations in such a society are the result of people, acting in their self-interest, adjusting to complex relations between prices and costs, to change such relations to their own benefit. Successful innovations are subject to economic forces. In fact, the relations between prices give a strong incentive to producers to anticipate wants, to change their habits, to eschew complacency, and to use opportunities of whatever kind to meet market demands.

The use of new ways to produce goods and services leads to higher real incomes for society. The scientific revolution of today is marked by waves of innovation as

[14] L. V. Berkner, The Scientific Age 129 (1964).

new industries emerge and grow, displacing older ones with multiplied productive power. The record of history confirms this development. Populations are growing at rates of two per cent per year, a doubling time of forty years compared to 200 years at the time of our American Revolution. Science and medicine, joined together, have reduced death rates faster than birth rates can be checked, multiplying mouths to feed.

Yet standards of living have risen dramatically in industrial countries. U.S. agriculture is almost wholly mechanized, its productivity having risen many-fold through intensive use of biology, chemistry, and mechanics in farming. From 1860 to 1960 the farm population declined from seventy to seven per cent of the U.S. total. We enjoy enormously increased production of basic fuels and minerals, employ exotic ones, and create new ones. The ability to produce of industry gains steadily at rates estimated at 2.5 to 3.5 per cent per year.

The impact of innovation has produced great changes in the labor force. The service industries[15] now account for more than half the nation's employment, now growing "far more rapidly than in the rest of the economy."[16] As manufacturing becomes more efficient, the labor force shifts to the expanding services sector, providing more convenience, professional and personal care, and government services, including education, to our people.

Fears that automation will produce mass unemployment and new poverty are a will-o'-the-wisp. After a year-long study, a blue-ribbon presidential commission on automation found that technological change presents no basic threat to employment that cannot be overcome by vigorous fiscal policies to spur economic growth.[17] The commission's conclusion recognizes the basic economic lesson of the Great Depression: that to achieve full employment in a progressive society, the total monetary demand of business, consumers, and government must match the society's productive potential. Aggregate desired employment levels can be achieved by appropriate monetary and fiscal policies that match total monetary demand with productive potential at a stable price level.

The presidential commission's views are supported by many other studies.[18]

---

[15] The service industries are defined to include wholesale and retail trade, finance, insurance, real estate, professional services, repair services, personal services, and general government.

[16] Fuchs, *Productivity in the Service Industries*, in NATIONAL BUREAU OF ECONOMIC RESEARCH FORTY-FOURTH ANN. REP. 11 (1964).

[17] NATIONAL COMMISSION ON TECHNOLOGY, AUTOMATION, AND ECONOMIC PROGRESS, TECHNOLOGY AND THE AMERICAN ECONOMY, REPORT 189-92 (1966).

[18] Such scholars include staff experts of *Fortune* magazine, in a series of articles on technology, "Technology and the Labor Market," Jan. 1965 to Aug. 1965; George Terborgh, economist of the Machinery and Allied Products Institute, in his book, THE AUTOMATION HYSTERIA (1965); Ewan Clague, U.S. Commissioner of Labor Statistics; and the President's Council of Economic Advisers.

According to Mr. Clague, for example, "Technology as such does not result in a net loss of jobs in the economy. It does destroy the jobs and occupations of individual workers; but it creates new jobs and occupations which require workers." See *What Employment Statistics Show*, Automation, April 1964, p. 95.

According to the Council of Economic Advisers, "Technological change permits any given level of

Those who, in wild exaggeration, have created an automation hysteria have done
the nation a disservice by muddy thinking unsupported by factual evidence.[19] The
burden of proof that automation is a new threat auguring mass unemployment rests
on those who claim it vitiates all past experience with technological change.

It must be recognized, however, that technological change involves inherent
costs as well as benefits. Among these, such change in the short run and at the level
of individual industries destroys jobs. If the shift from old to new industries is slow
or inefficient, both economy and worker are penalized in loss of output and income.
Therefore, it is sound public policy to improve labor mobility, job market efficiency,
and structural adjustment of the labor force. Easing structural adjustments and
keeping total monetary demand roughly equal with national productive capacity
are closely related. It is important to promote the flexibility and adaptability of the
work force. It is also important to provide for those unable to meet the demands of
the labor market—the sick, the disabled, the aged.[20]

And it is important to keep fiscal and monetary policies effectively matching total
spending and productive capacity. There is no intrinsic reason that an increase in
our ability to produce should not lead to an actual increase in production. Indeed,
we need more and faster technological change in order to raise living standards; to
provide more goods and services, more leisure, a more satisfying work environment;
and to enable us to solve the problems created by technical advance.

Thus, the basic means of minimizing poverty is stable and rapid economic growth,
with more emphasis on human development to provide skills needed in a scientific
and service-oriented age, and with institutions that minimize disruptions caused by
increased mobility. It is our capacity to grow faster that gives the sine qua non for

output to be produced with less labor and, in that sense, destroys jobs. But it also provides a significant
spur to investment and consumption and thus creates jobs. . . . Historically periods of rapid technological change have generally been periods of high and rising employment." Council of Economic
Advisers, Annual Report 95 (1964).

[19] Examples of wild exaggeration can be found in Donald N. Michael, Cybernation: The Silent
Conquest 15 (1962); in Hearings on the Nation's Manpower Revolution Before the Subcommittee on
Employment and Manpower of the Senate Committee on Labor and Public Welfare, 88th Cong., 1st Sess.,
pt. 5, at 1649 (1963) (prepared statement of John I. Snyder, Jr., Chairman and President of U.S.
Industries, Inc.); and The Triple Revolution (reprint of a statement by the Ad Hoc Committee on the
Triple Revolution, P.O. Box 4068, Santa Barbara, California, 1964).

The statement of the Ad Hoc Committee is perhaps the most extreme. The Committee includes
W. H. Ferry, Vice President, Fund for the Republic; Michael Harrington, author, The Other America
(1962); Gunner Myrdal, Swedish economist; Ben B. Seligman, Retail Clerks International; Linus Pauling,
chemist-pacifist; and Norman Thomas, Socialist leader. The Committee states that because of the
technical revolution, "the industrial productive system is no longer viable . . . the traditional link
between jobs and incomes is being broken. The economy of abundance can sustain all citizens in
comfort and economic security whether or not they engage in what is commonly reckoned as work."
Committee proposals include "a massive program to build up our educational system . . . massive
public works . . . a massive program of low-cost housing, and . . . the conscious and rational direction
of economic life by planning institutions under democratic control." The Triple Revolution, op. cit.
supra at 10-13.

[20] See Task Force on Economic Growth and Opportunity, Chamber of Commerce of the
United States, Poverty: The Sick, Disabled and Aged (1965).

alleviating poverty; it is upgraded human skills that makes ability out of capacity. Further, as John Dunlop has pointed out, our productive potentials "underscore the common gains to be shared by increasing productivity and the possibilities of insuring adequately those who bear the costs of the adverse initial impacts of some technological changes."[21]

III

Human development to combat poverty.is not a new concept in this country. From the vision of William Penn and Thomas Jefferson until today our public school system is an attempt to develop the human resources needed to build a great nation. And from the Northwest Territory Ordinance in 1787 until today, when ninety-nine per cent of our thirteen-year-olds are in school, Americans have followed the mandate laid down in that Ordinance, that "means of education shall forever be encouraged," as well as upholding—not without strife—its ideals of social and political democracy.[22] The Morrill Act of 1862,[23] fathered by Michigan farmers, set up land grant colleges to develop human resources needed to tap our food-producing potential and provide needed engineering skills to supplement humanistic and scientific education in private and state universities. The Smith-Lever Act of 1914,[24] setting up the Agricultural Extension Service, and the Smith-Hughes Act of 1917,[25] providing vocational education in agriculture, likewise fostered human development. The Elementary and Secondary Education Act of 1965,[26] though it places the federal government into traditionally state areas of responsibility, recognizes the national interest in the education of citizens, poor as well as not-so-poor.

But early efforts to develop human skills were focused on opportunity, not deprivation. Only since the poverty concept revolution of the Great Depression have we given serious thought to developing human resources as a specific way to fight poverty. In fact, we see the first national application of this approach in the George-Barden Act of 1946,[27] the Vocational Rehabilitation Act of 1954,[28] the Manpower Development and Training Act of 1962,[29] the Vocational Education Act of 1963,[30] and certain programs since then. If poverty is, however, a problem of specific individuals, families, and groups with "poverty-linked" characteristics, and if science promises further economic growth for the society, giving means to alleviate poverty and insure against disruptions of technological change, it follows that antipoverty

---

[21] Dunlop, *Introduction* to AUTOMATION AND TECHNOLOGICAL CHANGE 1, 3 (Dunlop ed. 1962).
[22] Northwest Territory Ordinance art. 3, 12 JOURNAL OF THE U.S. CONGRESS 85, 90 (1787).
[23] 12 Stat. 503 (1862), as amended, 7 U.S.C. §§ 301-05, 307-08 (1964).
[24] 38 Stat. 372 (1914), as amended, 7 U.S.C. §§ 341-43, 344-46, 348 (1964).
[25] 39 Stat. 929 (1917), as amended, 20 U.S.C. §§ 11-15, 16-28 (1964).
[26] 79 Stat. 27, 20 U.S.C.A. §§ 234-44, 331-32b, 821-85 (Supp. 1965).
[27] 60 Stat. 775 (1946), as amended, 20 U.S.C. §§ 15i-15m, 150-15q (1964).
[28] 68 Stat. 662 (1954), as amended, 29 U.S.C. §§ 31-42 (1964).
[29] 76 Stat. 23, as amended, 42 U.S.C. §§ 2571-2620 (1964).
[30] 77 Stat. 403, 20 U.S.C. §§ 15aa, bb, aaa, 35-35n (1964).

efforts should emphasize remedying personal deficiencies, imparting personal abilities, in order to help people become more productive and so share directly through their own efforts in society's economic advance. The purpose—as distinct from the programs—of the Economic Opportunity Act[31] reflects this concept, which has considerable merit.

A. Human Development versus Other Approaches

The debate about the merits of guaranteed annual incomes—a sophisticated version of relief doles—whether as "negative income taxes," for the poor, or "demogrants" making up universal grants to all citizens, or in other forms—challenges the human development approach. Proponents offer many reasons for such guarantees. Perhaps the most persuasive is that they are more efficient and less demeaning than present complex welfare programs with their often offensive and arbitrary eligibility conditions and hodge-podge benefit levels among states, counties, and cities.

Certainly, the need for such grants as a response to automation can be sharply questioned along lines argued above, and needs no further elaboration. Further, grants do not strike at today's poverty-causing conditions. Grants do not reduce job or union discrimination by color or sex, nor increase education, skills, or work discipline.

In effect, the guaranteed-income approach begs an important question if used for more than cutting red tape. The market system takes the individual as given—assuming the participants are rational, knowledgeable, and have initiative; and it promises favorable results on this assumption. Yet, in fact, individuals are complex and importantly influenced by their environment. It is callous to assume a degree of knowledge and initiative by today's poor which ignores environmental factors; to leave them isolated and dangling at the end of a new-fangled welfare check. Human development offers opportunity; while it is more expensive, it has merits recognized throughout our history.

Area development also challenges the human development approach. The Appalachian Regional Development Act sets aside eighty per cent of its authorized $1-billion-plus for roads. This comes when Appalachia requires more than 100 more vocational-technical schools.[32] The Appalachian Act concept raises several difficult questions. Why should high-cost roads in Appalachia, built in the hope of generating demand, yield higher returns to society than less costly roads built to meet pressing demands elsewhere? Why should road-building, that creates temporary jobs for skilled workmen and highly organized construction companies, help the *poor* in Appalachia? Indeed, why should the nation's poverty efforts go to help entire geographic areas and regions when it is specific people in them who are poor? Is it areas or people who are poor?

---

[31] 78 Stat. 508 (1964), 42 U.S.C. § 2701 (1964).
[32] See THE CONCEPT OF POVERTY 14.

Area development promises to become competitive for federal funds. Already, such regions as New England, the Ozarks, the Upper Midwest, and still others are prepared to follow the route of Appalachia. Government officials privately admit that in guiding the Appalachian act through Congress, roads were "easier to sell" than vocational schools. Current programs in urban renewal, farm subsidies, public works, and the like suggest that area redevelopment is far from taking a back seat. It hardly needs documenting here that public works tend to follow political influence. It is likely, indeed, that major federal subsidy programs have tended to redistribute income from the poor to the not-so-poor.

B. The Economic Opportunity Administration

As it is turning out, the Economic Opportunity Act may well be a poor vehicle for testing the human development concept. For one thing, it is not much of a test. Seen in the perspective of our country's great accomplishments in education, training, and welfare, the Office of Economic Opportunity (OEO), for all its strident publicity, is small potatoes. Beyond that, the act was hurriedly pieced together;[33] many of its offerings are old or duplicate existing programs;[34] it has spent its money mainly for administration;[35] it is deeply embroiled in what a former administrator terms "savage" politics;[36] it has been given a virtually impossible job of coordination;[37] its

---

[33] Reports in congressional hearings on the act indicate that it was drafted in six weeks; testimony of Sargent Shriver does not deny that it was put together in a hurry. A consultant serving on the task force that drew up the Economic Opportunity Act, in seeking cooperation from this author, replied to questions about the need for study: "We haven't got time to study; we have to act." The majority leadership of the House Committee on Education and Labor, when OEO legislation was reviewed and OEO's appropriation doubled in 1965, admitted that a complete study of the act was not possible—a study that had been assured the year before when the majority was pushing for quick passage of the act. 111 CONG. REC. 16872 (1965).

[34] The Job Corps duplicates in large part the Civilian Conservation Corps of the 1930s; it overlaps current measures such as the Manpower Development and Training Act, 76 Stat. 23 (1962), as amended, 42 U.S.C. §§ 2571-620 (1964), and the Vocational Educational Act of 1963, 77 Stat. 403, 20 U.S.C. §§ 15aa, bb, aaa, 35-35n (1964), which offer manpower retraining programs. The Work-Training (Neighborhood Youth Corps) program of the OEO also overlaps the same earlier acts. The College Work-Study program under OEO seems to duplicate the student loan program under National Defense Education Act §§ 201-03, 72 Stat. 1583 (1958), as amended, 20 U.S.C. §§ 421-29 (1964).

The Adult Basic Education program, the special programs to Combat Poverty in Rural Areas, Employment and Investment Incentives, and Work Experience programs duplicate in some degree programs existing before the act was passed. The inventory of programs to help people and groups in poverty, available from the federal government, released by OEO in December 1965, shows 57 separate federal programs for vocational education.

[35] Agency data are not available. This statement is based on the nature of the act and on press reports such as that in the Washington Evening Star, Dec. 23, 1965, sec. B, p. 4, reporting that of more than $600,000 granted Fairfax County under its community action program, only $20,000 was for nonadministrative expense, and in the Chicago Tribune, April 15, 1966, p. 5, reporting that 49% of federal war on poverty funds spent in Chicago is to pay salaries.

[36] See article by William F. Haddad, formerly assistant director and inspector general of OEO, Mr. Shriver and the Savage Politics of Poverty, Harper's Magazine, Dec. 1965, p. 43.

[37] The OEO enabling legislation provides that OEO is to coordinate all antipoverty efforts in the federal government. Economic Opportunity Act of 1964, § 611, 78 Stat. 532, 42 U.S.C. § 2961 (1964). Since poverty is a problem closely related to employment, race and sex discrimination, education, agriculture, depressed areas, and sickness-disability-old age, responsibility at the federal level is scattered

purposes are by definition apt to be confused;[38] and its independent life as of now seems likely to be short.[39]

Not only duplication with other federal programs but conflict with existing institutions and philosophy could lead to failure of the Economic Opportunity Act. Such conflicts are being more frequently reported publicly, ranging from views of Saul Alinsky[40] to Rutgers University consultants of the Camp Kilmer Job Corps Center.[41] Largely unreported are conflicts with existing welfare, public health, and educational agencies that are nevertheless real.

Job Corps centers, both rural and urban, give remedial education and job training in residential camps to poor youth sixteen to twenty-one in age, out of work and out of school. The average cost in fiscal 1965 for 10,000 enrollees was $8,000 per enrollee. For its second year the Job Corps plans for 30,000 and a budget request of $240 million—that is, about $8,000 per enrollee.[42] There have been reports that Job Corps enrollments are lagging; whether its training is job-related for the forty per cent of enrollees required to be in rural camps, or indeed, for the rest of its enrollees, will be tested only with employment of trainees.

There may be deeper conflict than meets the eye in severe criticism by Rutgers professors of Camp Kilmer and its business-firm job-training contractor. The criticism came close to condemning the whole concept of residential, private-industry approach. It called for central leadership from education, youth work, or welfare to replace business leadership.[43] In effect, the Camp Kilmer approach implies failure by (and, hence, conflict with) schools and welfare agencies in dealing with poor youth.

The largest of OEO programs in human development is the Neighborhood

---

throughout powerful government departments responsible to cabinet-level secretaries. To anyone familiar with organizations, it seems impossible for an independent agency head to "coordinate" policy of cabinet secretaries. As one example, OEO personnel have been reported in the press as proposing that the target for full employment, set by the Council of Economic Advisers to the President at an "interim" four per cent in 1963, now be lowered to three per cent. It is difficult to believe that, among the conflicting responsibilities of what Walter Heller called the "troika" of the old line Treasury Department, the prestigious Federal Reserve, and the influential Council, the OEO would, in fact, carry much weight.

[38] As Sargent Shriver explained on "Meet the Press," Dec. 19, 1965, the community action programs are locally directed by "some 700 or more" communities, and range from sponsoring newspapers (Ypsilanti, Mich.) to "work on beautification projects" (Providence, R.I.). As OEO says, "The door is always open for new programs with new approaches." *Community Action Programs*, I OFFICE OF ECONOMIC OPPORTUNITY, CONGRESSIONAL PRESENTATION 47, 48 (1965).

[39] In a front-page story, it was recommended by an inter-agency task force that the community action program should be transferred from OEO to the new department of Housing and Urban Development because of its deep involvement in the politics of cities. The Washington Post, Dec. 24, 1965, p. A-1.

[40] *The Professional Radical: Conversations With Saul Alinsky*, Harper's Magazine, June 1965, p. 37.

[41] N.Y. Times, Nov. 17, 1965, p. 1, col. 2.

[42] Address by George J. Vicksnins, *The War on Poverty and Federal Manpower Policies*, before the Washington chapter of the Industrial Relations Research Organization, Dec. 15, 1963, and *Community Development*, National Association for Community Development, Washington, D. C., March 1966, p. 2.

[43] *Trouble in the Job Corps—Report from a Showplace*, U.S. News & World Report, Dec. 27, 1965, p. 51.

Youth Corps (NYC), which served in its first year 278,000 teenagers at a cost of $134 million.[44] It provides part-time work in "newly created jobs in non-profit or municipal agencies." By Labor Department administrative decision, the jobs pay at the rate of $1.25 per hour. This means that some NYC youth may be receiving higher pay-rates than their parents, if parents are training under the Manpower Development and Training Act programs. The NYC programs, through the restrictiveness of work opportunities, are not immune from political abuse, inviting as they do municipal governments to hire young people in newly created jobs. Again, the existence of NYC implies failure of public schools in developing sound work habits and attitudes among poor youth.

The Work Experience program, for people on relief rolls, involved about 80,000 at a total cost of over $100 million in fiscal 1965. An example of the program is given by a million-dollar grant to Rhode Island for 1,000 men and women to receive, among other things, "training in good work habits and attitudes . . . and training through beautification activity as nurserymen, gardeners, and truckdrivers."[45] While these are valuable occupations in an increasingly service-oriented economy, it is not yet clear that, in general, training in the Work Experience program is well matched with market needs.

The VISTA (Volunteers in Service to America) program, with only about 2,100 enrollees, implies that a new corps of workers is needed to supplement the efforts of social workers, efforts that presumably fall short of the mark. However, VISTA has so far proved remarkably unsuccessful in attracting and holding volunteers, compared with initial claims.

If the above "war on poverty" programs are successful, they could lead to far-reaching changes in our traditional institutions. Buttressed by other federal manpower programs such as Manpower Development and Training, Vocational Education, and so on, the "war on poverty" programs could create a new educational and welfare concept and structure in our society. The controversy they create, even if moving in the right direction, could create formidable obstacles to OEO success.

An even greater source of conflict is title two of the Economic Opportunity Act,[46] the general Community Action Program (CAP), for here political organizations are being challenged. This is the title which, in many communities, is turning the war *on* poverty into a war *over* poverty. It is the title of the act which led Adam Clayton Powell to speak of "giant fiestas of political patronage," and which William Haddad linked with "savage" politics. To cost almost $500 million in fiscal 1966, CAP gives financial support for specific local antipoverty efforts in rural and urban

---

[44] Vicksnins, *supra* note 42.

[45] *Hearings on Supplemental Appropriation Bill, 1966 Before Subcommittees of the House Committee on Appropriations*, 89th Cong., 1st Sess., pt. 2, at 394 (1965).

[46] 78 Stat. 516, 42 U.S.C. §§ 2781-2831 (1964).

areas. What Haddad calls a "powder keg" is the provision that local programs must be "developed, conducted, and administered with maximum feasible participation of residents of the areas and members of the groups served."[47] It could mean a blank check for communities, anything from family planning to cultural enrichment field trips. It could also mean that, from the politician's viewpoint, the poor would be given not only money—as in the past—but also a voice in spending it—which, translated, in politics means power for indigenous leaders of the poor.

Title two departs from the traditional federal welfare programs by placing main responsibility on local communities for programs and by setting up a direct channel for funds from Washington to local community action groups, bypassing, if needed, local government (and political) organizations. In the view of some, CAP could evolve into a mid-twentieth century equivalent for the central government of *The Last Hurrah*, the "beer-bucket and coal-scuttle" local politics of some nineteenth-century city life. Others see CAP as challenging a source of power valuable to big-city administrations for a generation—namely, the power of doling out welfare through existing agencies.[48]

Reasons given for title two by its sponsors were the superiority of local leadership,[49] concern for the "state's rights" principle, and a desire to "unify" communities through broad local participation. Two "silent" reasons privately discussed were that the bill's drafters simply did not know what programs the war on poverty needed, and—perhaps more important—the act was designed as another layer of the Great Society's civil rights program. Because of growing distrust of established social and political institutions by increasingly vocal and powerful urban poor, particularly Negroes, such urban poor are to be the major beneficiaries, but under direct national administration leadership.

Few informed students can deny the ironic role of Negroes in the United States. European immigrants came here with the peasant's strength of family, full of hope in the land of opportunity, capable of "fading" into suburbs as language barriers fell before a new generation. The European belief that hard work could lead to fortune has been largely confirmed. Many urban Negroes, often of much longer American lineage and so more socially and politically sophisticated, feel trapped. Recognizing need for education and skills, they have been in the past frustrated by lack of opportunity and by unstable family life patterns set up purposefully earlier by the mores of slave ownership. Despite much progress in income that is closing the gaps between whites and Negroes,[50] the Negro faces the aroused expectations of mass media, on the one hand, and the realities of declining opportunities for the uneducated, on the other, all the while remaining "visible" on account of color.

[47] Haddad, *supra* note 36, at 44; §202(a)(3), 78 Stat. 516, 42 U.S.C. § 2782(a)(3) (1964).
[48] Silberman, *The Mixed-Up War on Poverty*, Fortune, Aug. 1965, p. 156.
[49] H.R. REP. No. 1458, 88th Cong., 2d Sess. 10 (1964).
[50] WATTENBERG & SCAMMON, *op. cit. supra* note 1, at 130-51.

Many of today's poor lack provision for that education, training, and environment that are needed. Central Harlem and other city school children undergo declines in measured intelligent quotient from third to sixth or eighth grades.[51] Urban renewal has often pushed urban poor into denser inner-core ghettoes.[52] Health of the poor is less robust; they are sick more and have higher infant mortality[53] and death[54] rates, suggesting preventive health care weaknesses.

Sophisticated leadership of urban poor—particularly civil rights organizations— know and protest such conditions. Equal opportunity is their main theme; relief programs of the past are considered an affront. The concept of economic opportunity has much validity, in line with the argument of this paper. Enhanced skills add to national output and income, to consumer buying power, to social and political stability—in short, to the means of reducing not only economic but also social, intellectual, and cultural poverty. This is why OEO has aroused interest and excitement.

In this context, the war *over* poverty is real and undeniable. It presses against the welfare and education status quo in cities, and thus also against city halls across the land. The U.S. Conference of Mayors noted last November that both "public and private agencies and interests are being combined and coordinated under community action program guidance"; and in view of this, the report said, ". . . the almost revolutionary potentialities of this new organizational unit become apparent."[55]

With the stakes so high, competition for CAP leadership is keen. Labor unions publish how-to-do-it pamphlets for their leaders;[56] Walter Reuther sets up a million-dollar "Citizens Crusade Against Poverty" to help involve labor. Austin Kiplinger writes that Reuther sees unions "as a vital cog in the coming power structure, with a unified voice, louder than any other, and able to run the show."[57] Part of the show may well be the powerful poor.

---

[51] Clark, *Education of the Minority Poor—The Key to the War on Poverty* (paper prepared for the Task Force on Economic Growth and Opportunity, Chamber of Commerce of the United States).

[52] See MARTIN ANDERSON, THE FEDERAL BULLDOZER ch. 4 (1964).

[53] U.S. NATIONAL CENTER FOR HEALTH STATISTICS, DEP'T OF HEALTH, EDUCATION AND WELFARE, SERIES 10, No. 4, DISABILITY DAYS, UNITED STATES: JULY 1961-JUNE 1962, at 9 (1965); U.S. DEP'T OF HEALTH, EDUCATION AND WELFARE, WELFARE ADMINISTRATION, DIVISION OF RESEARCH, CONVERGING SOCIAL TRENDS, EMERGING SOCIAL PROBLEMS, Chart 40, at 48 (1964).

[54] Handler, *Poverty No. 3 Cause of Death Here*, N.Y. Times, Oct. 10, 1964, p. 59, col. 2. The five causes of death included in the study were cardiovascular renal diseases, cancer, diabetes, pneumonia-influenza diseases, and accidents.

[55] Loftus, *Mayors Chide U.S. on Poverty Drive*, N.Y. Times, Nov. 28, 1965, p. 55. Last November's narrow re-election of Cleveland's Mayor Ralph S. Locher, who was nearly defeated by a Negro opponent, is possibly an example of what the Conference of Mayors was talking about. For months prior to the election, Locher, the OEO, civil rights groups and church organizations had been carrying on a battle over the composition of Cleveland's community action council. Until the election, the mayor had resisted demands that he increase representation of the poor. The groups that wanted more representation of the poor played active roles in the mayoralty election campaign and supported Locher's opponent, who came within 2,000 votes of defeating the incumbent mayor. Pincus, *Politics and Change in Poverty War, Interpretative Report*, The Washington Evening Star, Nov. 12, 1965, p. 2.

[56] See AFL-CIO, LABOR'S ROLE IN THE WAR ON POVERTY (pamphlet prepared by the AFL-CIO Antipoverty Office, Washington, D.C., 44 pages, undated).

[57] The Kiplinger Washington Letter, Nov. 26, 1965, p. 1.

The war over poverty creates troubles for the Johnson administration. On one side, the administration faces the angry big-city mayors, mostly Democrats; on the other, there are the civil rights groups and others whom the "establishment" frustrates. The conflict surfaced last November with a news report alleged to stem from what was said to be an intra-office Bureau of the Budget memorandum. The report claimed the administration plans to de-emphasize CAP in favor of NYC and Project Head Start. The Vice President's "informal" talks to reporters were soon in print with a similar line—hardly a coincidence in such a tightly news-disciplined presidency.[58] Carl Rowan, Negro columnist, has since reported that to move CAP to the new Department of Housing and Urban Development, Sargent Shriver may have to be replaced.[59] Such a move, with what some hear as overtones of the Johnson-Robert Kennedy power struggle, would add merit to Haddad's appellation of "savage" politics.

C. What Is the Basic Philosophy of the OEO?

The real long-run weakness of the OEO is lack of a basic philosophy. In the absence of strong intellectual underpinnings or vision of purpose, the sponsors of the Economic Opportunity Act created what Silberman aptly calls "a mixed-up war on poverty."[60] Defenders of the act and of the OEO as "pragmatic" overlook the wide gulf which separates the pragmatism of confusion from the pragmatism of hypothesis explored through scientific analysis and testing.

Many of the troubles in the war on poverty stem from its clouded vision and activist posture: Weak and distorted factual bases are too often defended instead of probed. Legislative devices such as "coordination" are substituted for strong policy direction to federal antipoverty efforts, vastly overlapping and duplicative. Existing welfare and educational institutions and concepts are naïvely attacked rather than firmly challenged on logic, quality and results. Indeed, issues which are at base substantive and analytical are exploded into political battles, rather than the desired reverse "implosion" of potential political issues into technical and substantive questions.

A meeting on December 5-8, 1965 of 286 representatives of community action and development programs—the National Association for Community Development—reflected in its resolutions concern over the conceptual shape of OEO administration as follows:

[58] As two experienced newsmen on the Washington scene later pointed out:

"The Vice President and the Budget Director are anything but bureaucratic adventurers who go off on policy tangents. High officials here just can't believe Humphrey and Schultze have crawled out on a limb without a nudge from President Johnson."

Evans & Novak, *Inside Report*, The Washington Post, Dec. 1, 1965, p. 17.

[59] Rowan, *Shriver Likely Poverty War Victim*, Washington Evening Star, Dec. 22, 1965, p. A-15.

[60] Silberman, *supra* note 48.

Judged in the light of its CAP funding actions, the OEO has not recognized the centrality to the community action effort of manpower development and employment programs.

. . . .

Attempts to carry out this [OEO coordinating] responsibility have proven especially difficult in the area of manpower development and employment programs in large part because this central planning and coordinating role is not afforded priority in federal bureaucratic practice.

. . . .

. . . greater recognition than ever should be given . . . to the realities of the current and future labor market, occupational demands, and labor force. . . . These realities include . . . a heavy concentration of hard-core unemployed young men and women without the formal or the actual qualifications for acceptance by employers.

. . . .

Almost one-half of those persons who make up the poverty population reside in rural areas and a large segment of the impoverished in urban areas have their origin in rural areas . . . . But only about 10 per cent of CAP funds have gone to rural programs.[61]

Too much of OEO efforts aim at offering people of good will a cause. John Fischer, editor of *Harper's* magazine, argues that since many of our youth lack substitutes for violence because of the comforts of modern life, we should start projects based on what William James long ago called the "moral equivalent of war." To some extent, Fischer points out, Project Head Start, VISTA, the Peace Corps, and such programs aim in this direction.[62]

One cannot help a feeling of disquiet, however, with such approaches by central government in questions affecting the lives and hopes of the poor. For one thing, the moral issue insists on turning around—are these programs aimed at doing good to the poor, or at doing good for those doing good to the poor? Next, is the issue of fighting poverty only an issue of *doing good*? If rich men in India gave all their goods to feed the poor, perhaps moral wealth would be enhanced, but certainly poverty would not be conquered. To those who argue that such programs help both helped and helpers, one can recall the haunting remark of Jane Addams: "One cannot do good to the poor; one can only hope to do good with the poor." Historically the supply of saints has always been scant.

These unhappy questions need facing, above all, because the war on poverty could conceivably only mislead, misinform, and misdirect the hopes of our most inarticulate people. What could be more regrettable an outcome of the war on poverty than to turn the stigma of "deprivation" in a loosely-defined barrage across major groups, areas, and regions? In a recent article "A Federal Study Finds Unrest Among Negroes Rising in Many Cities," the *Wall Street Journal* reports: "Federal officials who have felt the pulse now possess a closely guarded list of 'high tension' cities where

[61] NATIONAL ASSOCIATION FOR COMMUNITY DEVELOPMENT, EIGHT RESOLUTIONS PASSED AT NACD CONFERENCE (Dec. 5-8, 1965).
[62] Fischer, *Substitutes for Violence*, Harper's Magazine, Jan. 1966, p. 16, at 19, 24.

it's said the threat of violence is raised by Negro resentment over lack of jobs, inadequate schools and housing, and the attitudes of police and local officeholders."[63] Is mounting resentment and frustration, is more disrespect for law and order, either a desired or necessary result of antipoverty efforts? It would not appear so.

Lacking a clear philosophy, the war on poverty has nonetheless created a powerful rhetoric. No one who reads newspapers can escape realizing that the war on poverty has yielded tons of news releases. OEO has had more than one hundred ex-newsmen in its evaluation unit, to check complaints, while its research staff amounted to about forty. The public information staff of the war on poverty includes federal, state, and local manpower, throughout the country. The danger of powerful public information is that its output can be no better in the long run than its input. Thus, powerful rhetoric amplifies trouble with the war on poverty as much as accomplishment. It also runs the risk of demeaning its clients with the stigma of deprivation, while blotting out solid news of progress against poverty (in facts about income, jobs, and wealth) with the minutiae of OEO grants and administration.

D. Toward a Philosophy of Overcoming Poverty

The National Association for Community Development, earlier quoted, held in one of its resolutions:

> . . . we feel that the private and public institutions of America must not be led to believe that the usual market mechanisms and general fiscal and monetary policies can be expected to contribute *a direct or even an indirect* solution to these [hardcore unemployment] problems. Specific, tailor-made programs of manpower development, job development, and economic development must take up the attention and energies of employers, unions, and government in order to provide solutions and techniques congruent with the realities of the labor market today, and in the future.[64]

It is puzzling to determine who it is that contends that the market plus monetary and fiscal policy—alone—solve hard-core unemployment. It has been the National Chamber view that much unemployment in recent times is structural—that is, the result of job-upgrading not yet matched by skill-upgrading, or of other shifts in employment producing mis-matches of jobs and skills.[65] Further, businessmen have historically supported both public and private education and its expansion, as well as spending perhaps today as much as $15 billion yearly for training on-the-job.

The National Association for Community Development seems to raise a strawman issue in its premises. Signs of progress in education led *Time* magazine to write of "the education explosion." A few sentences put its essence briefly:

---

[63] Wall Street Journal, Jan. 5, 1966, p. 1.

[64] NATIONAL ASSOCIATION FOR COMMUNITY DEVELOPMENT, *op. cit. supra* note 61. (Emphasis added.)

[65] See CHAMBER OF COMMERCE OF THE UNITED STATES, UNEMPLOYMENT: THE NATURE OF THE CHALLENGE (1965).

Sixty-five years ago, when the U.S. population stood at 76 million, a thin 6% of the nation's 17-year-olds graduated from high school, and only 4% of the college-age youths were in college. Today, with the U.S. population grown by nearly 40% [*sic*], to 195 million, an impressive 71% of the 17-year-olds are getting their high school diplomas, and about 30% of the college-age population is in the classroom.[66]

The market mechanism and general fiscal and monetary policy have never alone solved human development problems in this country. They create conditions of high employment; the educational system, stimulated by a free and enterprising people bent on a better life for their families and children, has done so.

And given our great educational plant, still abuilding, why should we not ask about its quality in serving the poor? Is the issue not falsely drawn which leaps from hard-core joblessness to OEO-type programs, bypassing schools?

In seeking a philosophy of overcoming today's remediable poverty, are not probing questions needed about our concepts and practices in this great educational system? For example, might we not require schools to develop, use, and report on measures of their own productivity? We need a system of testing which would serve as a quality control for local school boards. Might public schools be subject to more competition, to improve quality for children of the poor? Why should educators not be required to produce results?

Indeed, if we are serious as a society in striving to enter the age of science—wherein results are tested formally and self-consciously—might we not also demand higher standards of accomplishment in government welfare-type programs such as OEO? Most such programs report results in numbers of cases served or in dollars spent, rather than in the achievement of specific purposes. Industry and commerce cannot survive through such primitive reporting methods.

Social innovations at once consistent with our ideals of freedom, enterprise, opportunity—and at the same time fit for the coming age of science—will require unleashing the mind of our age from depression-born manacles still evident in the war on poverty. It is hard to hear America singing tunes of negative income taxes, guaranteed incomes, or songs written by federal bureaus of economic opportunity, in such an age. A clearer theme emerges from phrases such as "the means of education shall forever be encouraged." Ours is the semantics of individual opportunity and know-how—not of individual dependency and deprivation. Those who write the new philosophy of poverty must hear America singing.

---

[66] Time, Oct. 15, 1965, p. 60.

MISPLACED EMPHASES IN WARS ON POVERTY

The current preoccupation with poverty and the construction of policies to alleviate it is only a recent link in a long historical chain. The beginning is shrouded in antiquity but it is known, staying with the Anglo-Saxon world, that in the Middle Ages there were associations of begging friars, monastic provision of food and shelter for poor wanderers, and networks of hospitals for lepers, the diseased poor, distressed women big with child, and for the infirm and impotent poor. The Church also organized private charity and the guilds operated on the principle of mutual self-help. When the medieval institutions disappeared, they were replaced by the Elizabethan Poor Law which assigned parochial responsibility for the care of the poor, and by a supplementary system of private philanthropy.

The condition of life of the people in this country was so commonly bad in its early years that not much explicit attention was given to *the* poor, but the New York Society for the Prevention of Pauperism had already published its Second Annual Report in 1819, and "sanitary reformers" were active by the 1840s. Many of the public policies now being executed under the descriptive euphemism "economic opportunity programs" have antecedents that are old in American experience.

The poor are defined in terms of the quantity of real goods and services they consume, relative to some standard. This standard for distinguishing the poor from others in society has been constructed in a number of different ways. Eugene Smolensky says there are two sets: those that aim to "determine the number or proportion of the population living at, or below, some insufficient welfare level (minimum decency estimates)" and those concerned with "the way in which the total available supply of goods and services is distributed between the rich and the poor (distribution estimates)."[1]

Minimum decency estimates are produced by the design of some basket of commodities and services which are considered to be the minimal requirements for "subsistence," "comfort," or "decency." The basket is then priced in the marketplace and this yields a dollar-number which can be used, by observing the incomes of all families, to differentiate the poor from others. It is such a procedure as this, employed by the Social Security Administration, that produced the numbers $3,000 for a family and $1,500 for an individual living alone (sometimes $3,130 for nonfarm

---

* A.B. 1939, George Washington University; A.M. 1948, Ph.D. 1950, Harvard University. Professor of Economics, Duke University. Contributor of articles and book reviews to professional journals.

[1] Smolensky, *The Past and Present Poor*, in TASK FORCE ON ECONOMIC GROWTH AND OPPORTUNITY, CHAMBER OF COMMERCE OF THE UNITED STATES, THE CONCEPT OF POVERTY [hereinafter cited as THE CONCEPT OF POVERTY] 36 (1965).

families of four, $2,190 for farm families of four, $1,540 for nonfarm individuals, and $1,080 for farm individuals) that are used in current discussion to define the margin of poverty.

Distribution estimates of poverty can be made only if income is unequally distributed. They may define the poor as those in the lowest twenty per cent, say, of all families ranked by income, and proceed one further step to define the extent of poverty by observing the distance between the sum of the incomes of those families and the number which is twenty per cent of the incomes of all families. Victor Fuchs offers a variant of the same set. He defines the poor as those families with incomes less than one half of that of the median family.[2]

The standard that is used will determine the number of the poor. Fuchs' procedure says that poor families were a constant one-fifth fraction of all families in all years 1947 through 1960, while the $3,000 standard (adjusted for differences in prices of each year from those of 1959) says that the poor were thirty-four per cent of all families in 1947 and twenty-two per cent of them in 1960. It is significant that one measure showed the quantity of poverty to be stable over time and the other showed it to shrink.[3]

It can be seen that some distribution estimates will say there is poverty even if we are *all* as rich as Croesus, and others will say it if we are all as rich as Croesus but only if income is sufficiently unequally distributed.

The words "comfort" and "decency" in the minimum-comfort estimates have the property of temporal one-way elasticity. They always expand and never contract, even when adjusted for changes in prices. And at any given moment of time fair men will differ over the content of the appropriate minimal basket. G. J. Stigler calculated, for example, that a minimum-cost diet containing all the nutrients recommended by the National Research Council for a "moderately active man" would have cost in 1939, for a full year, about $40.[4] This was only one-third to one-half of the costs of food intended to serve the same object in the same year that were calculated by others, including statisticians and dieticians of the U.S. Department of Agriculture. The cost differences derive, of course, from differences in the composition of the baskets. It cost, in 1939, twenty-one times as much to get as much protein from chuck roast as from dried navy beans. If "decency" requires the appearance of chuck roast in the diet, the income necessary to classify a family as outside the poverty line is higher; if navy beans suffice, it is lower.

How well do the American poor live? H. P. Miller reports[5] that of families with incomes of less than $3,000 per year,

[2] Fuchs, *Toward a Theory of Poverty*, in THE CONCEPT OF POVERTY 74.
[3] *Id.* at 75.
[4] Stigler, *The Cost of Subsistence*, 27 J. FARM ECON. 311 (1945).
[5] Miller, *Major Elements of a Research Program for the Study of Poverty*, in THE CONCEPT OF POVERTY 122.

79 per cent own a television set

51 per cent own a television set and a telephone.

73 per cent own a washing machine

19 per cent own a home freezer

65 per cent have a dwelling unit that is not dilapidated and has hot running water and a toilet and a bath for their exclusive use

14 per cent bought a car last year.

The conditions of life of these poor can, with some interest, be compared with those of the London poor at the beginning of the nineteenth century:[6]

> Persons of the lowest class do not put clean sheets on their beds three times a year; . . . curtains . . . are never cleaned but suffered to continue in the same state until they fall to pieces; . . . from three to eight individuals of different ages often sleep in the same bed, there being in general one room and one bed for each family. . . . The room occupied is either a deep cellar, almost inaccessible to light, and admitting of no change of air; or a garret with a low roof and small windows, the passage of which is close, kept dark, and filled not only with bad air, but with putrid excremental effluvia from a vault at the bottom of the staircase. . . . Some unsavoury victuals are from time to time cooked. . . . The apartments are clogged . . . [and] favour the accumulation of heterogeneous filth.

Dr. Southwood Smith wrote of the neighborhoods of habitation of the London poor in 1839:[7]

> While systematic efforts on a large scale have been made to widen the streets, to remove obstructions to the circulation of free currents of air, to extend and perfect the drainage and sewerage, and to prevent the accumulation of putrefying vegetable and animal substances in the places in which the wealthier classes reside, nothing whatever has been done to improve the condition of the districts inhabited by the poor. . . . Such is the filthy, close and crowded state of the houses, and the poisonous condition of the localities . . . from the total want of drainage, and the masses of putrefying matter of all sorts which are allowed to remain and accumulate indefinitely . . . . In these pestilential places the industrious poor are obliged to take up their abode; they have no choice. . . . The present returns . . . show that out of 77,000 persons (in- and out-door paupers) 14,000 have been attacked with fever . . . and that nearly 1,300 have died.

Other reports of the period were said to show that the slums of London "were in no way exceptional; they were indeed surpassed in horror by the courts of Glasgow, the cellar dwellings of Manchester, and the common lodging houses of Birmingham."[8] Rowntree's investigators found, in the late 1930s in York, slum housing of which the following is not unrepresentative:[9]

---

[6] ROBERT WILLAN, REPORTS ON THE DISEASES IN LONDON 255 (1801), quoted in M. DOROTHY GEORGE, LONDON LIFE IN THE EIGHTEENTH CENTURY 86 (1951).

[7] SIR JOHN SIMON, ENGLISH SANITARY INSTITUTIONS 183-84 (1839), quoted in GILBERT SLATER, POVERTY AND THE STATE 108 (1930).

[8] SLATER, *op. cit. supra* note 7, at 110.

[9] B. SEEBOHM ROWNTREE, POVERTY AND PROGRESS 253 (1941).

The house (occupied by a family of four) shares a common yard with ten other houses. It shares a w.c. with another house and a water tap with two others. There is no water or sink in the house. The house is verminous.... Much of the brickwork is perished. The roof is sagged and defective. The kitchen floor has sunk and is broken.... The plaster has perished owing to ground dampness. The woodwork is ill-fitting and rotted. The pantry has no external light or ventilation.

It is clear that the poor were once more easily identified than now. The discussion in the recent literature over the proper definition of poverty is perhaps evidence that tortured processes must be resorted to if people who are really quite affluent, even in a relatively short historical context, are to be called "poor." Assume, however, that definitions that have come to be accepted in political discourse are sensible. How many poor are there and what are their qualities?[10]

PERSONS IN POVERTY STATUS IN 1963 (MILLIONS)

Type of unit	Total U.S. Population	Below the Poverty Level	
		Number	Percent
Total number of persons	187.2	34.6	18
Farm	12.6	3.2	25
Nonfarm	174.6	31.4	18
Unrelated individuals	11.2	4.9	44
Members of family units	176.0	29.7	17
Children under 18	68.8	15.0	22

About thirty million people in 7.2 million families and almost five million unrelated individuals—in all, 34.6 million persons, or eighteen per cent of the whole population of the country—were in a state of poverty in 1963.[11] If one examines the characteristics of poor families, it is found that the incidence of poverty falls especially heavily upon farm families, nonwhite families, families whose head is either relatively young or relatively old, families with a female head, families with large numbers of children, families without income-earners, and families whose head was unskilled or who did not work during the year or worked only part time.[12] Many of these are not simply accidentally correlative characteristics but are rather causally associated with low income. On the average, farmers, women, young people and old, unskilled workers, the unemployed and part time workers are low-income earners. They are, therefore, more likely to be found among the poor than others. It follows that whatever tends to increase the incidence of these

[10] The numbers that follow are taken or derived from Orshansky, Counting the Poor, Soc. Sec. Bull., Jan. 1965, p. 3.

[11] The President reported in January 1966 that the quantity of poverty, measured in numbers of poor people, had been reduced to 17 per cent of the whole population or 32 million persons. N.Y. Times, Jan. 28, 1966, p. 14, col. 3.

[12] "Heavy incidence" does not necessarily mean that families with the indicated characteristics are a large fraction of all poor families, but rather that of all families with these characteristics, a large fraction of them is poor.

characteristics in the whole population will also tend to enlarge the number of the poor. Similarly, whatever tends to cause low income to be associated with these characteristics will also tend to enlarge the number of the poor.

An examination of various facets of public policy in the United States will show that some fraction of poverty which we encounter among the people is, in fact, produced by government. Those who promote these policies do not, of course, intend nor desire that they shall have these effects; indeed, some of them are thought to promote progress and ameliorate poverty. Their enactment and execution is a tribute to the power in the world of the naïve cliché. Only some of these poverty-producing policies will be discussed.

1. The Fair Labor Standards Act of 1938[13] establishes a legal minimum hourly wage for those employed in a large sector of the economy. This minimum is probably irrelevant for most workers who, even in the absence of the law, would be paid more than the law requires. It is not irrelevant, however, for those in the lowest-skill classes. The law requires that wages paid in some unskilled occupations be higher than the level at which the market would set them. The consequence is that a smaller number of workers is employed in those occupations than would be if there were no minimum wage law, because firms seeking lowest-cost resource combinations are given an incentive to use substitutes for now more expensive unskilled labor. Workers who would have been employed in those occupations but who are kept from them by the law's higher-wage standards are either forced into unemployment or enter occupations that are not covered by the law. In these occupations they are worse off than they would have been (it is for them a second-best option which they take only because the law shuts off preferred opportunities) and, in addition, larger numbers entering these occupations—where the wage paid is already less than the legal minimum—depress wages there for all, including incumbents in the occupations.[14]

2. The National Labor Relations Act[15] establishes procedures to determine whether workers in a "bargaining unit" desire to be represented by a trade union and, if their decision is affirmative, requires that firms negotiate with the relevant union the terms of employment. The act promotes trade unionism. If a union is effective (*i.e.*, if it is not innocuous), the rate of wages in the occupations to which it has reference will be higher than the rate that would have prevailed in the absence of unionism. This is equivalent to saying, definitionally, that the union has and exercises monopoly power. Such a higher wage rate has the same adverse employment consequences and the same depressant effects upon wages paid in other occupations as do minimum wage laws. Some workers (those who *are* employed at the higher rates) are privileged at the cost of other workers. Unions often ad-

---

[13] 51 Stat. 1060, as amended, 29 U.S.C. §§ 201-19 (1964).

[14] Stigler, *The Economics of Minimum Wage Legislation*, 36 AM. ECON. REV. 358 (1946).

[15] 49 Stat. 449 (1935), as amended, 29 U.S.C. §§ 151-68 (1964).

minister rationing instruments or rules to distribute the smaller quantity of employment offered among workers who aspire to them. Sometimes the rationing rule implies an equal sharing of adversity and this finds expression in the form of a short work week for all. Short work weeks have, of course, the outcome that output is diminished and smaller output means more poverty. Sometimes the rule involves unequal sharing of adversity, as when some are excluded entirely. This may take the form of excluding some from the union and, therefore, excluding them from occupations for which entry into the union is a condition for entry into the occupation. When this tactic is employed, not infrequently it is Negroes who are excluded. Or the rationing rule may be some seniority system which distributes privilege in proportion to longevity of service with the firm. Here, too, it is Negroes, who are the late entrants into the lower ranks of an occupation, who are disadvantaged.

3. Farming in the United States is a declining occupation, measured by the relative numbers of persons employed in it. The outmigration from farming is responsive to superior earnings in other sectors, and the relatively low earnings in agriculture can be taken as a proxy for relatively low productivity of employment in agriculture. Output for the economy as a whole would be larger if fewer persons were employed in agriculture and more in other sectors. At least since the middle of the 1930s, public policy has subsidized farmers at the expense of the rest of the community and this has had the effect of diminishing the rate of outmigration from agriculture. Whatever induces people to remain in agriculture will have adverse output consequences and, thus, will tend to enlarge the quantity of poverty.

4. The Social Security Act[16] requires most employed persons to purchase an annuity which is paid to them after they have reached a qualifying age but only if they substantially retire from employment. The annuity is withheld from those older persons who continue to work. The specific form of the rule is that the annuity will not be paid to those whose earnings from employment exceed a specified number of dollars in a year. The law essentially prescribes a lifetime distribution of expenditures of earnings which is different from the distribution that would be preferred by some people. In different words, the law requires the deferment of consumption from earlier to later years of life. On equity grounds, it is questionable whether deferred income earned by rendering services when young should be denied older persons, so long as they continue to work. It can be sensibly argued that it is theirs by right and they should have it. But set this aside. It is surely correct that the present policy creates an incentive for retirement. Some older persons who would be otherwise disposed to continue to work are induced by the law to stop. If they do not stop, they may not have their annuity benefit. The output of the whole economy is, therefore, less by some magnitude; the smaller the output, the larger the quantity of poverty. And the policy precisely induces older people to earn less. The act generates poverty among the aged.

---

[16] 49 Stat. 620 (1935), as amended (codified in scattered sections of 42 U.S.C.)).

5. The regulation of some industries by government inhibits entry into these industries. Artful defenses for these policies are constructed in terms of the public interest, but it is clear that the result and sometimes the object of this exercise is to cartelize the relevant industry. The consequence is that some industries are too small and, therefore, that others are too large, in terms of some optimal allocation of resources among industries. The final effect is that output is less and poverty deeper.

6. Public monetary and fiscal policy had generated almost continuous inflation; that is to say, the general level of prices has almost continuously risen. Such a policy disadvantages fixed-income earners, among them receivers of annuity payments and holders of relatively risk-free securities. Such persons are, of course, especially the aged, and a policy of inflation tends to impoverish them.

7. A policy of equal-pay-for-equal-work for men and women is common among the states. Such a policy makes it less attractive for firms to employ women rather than men. It is a policy that favors men over women by assuring men that women will offer them less competition for employment and that damages women by driving them to unemployment or to second-best employment options. Women who are heads of families are made worse off by it.

8. The incidence of poverty rises with rising numbers of children in the family. Whatever encourages parents to produce more offspring will produce more poverty. While the magnitude of the effect may not be large, the policy of granting exemption from income for children when computing tax liability will tend in that direction.

9. The amount of poverty in a community is a function of the quantity of goods and services it produces in some time period and of the distribution of income. Given the distribution, the more that is produced the less poverty there will be. Whatever creates production disincentives will increase the number of the poor. A system which distributes rewards in proportion to knowledge, effort, and skill will tend to cause output to be larger; some other system will diminish the quantity of knowledge assimilated, effort exerted, and skill learned and will have adverse effects upon output. Some welfare payments to the poor and some unemployment benefits, by providing substitute "earnings" for those that would be yielded by work, diminish incentives to work and cause output to be smaller. The welfare payments and benefits need not be as large as prospective earnings from work to have these disincentive effects, since leisure is a preferred good that is incorporated in the calculus of decision. Unemployment benefits received under some insurance system are especially vulnerable in this respect since the failure to work is precisely a condition for their payment. They are significantly different from savings from prior earnings by individuals to "tide them over" periods of unemployment. These are assets which the individual has whether he works or not; in an insurance scheme, he is given the benefits only if he does not work. Thus the policy encourages less work by making leisure less costly.

10. The earnings of skilled workers are higher than those of the unskilled. These higher earnings are, in part, payment for the investment of time, effort and money in the acquisition of the skill. Given the cost of acquiring skill, the larger is the difference in earnings at the two levels of skill, the larger is the incentive to make the investment, and the larger is the number who make this investment. Public policy makes welfare payments to the poor. We may think of the whole receipts of the skilled as being the wage payments made to them for the services they render; they receive no welfare payments because their wage earnings are high enough to disqualify them. The whole receipts of the unskilled, however, are the sum of their lower wage earnings *and* their welfare receipts. The welfare payments for which only the poor (say the unskilled) qualify serve to diminish the size of the difference between the earnings of the skilled and the unskilled and reduce the incentive to invest in the learning of skill. In a sense, the system pays people to refrain from investing in themselves. The mean level of skill in the whole population is less and, therefore, so is the output of the economy. The policy has poverty-generating effects.

11. Some of the poor are in declining regions. They may live in the vicinity of cutover forests or exhausted coal mines, for example. The population of these regions may rise while opportunity in them falls; or opportunity may rise at a slower rate than does population. There are too many people there, from the vantage point of income earned. If outmigration from such regions is large and rapid enough, those remaining need not endure poverty and those who go are more productive and have higher earnings than if they had stayed. If prospective outmigrants are induced to stay, the condition of regional poverty is reinforced and the country as a whole is made poorer. There are, of course, public policies to make "welfare" payments to residents of these distressed regions which they receive only if they remain there. This tends to perpetuate poverty by diminishing the magnitude of corrective action that goes to its root cause.

12. A significant fraction of poor families are those without a male head. It is not clear that the law has worked well to compel fathers to provide for the care and maintenance of their children, when they are disposed to abandon them.

This is not, of course, a complete catalogue. It is, however, a sample that is sufficiently large to suggest that some not insignificant fraction of the poverty which is experienced in this country is produced by governments executing policies whose consequences have perhaps not been fully foreseen. At least marginal behavior is responsive to incentives, both positive and negative. People will attempt to capture gains and to escape costs. Policy-makers seem always to ignore the fact that policies have consequences, or they forecast the future falsely because some other object than utility-maximization is assumed to explain behavior.

The war on poverty which, it is said, is now being waged in the United States is a melange authorized by the Economic Opportunity Act of 1964[17] and administered by the Office of Economic Opportunity. For the most part, the Office of Economic Opportunity acts as though it were a granting endowment or a contractor rather than executing programs itself. The most important programs, measured by cost, are Community Action, Job Corps, Neighborhood Youth Corps, Work Experience, College Work Study, Small Business and Rural Loans, and Literacy.

The condition of being poor is the same as receiving relatively low income. If one reviews the circumstances that cause income to be low, it is clear that there are many causes that are left apparently untouched by the Office of Economic Opportunity. Who are the low-income receivers? They include the sick, the disabled and infirm, the aged, the young, families abandoned by fathers, the self-employed in declining industries, those who suffer racial disabilities, those without skill, and families with many children.

There are two roads to raising the incomes of people—make transfer payments to them, as when they receive "gifts"; and cause them to earn more, either by working more or by becoming more productive. Becoming more productive can be achieved either by removing to a more productive occupation (given skills possessed) or by acquiring additional skills.

There are some among the poor whose condition cannot be improved greatly except by making transfer payments to them. It cannot be said with certainty that the war on poverty excludes these classes because it is not clear what the "community action programs" are and some of them could, possibly, make payments in kind to members of these classes. Other public programs, not encompassed by the Economic Opportunity Act, do make payments to certain of them.

But it seems in general to be true that many of the causes of low income lie outside the programs authorized by the act or are touched by them only tangentially. The war on poverty is not essentially a health program to reduce the incidence of morbidity or the mean duration of illness; it does not offer incentives for people to leave declining occupations, industries, and regions; it does not attempt to prolong the duration of *working* life; it does very little to reduce family size, family abandonment, or the disabilities that attach to race. Indeed, in some respects, the act fosters poverty. When the act provides for subsidies to farmers (low-interest rural loans) it reduces the incentive to leave agriculture; when it provides housing, sanitation, and child care services to migrant workers, it reduces the incentive to take regular employment (and incidentally cheapens the cost of labor to employers of migrant labor); when it offers services to young children, it diminishes their cost and reduces the incentive to parents to have more care.

A large part of the funds appropriated for the war on poverty are said to be

---

[17] 78 Stat. 508, 42 U.S.C. §§ 2701-981 (1964).

devoted to the promotion of education of young people. The literature of the OEO offers these programmatic descriptions:[18]

> *The Job Corps*: A program of remedial education and job training for young men and women.
> *The Neighborhood Youth Corps*: . . . provides full- or part-time work experience and training for youths . . . enabling them to stay in or return to school, or increase their employability.
> *College Work Study*: . . . provides part-time employment of college and university students from low-income families.

Because this cohort of programs is quantitatively so important, it is deserving of special critical attention. These programs seem to be intended to treat the problems of school dropouts, actual or prospective, by subsidizing continued schooling or re-entry into school of those who have already withdrawn, and we shall discuss these programs in this light.[19]

Students enrolled in school are engaged in one or another of two distinct economic activities, or some combination of them in variant proportions. They may be consuming; that is to say, deriving utility (as a first approximation, satisfaction) from the act of learning. And they may be investing; that is to say, learning some "skill," either general or specific, that will cause their output (and earnings) to be higher in the future than they would then be, if they had not been enrolled in school. Both the consumption and the investment gains of schooling are acquired at what economists call an opportunity cost. Something is given up or sacrificed in exchange for them. The opportunity cost of schooling is the output (earnings) foregone. If the student had not been enrolled at school, he could, in principle, have let his services out to hire and they could have been used to produce goods and services. This would have produced income for him. A student loses this income and the community loses the output he would have produced. If the student had dropped out of school and worked instead, he could have converted the income he would then have earned to goods and services produced by others. These would have produced utility for him.

With respect to the current consumption calculus, every student, by choosing to study rather than work, decides, at the least implicitly, that the bundle of utilities yielded to him by consuming education as well as other things is larger than some alternative bundle which included the consumption of less (including zero) educa-

---

[18] I OFFICE OF ECONOMIC OPPORTUNITY, CONGRESSIONAL PRESENTATION 13, 23, 29 (1965).

[19] Jobs Corps and Work Experience on-the-job training will be referred to, for convenience, as "schooling"; this is consistent with their announced object. Subsidizing the continued enrollment of students (prospective dropouts) in formal schools is the same in principle as subsidizing the re-enrollment of dropouts. They will be collapsed, for simplicity of exposition, to the single cases of subsidizing the re-enrollment of those already withdrawn. Some of the discussion that follows was suggested by Eugene Smolensky in "Investment in the Education of the Poor: A Pessimistic Report," a paper read at the meetings of the American Economic Association in December 1965. He is not responsible for what follows.

tion and more of other things. With respect to the lifetime individual consumption calculus, every student decides that the lifetime bundle of utilities he will consume is sufficiently larger, if he enrolls at school than if he does not, to warrant his sacrificing some utility in the present, by consuming less, for the sake of having more of it in the future. The solution to this problem is complicated by the influence of a time preference variable. There is less uncertainty in the present than in the future and the quantum of uncertainty is a function of time, so that the farther one peers into the future, the more uncertainly is it seen. Partly for this reason, and for others as well, the present is preferred to the future. If one is asked, "Shall I give you $100 now or $200 x years from now or 300 $2x$ years from now?," the response will vary among individuals, some of whom have a stronger preference for the present over the future than others and, correspondingly, have a stronger preference than others for the near future over the distant future. All individual time preferences are aggregated by the market and they are expressed by a market rate of discount.

The payment of a subsistence scholarship to school dropouts who re-enroll in school changes the magnitudes of the variables that would otherwise govern for each individual the choice for which he opts between the two alternatives: enroll in school or work. The subsistence payments diminish the opportunity costs of schooling and the extent to which they are diminished depends upon the size of those payments. If, for illustration, they are as large as his earnings would have been, if he had worked, they reduce his opportunity cost to zero. He would then be permitted to consume in the present as much of goods and services other than education as he would have consumed if he had sold his labor services during the hours of school and, *as well*, to secure the consumption utilities of schooling and the enlarged future income that the schooling will produce for him. He has the best of all possible worlds. If the subsistence payments are less than this, but still some positive number, the magnitude of the effect will be less, but the direction will be the same. Each additional increment in the size of the subsistence payment above zero can be expected to cause some additional persons to withdraw from the labor market and to enroll in school.

Does a policy of granting subsistence scholarships to induce school dropouts to re-enroll in school serve the social purpose? Every individual makes a large number of sequential decisions that will serve his own purposes in selecting among alternative bundles of consumption goods confronting him and in distributing his consumption over his lifetime. His behavior is responsive to a set of incentives, which may be positive or negative, and which are in the nature of signals to him. One set of these signals takes the form of market prices. If some good becomes more costly to make, or if it requires a resource for its making which has become more scarce, its price will rise and this is a signal to some to forego its consumption. For if the decision were made to consume it, more of other things that could be purchased for the same amount of money would be foregone. Thus, the signaling system suggests that what becomes more costly or scarce should be economized more.

In the same way, market prices signal what a student at the margin of deciding whether to continue in school or drop out should do. The cost of continued schooling for a high school student is something like the product of the price paid for the services of relatively unskilled labor and the magnitude of the probability that, if the student should offer his services as an unskilled worker, he will be employed at all in that capacity.

When the wages of unskilled labor are high, relative to those of skilled labor, and when the rate of unemployment among young people is low, the cost of continued schooling is relatively high and some young people are signaled to drop out. Relatively high unskilled wages is the same as relatively low skilled-worker wages; relatively low skilled-worker wages means that the payoff to the acquisition of skills (as from schooling) is low. Thus when the cost of schooling is high, the expected gain from schooling is low. The signal on the gain side of the ledger also says "drop out." Oppositely, when the wages of unskilled labor are a smaller fraction of those of skilled labor and when the rate of unemployment among the young is high, the cost of schooling is relatively low and the signal is "continue in school." This is reinforced by the signal with respect to the gain component of the calculus; skilled-worker wages are now relatively high; it pays some to stay in school who would otherwise have withdrawn. These signals are not randomly generated. They express, through market aggregation processes, the social will.

We can assume, a priori, that no community desires that all of its members spend all of their days for the whole of their lives at school in every generation, for if it did, in that society nothing would be produced and, therefore, nothing would be consumed other than the commodity, educational services. Similarly, we would not expect to find any communities that were unwilling in any circumstances to have any of its members at school for any days at all, for such a community would be willing to sacrifice nothing in the present for the sake of more in the future, however small the current sacrifice and however large the future gain from the formation of human capital. All communities can be expected to fall somewhere on the continuum between the polar extremes. This is equivalent to saying that all communities desire that some fraction of its population be enrolled at school. The fraction that corresponds to the social will can be called the optimal fraction. The optimal fraction will vary from time to time in any society. The signaling system that is the instrument for causing the optimal fraction to occur in the world is the cost of continued schooling and changes in that cost over time and the payoff to continued schooling and changes in that payoff over time.

We observe that the wages of unskilled workers are relatively high in good years and relatively low in bad years. We observe also that the rate of unemployment among the young is low in good years and high in bad years. We would expect, therefore, that there are more school dropouts in good years and fewer dropouts in bad years and this is exactly consistent with what the society has signaled, through the market, that it desires to occur. If, now, in the good years of large-scale withdrawal from school, public policy pays dropouts to return to school, it frustrates the achievement of the optimal solution to the problem of finding that fraction of the population to be enrolled in school which the community desires. It causes the community to consume more educational services currently than it desires and less of other things; and it causes the community to sacrifice more in the present than it desires so that it will have more in the future than it desires, given the cost.

It may be argued that the social purpose is being given utterance through politically collectivized processes of modifying market signals but this is defensible only if the market does not function efficiently to express the whole of this purpose in the first instance. Nowhere in the literature that generated the scholarships-for-dropouts policy is such a defense to be seen. What seems more likely is that the public policy-makers operated from simplistic and naïve premises: education is a good thing; ergo, the more of it the better. It may be, of course, that a dropout was misinformed; he believed that unskilled-worker wages were higher than he later found them to be, or skilled-worker wages lower, or he believed he would be employed and was not. But experience teaches and, having once assimilated the information that he was mistaken, one would expect him to return to school. If one wants to cheapen these costs, then it would seem appropriate to establish some instrument to disseminate information that would diminish the probability of error. But this is immensely different in its effects from subsidizing re-enrollment. The production of information tends to produce phenomena that coincide with community goals; re-enrollment subsidies tend to obstruct the occurrence of this coincidence.

Antipoverty policy perhaps has its genesis in estimates that it can be turned to political capital because the lower-income classes are finding new and more aggressive instruments of expression and in feelings of guilt and compassion of the middle classes. The object of this critical exercise has been to suggest to the latter that Pavlovian responses to word signals is a poor substitute for the use of rational intelligence. The words "war on poverty" are no exception to this rule.

POVERTY'S CHALLENGE TO THE STATES

> Anticipate charity by preventing poverty; assist the reduced fellow-man . . .
> by teaching him a trade or putting him in the way of business, so that he may earn
> an honest livelihood, and not be forced to the dreadful alternative of holding out his
> hand to charity.
>
> —MAIMONIDES

I

POVERTY AND THE AMERICAN SYSTEM OF GOVERNMENT

The American Society has begun a significant shift in its philosophy toward "the reduced fellow-man." In the affluent sixties, the faces of poverty haunt our consciences as we discover its many moods and sources. Poverty can be the family suddenly fatherless, the handicapped individual with insufficient means to relieve his suffering, the child born into life without family, the blue-collar worker pushed out by the machine, the Negro struggling in a white man's world, the marginal farmer in an increasingly urban America, the coal miner in the age of nuclear energy, and the ill-educated in a time which increasingly demands education.

Early America left the treatment of the poor to private charity and scattered government aid and activity. The aid was usually dispensed with a charity philosophy and the most common method of treatment was the poorhouse or other specialized institutions which segregated the extreme cases from society's view. Some communities drove the poor from the city's gates. As time passed, political organizations in the large cities developed welfare programs suited to their own purposes more than to the poor. Later some cities and states developed specialized programs to aid the most appealing groups of the poverty-stricken—the abandoned mothers, the elderly, and the blind.

The depression of the 1930s focused the nation's attention on the poverty question as America realized that private and local and state governmental efforts were inadequate. The New Deal stimulated new federal programs which embodied a "work-for-relief" principle and direct support for certain categories of our poor—such as those over sixty-five, the needy blind, and dependent children. The challenge to the whole American system caused a re-evaluation of the role of government and the development of the concept of government as the guardian of the economy. The federal government instituted safeguards for the investor, the banks, the housing industry; it provided loans, regulated the monopolies, assured the compensation of the unemployed, and stimulated the economy by conscious government policy.

* A.B. 1939, LL.B. 1946, University of North Carolina. Governor of North Carolina, 1961-65; currently heading "A Study of American States" at Duke University under grants from the Ford Foundation and the Carnegie Corporation. Author, BUT WHAT ABOUT THE PEOPLE? (1966).

Recovery was the byword, but there was a strong feeling that the government should never let a depression happen again.

Several states began serious efforts at developing their industrial base through campaigns to attract new industry into the states. But within the states the areas of economic need could not compete for industry with the areas where life was better, and the neglect continued.

A. Where We Are

How far has America come? It is difficult to measure the success of America's efforts against poverty in individual terms, but some facts can be stated. In 1962, the Conference on Economic Progress issued a detailed analysis on the condition of poverty as of 1960 in the United States. Using the annual income guidelines to measure poverty—that is, under $4,000 for families and under $2,000 for unattached individuals—the Conference found that over one-fifth of the nation's population was living in poverty. While this number had been decreasing at a rate of 2.2 per cent per year between 1929 and 1960, there still were in 1960 nearly 37 million impoverished Americans—one-third of them children.

But these gross figures paint only a partial picture. In the last few years it has become increasingly apparent that entire segments of our society have been unable to elevate themselves above a poverty situation. There are those living in the Appalachias and the Ozarks, in the stifling ghettoes of New York, Chicago, and Los Angeles, and those who must hang tenaciously to the crop-weary lands which can no longer produce a living wage. All of these and more have been bypassed and left behind by our society. These are not cases. They are people—our people.

And what is the cost to us? We can measure the cost of lost productivity, of lost purchasing power, and of the relief rolls. But how do we measure the cost of a crushed spirit or a dead dream or a long-forgotten hope? What is the incalculable cost to us as a people when the children of poverty become the parents of poverty and begin the cycle anew?

The evidence seems to indicate that our governmental system has coped with only part of the poverty problem. In the past few decades, it has provided programs which maintained many people at or below a minimum subsistence level—while not reaching others at all.

With all of the effort in the New Deal and since, with all of the postwar economic boom in this country, still one-fifth of the American people do not earn enough to feed, clothe, and house themselves. Why? Why haven't we done the job by now? Where have we failed?

B. The Myths That Block Us

There are many answers, but at least part of the answer lies in a number of myths that all of us have shared about our economy, our society, and ourselves.

The first is the explicit faith that so many of us have held that our economic system will overcome, in the long run, most of the obstacles facing our society. By developing our economy fully, and using the resources of the government wisely, we believed that unemployment would fall, incomes would rise, and poverty thereby would automatically be reduced. While there is evidence that economic development has much to do with helping some of the poor, there is also ample evidence that an increase in economic growth does not touch most of the poor. Increased opportunities do not help those who are unable to take advantage of them. There are some obstacles which our economic system alone will not overcome.

The second myth is the myth of Horatio Alger—that if a person has the energy and the will to work, he will be able to make his way. In a sense, this means that poverty and unemployment are a result of choice, not a condition of society—a manifestation of laziness, not economic isolation. The depression jolted this belief when millions of Americans, who were left jobless through no fault of their own, were also powerless to help themselves at all. The economy had let them down and so had the American way of life. Government assumed the role of the protector—of the old, the very young, the unemployed. But even with Social Security, Aid-to-Dependent Children, Unemployment Compensation, and others, the feeling has remained that a bit of Horatio Alger exists in us all, if each of us only will work hard to succeed.

A third myth which has held back action against poverty is the status quo myth—that things are basically fine, we have the tools to conquer the problems we face, and really only need to change or adjust some minor mechanism of government to reach those few people who need help. Therefore, governmental agencies and their programs, operating for years, do not need changing or redirection but just need more money and more people to work for them. Consequently, when government acts, it usually turns to more of the same, solidifying the old structure and programs rather than seeking possible new solutions to the problems of a changing society. And this old structure has given birth to new problems: a housing program which eats up suburban land while the inner city slowly crumbles and decays; a welfare program which does not give enough to get by nor provide a path out; an agricultural program which thrusts vast changes on our farm population while failing to prepare the farmer for his withdrawal to the cities; and an educational system keyed to college and middle-class goals, leaving many behind who do not share those goals. And this does not exhaust the examples.

Government must be flexible, alert to change, coordinated and personal. The old textbook three-layered system of government with state, local, and federal governments clearly assigned their tasks has already given way to a compartmentalized approach based on government responsibilities. Communication up and down the line is much better than communication between activities—a county welfare agent talks easily and often to his superiors at the state and federal level but rarely to the county health agent. Today problems span the responsibilities of government and yet administrators and the departments see these problems in their own terms. The poverty problem is seen as a problem of welfare by welfare departments, as a problem of education by education departments, as a problem of health by health departments, and so on. While elected officials like the governor are held responsible for carrying out these programs, in fact they have little or no control over these segmented activities.

What is needed is a multi-pronged, coordinated attack rather than an attack by parts of government on parts of problems. Michael Harrington, America's foremost analyst of the poverty program, has said:[1]

> In case after case, it has been documented that one cannot deal with the various components of poverty in isolation, changing this or that condition but leaving the basic structure intact. Consequently, a campaign against the misery of the poor should be comprehensive. It should think, not in terms of this or that aspect of poverty, but along the lines of establishing new communities, or substituting a human environment for the inhuman that now exists.

The fourth myth which has blocked effective action against poverty revolves around the ready tendency of Americans to believe that money will solve all our problems. Too often the initial governmental action has been a reflex to a symptom rather than a thoughtful response to the actual problem. Too little pre-planning goes into our governmental actions, and too often we find ourselves investigating a crisis rather than anticipating it. Examples abound in our history, but none seems as potent as the fact that there are still over one-fifth of our citizens living in poverty, despite all the programs and economic development we have achieved in the last three decades.

But a government alert to change is not enough. It must be responsive to the voices of those who need its help. When it is not representative, it cannot listen—and when it cannot listen, it ceases to be responsive. Increasing malapportionment of legislative bodies and the disfranchisement of segments of our population has undoubtedly had the effect of reducing or restricting the voice of the poor. Thus, we are just beginning to heed the cry for a fair share of tomorrow's blessings.

For all of these reasons and more, our governmental system has been doing only a partial job on the problem of the impoverished American. No level of government is exempt from this indictment. The federal government, active in the general field of welfare for several decades, chose the year 1964 to declare war on poverty. The states, active in this area for a longer period, have a spotty record of achievement—for only a few have exerted any great effort or shown much initiative in this problem, except recently in response to the new federal program. Generally, the problem has fallen to the local community, with its limited resources and abilities. Local response has been equally uneven: extending from the Community Chest approach to the "100 Neediest Cases Fund" each Christmas; from the private efforts of the neighbor-

---

[1] MICHAEL HARRINGTON, THE OTHER AMERICA: POVERTY IN THE UNITED STATES 168 (1963).

hood church to the overtaxed, understaffed and underfinanced local welfare agency.

But no level of government has done enough, for massive problems demand massive support.

II

FORMULA FOR THE FUTURE: COMMUNITY ACTION AND INNOVATION

The new approach to the battle against poverty had to be unique. It needed to be able to overcome the shortcomings of prior efforts while at the same time using the very positive parts of existing programs. It needed to involve all parts of the community and not segments. The whole problem needed to be tackled and not just parts of it. The new technique would be community action, the keystone of a broad-based antipoverty effort, and innovation preserving the best of the old with the promise of the new.

By innovation in approach I do not mean a whole new series of programs suddenly pressed into service. This is not what innovation means. Innovation in the anti-poverty program takes the best of the broad variety of programs now available, combines it with new ideas to provide the total effort with flexibility to fit all the problems. The approach might be likened to a supermarket, with a varied display of programs from which to choose, along with the ingredients to mold a whole new program. The particular mix desired and developed depends on the definition of poverty brought to the market by the community. This allows for initiative, innovation, and diversity in the development of programs rather than preconceived and pre-structured answers to a dynamic and changeable problem.

In addition, the new definition of community action stresses an inclusive definition of community—including representation from the poor themselves. This means that a new umbrella organization would be created to cut across all the vertical strands of government, such as welfare, health, education, and so forth, and to join with those in the non-governmental sphere, such as churches, private philanthropic agencies, and a cross section of the citizenry. This community action organization was to look into the community mirror and devise its own answer. Not only did this broad-based organization force some of the rigid professional boundaries to be breached and questioned, but it also allowed the entrance into the market of many of those previously excluded. In this way, new voices would become part of the process. That this was a revolution is obvious—but a revolution within a structure established to encourage revolution.

We in North Carolina recognized these two components when we established The North Carolina Fund in the summer of 1963, with grants of $7 million from the Ford Foundation, matched by grants from Reynolds and Babcock foundations, and state and local funds. In announcing the establishment of the Fund, I said,

There are tens of thousands whose dreams will die. Some of this poverty is self-imposed and some of it is undeserved. All of it withers the spirit of children, who

neither imposed it nor deserve it. These are the children of poverty who tomorrow
will become the parents of poverty. We hope to break this cycle of poverty. That
is what The North Carolina Fund is all about.

We wanted to have the freedom to go into the communities of the state and say to
the leaders of schools, government, welfare, health, charity: "Look, let's work together; let's see if together in a few neighborhoods near here we can't break the
cycle of poverty and give these children a better chance."

We wanted the community, the entire community, first to analyze its own situation and then to come up with what it felt would alleviate the problems. We were
gratified that sixty-six of our 100 counties were represented in such self-analyses
and submitted proposals. Some proposals called for more of the same; others wanted
striking new approaches. Some proposals could best be implemented by tinkering
with the existing governmental machinery; others needed new machinery established.
When there was a pattern, maybe a statewide program was needed. When it was
unique, The North Carolina Fund would support the community in its innovation.
Unfortunately, our funds did not allow us to satisfy the tremendous response we
received, and we had to select certain proposals as pilot projects—both statewide and
community based. But all the communities were interested in a broader effort than
was being made at the time.

We already see results. The first impact was to upset the existing power structures within communities so that changes in the status quo could occur. In most
cases this amounted to radical changes in community relations and activities—but this
we did knowingly, realizing that positive results would occur when existing structures are challenged by the new.

This process of self analysis seemed to awaken the community conscience. The
important thing in my mind was that we established a vehicle by which a community approach in its broadest sense was undertaken, encouraged a new look, and
made provision for creative innovation in developing solutions.

The Economic Opportunity Act of 1964,[2] which embodies the nationwide commitment against poverty, was based on these same two components: community
action and innovation. The success or failure of the antipoverty program is in the
future, but the history of the national effort to date indicates that the existing order
is being challenged on all fronts and that communities are beginning to probe their
consciences. Critics charge mismanagement, unclear plans and goals, programs in
shambles, "politicos" using the poverty war for narrow purposes, poor communication, agencies and whole levels of governments being bypassed. Some complaints
are contradictory: too little coordination, too much coordination, no guidelines, too
many guidelines—all these and others represent the beginnings of the significant shift
we have taken in our philosophy toward the reduced fellowman in our midst.

But, regardless of objections, our governmental system is carrying this fight to

[2] 78 Stat. 508, 42 U.S.C. § 2701 (1964).

every community and every part of society in the nation, with the overwhelming commitment of the federal government serving as the stimulant. Local communities everywhere are evaluating their situations and submitting proposals to the Office of Economic Opportunity in Washington for approval and funding. The states are being asked to aid the local communities in this effort and to mobilize the states' resources to achieve the goals of the programs. And the federal government is providing the guidance and the funds for the massive effort.

III

THE ROLE OF THE STATES

The antipoverty program is less than two years old, and much is still in the definition stage. However, there appears to be a trend in development which, in the long run, may serve to reduce the potential results of the program. The trend I speak of is the unclear definition of the role of the states in the program and the fuzzy set of relationships between all the levels of the governmental system.

In many respects, the states are the key to the operation of the federal system of government. I am not arguing from the constitutional position that all other governments in our system derive their grant of authority from the states. Nor am I arguing from the political position that shows that our state political systems are the basis of the national political system. The position I am arguing from is based on an understanding of how our governmental system operates—that the states are a major partner in almost all the federal domestic programs, and are a vital resource which ought to be summoned to the front lines of the battle. Highway programs, health programs, the new recreation program, the new education programs, the welfare programs and others are all combinations of federal-state funds and standards. And many states were active in these areas before federal funds and standards were added.

Critics argue that the states have so often neglected their responsibilities in these areas that national programs were necessary. While this certainly is true of the need for national action in aiding urban areas, the voting rights bill, and the reapportionment question, there are many cases of states performing the role of the experimenter and the innovator, in which they have demonstrated the need for wider programs through their successes. The first antitrust statutes were developed by the states; the first maximum hours-minimum wage legislation was developed by the states; the states fashioned the first anti-discrimination statutes, the first child labor laws, the first unemployment insurance.

The point is that all levels of government are new to the problems of poverty, and that no level has a monopoly on solutions. The states, like all levels of our system, are already involved in the problems of poverty through their welfare, education, health, employment and other activities. They are providing many of these services now, and the concept of innovation which I have discussed previously does not only look to the new, but a mixture of the new with the old, to achieve the goals of the program.

For that reason the states have a crucial role in the development and administration of the antipoverty program, and this role may be the key to its success. To date, there has been little or no support for the states to take much of a positive role; and their role has been left vaguely defined. With such a national commitment to a program, it is time for the states to move fully into the fray. It may be true that the states neglected the area of poverty in the past, but they were not alone in this. And, as I have stressed throughout this discussion, success will be achieved by bringing to bear all the resources available on the problem. *The states can be a major resource.*

There are at least four types of activities for which the states are uniquely suited. Some are already being performed by a few of the states.

1. *Technical Assistance, Communication and Interpretation.* The states should be the fulcrum of the federal system. Halfway between the national and local government, the states are situated so that they can be either bottlenecks or positive participants in the overall process. Section 209(b) of the Economic Opportunity Act of 1964 recognizes the unique contribution that states can make and provides for grants to state technical agencies for coordination and communication.[3] The state agency in this case serves on call for the interested communities and agencies to aid them to understand the various provisions of the program and to apply for grants. For small communities, often mystified and discouraged by federal procedures, this state agency can make the difference as to whether many communities will participate in a poverty program at all.

Most states are doing this at the present time in their antipoverty programs, but it is not enough. With the high funding ratio (90-10 federal-state) in which the states' ten per cent can be in kind rather than cash, these agencies virtually become extensions of the federal Office of Economic Opportunity rather than state agencies adding the resources of the state to the battle. While this role is crucial in getting the nationwide poverty program underway and making its impact complete, it must not be the states' only effort. For once the program is interpreted, and the various communities and agencies are operating programs with grants from the federal Office of Economic Opportunity, the need for such an office at the state level may disappear. Thus, interpretation and communication is only the first step rather than the total role to be played.

2. *Stimulation of Antipoverty Efforts.* Using the same agency and funding available under section 209(b), the state agency can move out into the state at large and into the various governmental agencies and stimulate the necessary programs to be undertaken. It need not wait to be called upon. The agency can stimulate and challenge the communities and agencies to fulfill their responsibility. The state

[3] 78 Stat. 519, 42 U.S.C. § 2789(b) (1964).

agency can take the initiative in getting statewide efforts underway where a state-wide effort is preferable to a piecemeal community-by-community approach. Often the state agency will initially undertake the program itself and spin it off once underway when a suitable home can be found.

Several states have perceived their role in this manner. New Jersey, with the strong backing of Governor Richard Hughes, has been using an affirmative state office approach and thereby has been able to obtain a "greater variety of grants covering more of its people than any other state in the union," according to OEO Director R. Sargent Shriver. Some of the programs are developed and run directly by the state office. California, with an equally aggressive approach under Governor Edmund G. Brown, has been a leader in developing rural area programs and a very impressive migrant labor program—created and initiated in the State Coordinator's Office. There are other examples, but I fear too few. This type of an approach means an active commitment and involvement by the governor and the state in the program. There is nothing preventing the states from filling such a role except their own lack of imagination and leadership.

Many states have been distracted from this positive approach by the question of the governor's veto over community action program proposals within the state. The argument on the one side is that the veto involves the governor and thereby the state in the programs and allows for a certain degree of control. The other side of the argument is that the veto acts as a negative control rather than affirmative leadership. It is ex post facto, coming after the planning, development, funding and announcement stages—thereby presenting the governor with an unhappy choice of just going along or stopping a program which has the support and commitment of many people. Further, its use has stimulated reaction from Congress to restrict the governor in the future. The answer is that the veto can be used constructively if combined with a positive state approach. It can serve as another weapon in the governor's arsenal to prod and stimulate agencies and communities in the proper direction. It can serve as the entrée for the governor to become an active part of the planning and development process.

3. *Coordination of Governmental Activities.* Coordination of governmental activities is a concept which excites the reformer and frightens the participant. Although everyone pays it lip service, it is a concept which is ignored throughout our governmental system, and the poverty program is no exception. According to the United States Conference of Mayors,

> Most of the Community Action Agency Directors reported that they had not encountered meaningful coordination between (the federal) Office of Economic Opportunity and the so-called delegated programs operating through the Department of Labor, the Department of Health, Education and Welfare and various other departments. . . . If local communities are expected to achieve any effective program development of a comprehensive and coordinated sort, the OEO must take the initiative among the federal agencies which the local Community Action

Agencies are powerless to affect. *This administrative failure, if allowed to continue, constitutes the most serious threat to the effective operation of a local umbrella agency currently on the horizon.*[4]

This points out several important facts to be considered: first, coordination of effort by all levels of government is necessary for the success of the program; second, coordination at the federal level has not really occurred and without coordination at this higher level, lower levels cannot meaningfully initiate or influence programs; and, third, the local communities face an impossible task in attempting to coordinate all the governmental activities which focus on them. The local communities do not possess personnel or resources; they suffer from a more parochial view of the world which leads to an inability to relate local particular problems to broader trends; and they do not have political muscle to force other levels to coordinate efforts.

The states can do part of this coordination job with the programs and agencies concerned with the poverty effort. The states already are a key to the operation of the federal system of government, as a major partner in almost all the federal domestic programs. They are responsible for administering most of the existing services and have impressive resources to bring to bear on the various problems. As entities more regional than local communities, they have a broader view and are more able to relate particular problems to broader trends. They may not be the perfect regional entities to carry this out, but they exist with a considerable present administrative structure, a power base and loyalty.

The logical place to vest responsibility for coordination is in the office of the governor. The governor is the only man representing his state who is acutely aware of the problems it faces in education, health, welfare, finances, mental health, urban renewal and poverty. In almost every state, the responsibility for initiation of major statewide programs falls upon the governor. He must, like the President of the United States, energize his administration, search out the experts, formulate the programs, mobilize the support, and carry through with the idea. Few major undertakings ever get off the ground without his support and leadership. The governor sets the agenda for public debate; frames the issues; decides on the timing; and can blanket the state with good ideas by using his access to the mass media. His office is really the only place where statewide coordination can occur.

4. *Planning and the Setting of Priorities.* The major criticism of the antipoverty program to date is the lack of adequate planning and setting of priorities in the development of the various programs. The supermarket approach makes programs available to attack all types of problems—but it is up to the local communities to pick and choose as they desire. At times, what one community does in answer to its problems may add to the problems of the next community, the region, or the state. For example, in some rural areas, separate communities, each offering retraining programs for high school dropouts, could glut the market with similarly trained

[4] U.S. CONFERENCE OF MAYORS, SPECIAL REPORT: THE OFFICE OF ECONOMIC OPPORTUNITY AND LOCAL COMMUNITY ACTION AGENCIES 4 (1965). (Emphasis added.)

people—to the disadvantage of both the community and the people. Likewise, there is need to ensure the best priority of effort, so that programs build on each other rather than compete for the limited resources and energy at hand.

The local community sets its own priorities and the federal OEO reviews them, but who relates the priorities established by a series of communities within the same region, or just beyond that region? The problems of our society flow in major part from its complexity. Yet, the emphasis on local communities acting individually or at best with several other communities in defining their problem and in devising their answer may potentially be overlooking the very complexity it seeks to meet. I agree with the efforts to seek multi-county approaches such as Georgia and Indiana have used, and also with the increasing emphasis that the federal OEO places on this approach.

But poverty is too complex to yield to a one-dimensional approach. Our society is not made of neatly contained, self-functioning units. Problems often are not encompassed by political boundaries.

Look at the Appalachian Regional Development Program. Twelve states, the federal government, and the local communities are attempting to focus the resources of all on a common condition—poverty in rural Appalachia. The impetus came from the governors themselves, who had long known that poverty lurked in the valleys and the hills of this mountain chain that stretched over twelve states. But we had never defined the problem in quite that way. This new way of thinking about an old problem gave life to a whole new set of proposals and programs. The framework guided the effort. We soon came to realize that decisions made within one region have an impact well beyond its bounds, and events outside bring severe repercussions within the region.

With this sort of framework for action, the states could be turning to their own "Little Appalachias." They could be designing fresh approaches to meet the challenges of an era when populations and problems ignore the old city limits and county lines. As a funnel for funds, the states could act to bring together the strands of government. They should present the communities with an array of possible programs and aid them in fitting new approaches into the overall effort.

We need proper planning and the setting of priorities within an overall framework. Problems need definition and pinpointing. Trends must be discerned and areas defined. Programs like Appalachia must be meshed with the poverty program. Goals and the means to these goals must be set. Priorities and timing of activities should be suggested.

The states are in the best position to carry out this charge. The federal government looks at problems and programs in broad, general, aggregate terms. Local communities see the world in narrow, particular, individual terms. The states, as regional, territorial entities, are best equipped to bring these two viewpoints into focus to the benefit of those receiving the service. Further, they sit at a key point in the provision of services to the people and probably have the best chance to effectuate plans.

The future, however, will depend on the states' own action—their willingness to take on the responsibility and challenge this represents. Some states are taking the first steps in this direction. Illinois and Massachusetts have used portions of their state technical assistance funds to gather and analyze data relating to the poverty situation within their bounds. The North Carolina Fund, from its inception, has maintained a strong emphasis on the research and planning function, with its first publication setting out the profile of poverty in the state. The next step in all these efforts is to relate the data to policy and program decisions and to translate their meaning to the communities in the state. This is the major role which the states can play, not just in this program, but in all programs—and it really means making government more responsive and effective.

IV

POVERTY IN PERSPECTIVE

Whether we acknowledge it or not, the realities of American growth and the demands of the American people are recasting American government along new and more exacting lines. For America is, as James Madison prophesied, a system of interacting federalism—and the influence of the states will fluctuate with their responsiveness to the needs of the times and the demands of the people.

Most people do not realize that the states are spending more than $40 billion a year on services to the American people. In the two decades since the Second World War, their budgets have risen at a faster rate than the federal budget. They pass most of our laws; run our courts and our prisons; do most of what's done for the mentally ill; and have the largest responsibilities for education.

Despite the persistent arguments over the last twenty years that states have ceased to be progressive and should therefore be abandoned as obsolete, the facts remain: states are here, they are here to stay, and in terms of services and functions, they are stronger than they have ever been before.

But the future of the states will depend on the energy with which they attack the problems of the nation. As I said recently in a speech to the Midwestern Governors' Conference,

> It is when the states fail to meet their responsibilities in such areas as education, civil rights and liberties, enhancing the opportunities of the poor, and urban affairs that the federal government moves into the vacuum. It is when the states are not responsive, are not laboratories of experimentation, do not reach all the people because they are either oppressive or not representative, that the states forfeit their strongest argument for a future.

This is poverty's challenge to the states—to respond to the summons of the people. But it will take more than talk and more than interest and even more than a willingness to act. The states must be able to act. They must initiate a period of total reform which will do away with the weak governor, unrepresentative legislatures, chaotic administrations, and archaic judiciaries. To conquer the future, the states must first conquer themselves.

Most Americans tend to believe that there is something inherently good about the federal system. Our high school civics books teach us it is the best. However, no form of government is inherently good. It can be judged only in terms of the quality of the civilization it helps to produce and to sustain.

If the states can help to abolish poverty in America, they will have contributed to a more civilized nation. And by fueling the light of hope for millions of Americans, they can give fiber to the American dream and set a new course for themselves as active partners in a revitalized federal system.

THE ROLE OF A STATE-WIDE FOUNDATION IN THE WAR ON POVERTY

GEORGE H. ESSER, JR.*

The "war on poverty" is the most recent step in our search for a more perfect democratic society. Because this war reaches into every aspect of our national life, it requires a perspective broader than any one of us normally employs. It also seeks change on a broader scale than any single national effort.

As the pace of the war quickens, we are becoming more aware of the significance of essential interrelationships—the importance of economic growth for the success of antipoverty programs which must promise jobs; the weakness of the federal system in adapting to programs demanding close and intricate coordination between many federal, state, and local agencies; our middle-class failure to understand the poor of all races, and the resulting failure of our middle-class oriented social institutions to make an impact on poverty; the barriers in our economic, social, and political systems that keep the poor in a never-ending "cycle of poverty"; and the inability of communities to develop processes for defining and meeting the total needs of people in the community.

I

THE NORTH CAROLINA FUND AS A STATE-WIDE FOUNDATION

The North Carolina Fund was established as a small foundation to help North Carolinians find ways to break the "cycle of poverty." The Fund's conception and early history have been covered in the preceding article; that history reached a transition point in the passage of the Economic Opportunity Act of 1964.[1] At that point the Fund's initial mission, to seek solutions to the poverty problem through community action on a demonstration or experimental basis, was superseded in part by the new federal program.

Fortunately, both the Fund's proposal to its supporting foundations (the Ford Foundation, the Z. Smith Reynolds Foundation, and the Mary Reynolds Babcock Foundation) and the grant letter under which it received funds recognized the broad areas within which the Fund might have to act in seeking its objectives. The Fund's charter established a broad arena for action. It authorized the Fund:

a. To do all things necessary or proper to aid in improving the education, economic opportunities, living environment and general welfare of the people of North Carolina, either directly or through other private or public organizations.

---

* B.S. 1942, Virginia Military Institute; LL.B. 1948, Harvard University. Executive Director, The North Carolina Fund. Formerly professor of public law and government and assistant director of the Institute of Government at the University of North Carolina.

[1] 78 Stat. 508, 42 U.S.C. §§ 2701-981 (1964).

b. To study the problems involved in improving the education, economic opportunities, living environment and general welfare of the people of North Carolina, of all ages and in different parts of the state; to make and recommend grants for research, pilot experimental and other projects toward the solution of such problems; to make available professional staff services to private and public agencies, both state and local, seeking solutions to such problems; to encourage cooperative state and community action in devising such solutions; and to encourage wise use of public and philanthropic funds devoted to any of these purposes.

The grant letter from the Ford Foundation was more specific but still very flexible. Although it defined the Fund's major responsibility as the provision of support for a "limited number of comprehensive community development projects," it also permitted grants in support of innovative projects on a state-wide basis, and the use of funds in support of planning and technical assistance, education and training, and research and evaluation.

A foundation may act in a number of ways. In purely philanthropic fashion, it may provide the funds needed for a new program or facility. It may provide grants to help other institutions explore new programs or seek to bring about change. In serving as a catalyst, it may provide all of the funds or simply the critical, risk-taking share. But the foundation's function is not limited to grants of money alone. Depending on the situation, on need, and on opportunity, it may itself provide technical assistance to other institutions. It may itself sponsor and administer innovative and experimental programs on a demonstration basis. It may undertake research and evaluation to determine appropriate new directions or the validity of competing alternatives. It may sponsor, directly or indirectly, public information and educational programs. But these are means of acting; they do not define the foundation's role.

The passage of the Economic Opportunity Act of 1964, and other legislation aimed at creation of the Great Society, brought millions of dollars to bear on the very problems the Fund was created to support through experimental action. The board of directors of the Fund could not, in good conscience, spend its limited funds for the same programs which now could draw on ample federal resources. But as government takes over responsibility for programs whose need has been defined by foundation projects, the opportunity exists for the foundation to experiment in other areas and to explore new frontiers for action. Within the context of a concern for the problems of the poor in North Carolina, the Fund has sought to fill this sort of role.

If the Fund were an agent of government—either federal or local—its scope would probably be more narrowly defined, though its resources might well be more bountiful. That is, although it might be less limited in the time available to accomplish its objectives, it would be perhaps more limited in its freedom to define its roles and to investigate the choices available, and certainly more limited in defining its functions.

But as a foundation entitled to act in a number of ways, it still must act in the context of the possible. Yet, were the Fund to use this freedom merely in a day-to-day "expense of spirit"—use of energy and of funds in reaction to the problems that exist and in conquering the frustrations and limitations implicit in the complexity of government—its contribution to the welfare of people would again be "more of the same." Thus, coupled with its necessity to act within the *context* of the possible must be a responsible use of the *art* of the possible. The fact that administration of funds is a science requires that foundations, as public servants, be aware of the context within which they serve, and the most efficient, most valuable, most humanly remunerative use of those funds. The fact that administration of funds can also be an art requires that foundations be creative—that is, that they disturb that context.

The very limitation of time in which to act has to be used creatively. The Fund was financed under grants running for a period of five years, and the board has taken the position that the Fund should regard that period as terminal lest the temptation to institutionalize its functions become too great. The Fund finds itself required by this shortness of intended life to *create* the possible—in effect to examine the whole fabric of the war on poverty, the holes in imperfect weaving of programs, the knots where the complexity of government has impeded an effective process, the imperfections that signify the need for change. The Fund must point out these imperfections, must provide the assistance necessary to mend the tears, must sometimes accept the imperfect whole, and must sometimes force a reweaving—to join the separate threads of social agencies, or provide the means to change institutions. And at times, if the finished garment does not cover the body of the poor, while allowing the poor to flex their muscles, the Fund must be able, flexible enough, and willing to try to create a new one.

Action within the context of the possible, responsibility for using the art of the possible, and creation of the possible might well be called the roles of the Fund. These roles are not necessarily specific pledges in the proposal to the supporting foundations, but they are in the spirit of that document. The means the Fund must choose to carry out these roles thus flow from its objectives and, when the choice is deliberately and carefully made, determine its functions. The objectives are clear; the functions must vary with time, climate, money, community, and so on, and particularly with the means chosen or created before those functions are determined. It is these means with which we must deal, these choices which must be measured against our objectives, these innovations, if needed, for which we are ultimately responsible.

Although the Fund can extend its activities throughout the state, its initial emphasis on the community as the critical focal point for dealing with the problems of poverty has been continued. Before looking at the choices made by the Fund in how to deal with the problems of the poor, it is useful to look at both the opportunities and the limitations implicit in this selection.

II

THE CONTEXT OF COMMUNITY

The definition of "community" for purposes of antipoverty programs may be said to have begun with the concerns of the Ford Foundation "grey area" programs and the projects sponsored by the President's Committee on Delinquency and Youth Crime for the problems of people living in urban slums. The context for action in these projects was usually the political jurisdiction within which action affecting services provided in slum neighborhoods could be planned and implemented. Although the planning and implementation was generally through the new instrument of a non-profit corporation, the cooperation of existing governmental and voluntary agencies at the municipal or county level was essential.

A similar approach was followed in the statement of The North Carolina Fund's initial program, since the county in North Carolina is the smallest unit responsible for administration of educational, health and welfare functions. Administration of the Economic Opportunity Act of 1964 has followed essentially the same approach. While the focus of particular programs may, then, be the neighborhood where the poor live, planning, financing, and administration are through a governmental unit or corporation which can involve the cooperation of the basic service agencies concerned for the poor throughout the community. The definition of community for administrative purposes is therefore pragmatic and includes the flexibility to decentralize particular programs to smaller communities.

The assumption of the "community action" approach is that effective action to deal with the problems of the poor must take place in the community where the poor live and work, and that all the resources of the community—whether public or private, or of local, state or federal origin—can best be mobilized and focused on those who need help where they are. We must, the assumption goes, enlist the cooperation of the total community in examining the total problems of people in the community and in finding solutions built to the particular needs of those people.

The arguments in favor of this approach have much logic. The poor, the slums they live in, the problems of poor health and delinquency and insufficient income, are a reproach to the community. They are a drain on community services and governmental revenues. They are the Achilles' heel of a democratic society. Logic dictates that poverty must be eliminated or the impact of poverty on the community reduced.

Many resources to deal with poverty exist at the community level and within the systems of community power. Many of them were established to deal with poverty.

The clientele of the welfare department basically consists of the poor. Many of the services of public health departments are aimed at the poor. Most of the services of voluntary welfare agencies are for the poor. And if the answer to poverty is education, then the public school systems and the adult education agencies are directly concerned with the poor.

If something is missing, if we are simply failing to find the right combination to the problems of the poor, then it should be within the capacity of the community to find that combination. Is it more services? Then the answer is to find the resources to support those services. Is it a different type of service? Then the answer is to find the resources to experiment. Is it failure of the services mutually to support one another? Then the answer is coordination. Is it more jobs and higher wages? Then the answer is economic development.

Implicit in the community approach are the consequences of the failure to plan for maximum use of existing resources, the failure to establish goals to fix priorities, and to focus on these priorities. As problems of the poor are defined, and suggestions for action are set forth, the absence of planning and coordination becomes evident. The emphasis of existing programs on symptoms rather than causes is criticized.

There is much truth in this hypothesis, but also much naïveté. A brief look at the problems of poverty in the community, and the complicating factors lying beneath the surface of community life, helps make the dilemma apparent.

A. The Problems of Poverty in the Community

When the Fund was established in the summer of 1963, its first action was to define the dimensions of poverty in North Carolina. The enormity of the task the Fund had undertaken was reflected in the cold statistics which laid out the extent of low income, of inadequate education, of poor health and poor housing and delinquency. A review, without necessary order of priority, of some of the things we noted then and continue to face helps to clarify the dilemma of a rural state attempting to lift itself by its bootstraps into the mainstream of American life. In a time of a rising national economy and a rising gross national product, of declining unemployment, we find:

(1) about one-third of all North Carolinians living at an income level inadequate to provide a decent standard of living;

(2) rising unemployment in many low-income, particularly rural, areas while the national level decreases;

(3) increasing unemployment for non-white families while that of white workers decreases, and a wide range between the median income of white families in urban and rural areas as compared with non-white families;

(4) an increasing gap between the wages of the lower one-fourth of the popula-

tion and the remaining three-fourths, a gap that last reports suggest may have stopped widening but which is not yet narrowing;

(5) the threat of industry to bypass some North Carolina cities on the ground that there is no available labor force. (The fact may well be that there is no reservoir of the skills needed by industry, and in a few urban localities the labor force has been drained dry. In the state as a whole, however, there are thousands and tens of thousands either without a job or earning wages insufficient for adequate food, clothing and housing. And too many of these are Negroes who have heretofore been systematically denied access to skilled jobs);

(6) jobs going in many cities of the Piedmont, while in other parts of the state men who want to work have no jobs because the machine has made their labor on the farm obsolescent;

(7) despite the rate of industrialization in this state and the relatively high percentage of manufacturing jobs, North Carolinians earn less in average weekly wages than workers in any other state;

(8) for every person unemployed in North Carolina, between five and six employed work less than forty weeks during the year, lending some explanation to the information on inadequate income;

(9) about 400,000 adults twenty-five years of age or over who have less than five years of schooling, and almost a million who have less than eight years of schooling— at a time when industry is asking for a minimum of eight years of education and prefers a high school education;

(10) thousands of young men and women continuing to drop out of school before reaching, much less finishing, high school—when a high school education is an imperative in an industrial society;

(11) two out of every five housing units in North Carolina classified as inadequate, obsolete, or lacking essential facilities such as plumbing;

(12) continuing evidence of the inadequacy of health, welfare and other services to meet the needs of the poor—evidence in the form of hungry children, families suffering from multiple ravages of disease and despair;

(13) the barriers on every hand which have denied to the Negro the full benefits of society and, in denying opportunity, have helped keep a disproportionate number in the "cycle of poverty";

(14) evidence that the poor continue to have the largest families and that, particularly in the Negro community, the head of household tends to be the mother;

(15) the continuing, if somewhat declining, rate of migration to urban centers of the North and Middle West, including not only those who leave because they find opportunity elsewhere but those, unprepared for urban life, who hope unrealistically to find greener pastures elsewhere.

The list could go on. We knew that, however appalling the evidence, progress could not be made by focusing on any one problem. As Michael P. Brooks, Director of Research for the Fund, observed in 1963:

> Poverty exists for a number of reasons, and elimination of any one of these reasons will not in itself eliminate poverty. Inadequate education, low or non-existent income, limited job opportunities, dilapidated and overcrowded housing, poor physical and mental health, and inclination toward delinquency and crime—these and many other characteristics of poverty both cause and are caused by each other, interacting in a manner which renders it virtually impossible for the disadvantaged child, adult or family to break out of the "cycle of poverty." It is essential, therefore, that any attack on the problem of poverty must be comprehensive, bringing the forces of state and community action to bear on all the characteristics of the problem.[2]

As we looked at the problem of poverty, the children and the parents of poverty, we could best pose for all North Carolinians the simple question: How can we in North Carolina reverse trends, motivate people, re-orient attitudes, supply the education and the public services and the jobs that will give all our people the chance to become productive, more self-reliant, and able to compete in the complex but dynamic, exciting but perilous world of today and tomorrow?

III

SHORTCOMINGS OF THE COMMUNITY ACTION APPROACH IN THE "WAR ON POVERTY"

In the fall and winter of 1963-1964, the Fund asked for proposals for demonstration projects from each of North Carolina's one hundred counties.

When Fund staff and board members, encouraged by the response of sixty-six of the one hundred counties to this initial statement of the community action program, sat down to review the fifty-one proposals received, some of the limitations of the community action theory began to be evident. Making allowances for the short length of time provided for the preparation of proposals, it was still clear that communities in North Carolina had not generated many truly creative ideas for dealing with the problem of the poor. It has been no particular source of gratification, though perhaps one of relief, to find that the state and its communities were not unique in this respect.

The coming of the Economic Opportunity Act, and the other legislative milestones on the road to the "great society," interrupted the effort of the Fund to encourage the eleven communities selected for Fund suppport to go back and carry out a more realistic planning process with the help of consultants. No board member could conscientiously spend private dollars for experimental programs when public dollars were available for the same purposes. Instead, the board decreed, the Fund should help the state and its communities take maximum advantage of the

---

[2] THE NORTH CAROLINA FUND: PROGRAMS AND POLICIES 10-11 (1963).

new resources—now on a community-wide basis rather than on a more limited demonstration basis.

In that first year of an approach to an experimental and demonstration program, and in the succeeding year or more of efforts to help communities take maximum advantage of new federal resources, the shortcomings and complexities of the community action approach have become more evident. Some of these shortcomings are beyond the power of any community to deal with without help from state and federal levels; some of them are built into the community process.

A. Confusion in Objectives

Despite this nation's declared all out "war on poverty," one thing is clear from the experience of less than two years. The legislative programs enacted by Congress are not at all clear on the objectives of the "war on poverty." In effect, there is a confusion of goals, and because of the confusion of goals there has been a significant confusion in the aspirations and expectations of the poor. For example, the poor as defined by inadequate income fall into several classifications; and many of those who are most poor are not able to increase their income to an adequate level of living through their own efforts. These groups include the aged, the permanently and totally disabled, and young children in families qualified for aid to dependent children. All of these poor live on grants which are demonstrably not enough to provide the minimum standard of living which we are attempting to reach. The grants merely provide for a marginal existence; and, particularly for young children, this marginal existence may build in for the rest of their lives those factors which result in poverty.

Another interpretation of new and existing legislation is that we can best attack the problem by more adequate services. While the need for more educational, health, welfare, and other services must be acknowledged, there clearly is doubt whether services alone meet the needs of those living in poverty—particularly those services that cannot result in increased employment or income. Thus, while services may help people face some of their problems, an increased package of services does not necessarily assure an end to poverty.

Another goal which underlies many of the programs in the "war on poverty" is the opening of opportunity structures for young men and women and for adults displaced from employment or adequate employment by the effects of automation and technology. This is clearly the objective of Job Corps, Neighborhood Youth Corps, various manpower programs under both the Economic Opportunity Act and the Manpower Development and Training Act of 1962,[3] and the work experience programs provided under title five of the Economic Opportunity Act.[4] While these programs are aimed at helping people overcome their inability to compete through

---

[3] 76 Stat. 23, as amended, 42 U.S.C. § 2571-620 (1964).

[4] 78 Stat. 527, 42 U.S.C. §§ 2921-23 (1964).

education and skill training, they do not assure that there will be a job on the other end of the pipeline. They do not insure that the training provided is for skills that will be in demand. And even if the skills lead to jobs, there is no assurance that the jobs will pay a wage calculated to lift the family or the individual out of poverty. Some critics have questioned whether the continued existence of millions of jobs that do not qualify for the minimum wage can ever permit us to lift a significant portion of our population out of poverty, particularly when the minimum wage itself is not sufficient to meet the income required for the minimum standard of living we seek.

Some provisions of the Economic Opportunity Act, particularly those requiring the "maximum feasible participation"[5] of the poor, suggest that motivation is the problem and that we will not secure motivation until we either make our class structure more open and flexible, permitting an increasing number of individuals and families to move into the vast middle class, or unless we strengthen and expand the democratic process itself at all levels, so that all our people can play an active part in the shaping of their own, and the nation's, destiny. This latter approach suggests that our service state is not providing the services that the poor themselves define as necessary or needed, and suggests that we need an immediate re-evaluation of our society and the philosophy under which it attempts to help those who lack the income or education to help themselves.

Obviously the formulation of goals at any level is difficult. Congress must question whether public opinion would support more precise formulation of goals. Furthermore, the inertia of old programs and the demand to get new programs under way make careful formulation of goals at any level difficult. But confusion in goals leads to confusion of expectations. And unless we have specific goals, it is going to be difficult for the "war on poverty," as it is carried out at local levels, to meet the full range of expectations. Frustration of expectations can be as dangerous to the success of this war as inadequate achievement of well-defined goals.

B. The Problem of Approach

Even if there were clearly formulated goals, we would have a serious problem because of differences of opinion in how to approach those goals. And the problem of approach has many facets, not just one.

For example, there is the dilemma posed by the language of title two of the Economic Opportunity Act itself.[6] The concept of mobilization of services assumes that there are those who have the professional training and commitment and understanding to give the help and assistance to the poor which the poor themselves cannot provide. On the other hand, there is the concept, one of the cardinal American virtues of self-help, that given the opportunity, every individual can find ways in

---

[5] Sec. 202(a)(3), 78 Stat. 516, 42 U.S.C. § 2782(a)(3) (1964).

[6] 78 Stat. 516, 42 U.S.C. §§ 2781-831 (1964).

which to help himself. Related to this concept is the concept of "the maximum feasible participation of the poor," which suggests that our system of services discourages self-help, that the poor themselves must be involved in the definition of problems and the implementation of programs in order to find the ways in which society can open up avenues through which the poor can move to greater self-reliance.

At another level, we have another dilemma. The concept of mobilizing community resources to focus on the problems of the poor at the local level conflicts with existing methods for dealing with these problems. Existing bureaucracies, which we can lump together as the various state and local agencies and professional groups which have traditionally dealt with problems of the poor, have characteristically been concerned with only a single segment of the poverty problem as it affects individuals; and each discipline—be it education, health, welfare, or recreation—feels that it has understandably acquired a vested interest in how to deal with that segment of the problem with which it has had experience. These professional people find it difficult to react when they are asked to participate in a process wherein the community, the family, and the individual are to be looked upon as a whole, rather than as fragmented entities. Because the credentials of the person doing the asking are occasionally suspect, and because the agency official has a stake in protecting the significance of his graduate degree and his position in the agency, the reaction of the bureaucracy is often negative. The community action organization claims it wants to coordinate the efforts of the bureaucracies, which, in turn, sense this as a threat to their autonomy. The community organization claims that it wants to start *new* programs; the bureaucracies respond that they themselves would have undertaken such programs long ago were it not for their lack of funds and statutory authorization. These agencies say "Give us the money, and we will run the program; we, after all, are the 'professionals.' "

Thus, we not only have the problem of whether we rely on professionals or the poor, but we also have the problem of which professionals. We have the problem of how to introduce a single comprehensive process for the planning of human resource development into an arena already characterized by a variety of planning processes, each with its traditional, carefully-guarded boundaries.

There is still another facet to the question of approach. While this problem is central to the problem of complexity noted below, it also relates to the basic philosophy of the federal system. Although most of the new legislation encourages and requires local community initiative in the definition of needs and ways to meet needs, there is substantial evidence that many administrators of the new programs believe that there are tested ways which should be imposed on communities, whether or not the communities agree. This is reflected in the preference of the Office of Economic Opportunity for some types of prepackaged national efforts. Project

Head Start is such an example. It was easy to define; it was easy to administer as a uniform program. But there is lack of evidence that a uniform approach to programs for preschool-age children is the best way to meet the very real needs of those children who come from poverty families.

C. The Problem of Complexity in the Federal System

Underlying all the problems in the "war on poverty" is a concern for the adequacy of the combined public and private systems that are a part of a functioning democracy.

Our nation of nearly 200 million people is committed both to free enterprise and to government as advocate of the public interest. We do not expect—and certainly do not want—governmental planning and efficiency which theoretically would best utilize our resources, but which, practically speaking, would result in inertia, slavery to a system, and a totalitarian role for federal government.

Serious questions are being raised, however, and are implicit in several pieces of new legislation, as to whether existing governmental and private systems are producing the results that a free people should expect. The question is raised whether a democracy can afford poverty for one-fourth of its people, a poverty that infects the social system and builds in the concept of a disaffected minority.

When we look at the organization of this country, we can identify several operating systems which affect the status of individuals. There is the economic system, in all its variety and complexity, which keeps the wheels of production and distribution of goods in motion. There is the system of government, a federal system, which operates in different ways in fifty different states to serve both national and local concerns. And there are other systems, albeit more informal ones, which provide the mechanism through which both public and private agencies achieve local and national objectives. From this point of view, we can define systems of informally related agencies which deal with such problems as land development, transportation, communication, urban renewal, education, provision of health and welfare services, provision for housing, and so on. We can also, from another point of view, identify the multitude of governmental and private agencies which together focus on the community, whether defined in geographic terms, in terms of areas limited by local governmental boundaries, or defined on a regional or state basis.

It can be said that, however we define the responsibilities of government in cooperation with the private sector, these systems are not doing the job when one-fourth of our population lacks the income, the education, the employment, and the opportunity to participate in the wealth of a free society.

Here again the existing "great society" programs complicate rather than clarify goals. At one and the same time they (1) encourage further development of the federal-state-local approach to the provision of services such as education, and (2) encourage federal-local relationships which squeeze out the potentially valuable and essential mechanism of the state. This is particularly confusing when the concept of "mobilization of resources" under the federal-local program in the Economic Opportunity Act requires coordination with significant services which are primarily state-administered or state-coordinated.

Thus, we have a series of basic questions. If the "war on poverty" is to be successful, we need to redefine the proper roles of several levels of government. With a substantial increase in federal assistance for locally- and state-administered programs, can the federal government provide a framework for action which is appropriate for all states and localities? To what extent must the federal government adopt common restrictions and regulations which limit local initiative but without which the intended benefits may not reach those who need to be helped? Or can the federal government coordinate its own policies and services, emanating from several major departments, in such a manner as to permit rational planning at state and local levels? There is no source of greater frustration for the state or local official than to try to determine a policy consensus for programs which involve two or more federal agencies.

Similarly, questions must be raised about the role of the state and the role of the local government.

The state *does* have a strong role to play. Ideally, it can serve as a countervailing force against the rigidity of federal agencies, on the one side, and against the occasional parochialism and short-sightedness of local governments, on the other side. The state can provide expanded technical assistance and expertise to communities which need it. It can increase its sensitivity to problems as they are defined locally, and can formulate programs and policies accordingly. It can develop experimental or demonstration projects in problem areas which transcend the boundaries or resources of a single community—for example, in the areas of manpower and economic development. It can pioneer in the usage of sub-professional personnel in service agencies. There are, in short, a number of potentially valuable functions for the state. Whether or not the states *will* carve out significant roles for themselves—and in fact, whether the concept of federalism is to remain viable in the face of contemporary problems—remains to be seen.

There are also questions to be asked about the role of local government in the "war on poverty." *Does* it have the power to coordinate an effective attack on the problems of low-income families? Can it bring to bear on local problems the information necessary to analyze and plan? Can it find, within its own boundaries, the expertise needed for the design and execution of effective programs? While the nation's metropolitan areas undoubtedly have this expertise, there are hundreds of small cities and towns which do not. How—if at all—can the necessary skills be brought to bear on such communities in a manner which is consistent with the principle of local autonomy?

And finally, how is local government to respond to the charge that its antipoverty programs must indeed be based on the democratic process—that is, that the poor must be given an active role in programs aimed at improving their circumstances?

In terms of the combined public and private systems, such as manpower and economic development, and housing, and education, there is a demonstrable need for more careful evaluation of how these systems operate, of how they succeed, and of how they fail to achieve desired results. There is also need for a continued dialogue between governmental and business leaders and representatives of the poor on how best to achieve results in terms of jobs, homes, and educational opportunities. But these cannot be discussed without the availability of more information defining the boundaries of the problem. At the state and local, as well as at the federal level, we need more information on which to base further definition of the problems, and thus the policies, that today are not working but which must be changed.

We also need a setting in which there can be innovation in development of the things we try and subsequent evaluation of the techniques chosen. There is a limit to the development function of government, and of the universities, as they have dealt with the problems of human resource development. We need to find additional institutions, similar to the Learning Institute of North Carolina, which can define new solutions and try out new ways of dealing with the problems of people.

D. Role of the Poor

The Economic Opportunity Act of 1964 not only emphasizes mobilization of resources to meet the needs of the poor; it also requires "maximum feasible participation" of the poor in planning and administering community action programs.[7] In establishing community action organizations under the Economic Opportunity Act, there is a requirement that these organizations be broadly representative of the entire community, including representation from business and labor, from public agencies and private agencies, from representatives of minority groups, and from representatives of neighborhoods and groups where the incidence of poverty is highest. In administering programs, the employment of the poor in sub-professional roles is encouraged, both as a source of employment and as a means of reaching more successfully the poor.

These latter concepts are new to most of us. As *Fortune* magazine has pointed out,[8] this concept is one of the really new things in the "war on poverty." It does not seem to make sense to many people, for how can the poor, who are the least able to produce, help plan and coordinate and administer complicated services? The answer lies in understanding history and understanding people.

First of all, our nation has traditionally acted *for* the poor. *We* have decided what *they* needed. *We* have expected *them* to think as *we* think, to act as *we* act.

---

[7] Sec. 202(a)(3), 78 Stat. 516, 42 U.S.C. § 2782(a)(3) (1964).

[8] Ways, *Creative Federalism and the Great Society*, Fortune, Jan. 1966, p. 121.

And if all that our scientists tell us is true, we were totally and abysmally wrong. We not only misunderstood them. We lost their respect and confidence. In particular we lost the respect and confidence of minority groups.

If the poor lack respect and confidence for government, and for community agencies, how can that confidence be restored so that there will be the desire to get an education, the motivation to work, and the assurance that work and education will pay off in jobs that pay good wages? The assumption of the Economic Opportunity Act is that, initially, respect and confidence can best be restored by bringing representatives of the poor and the poor themselves into the planning of programs aimed at the poor, by letting them speak up concerning what is needed, by giving them the assurance that comes from participation. Does it work? It is hard to say concretely, but all of the evidence is that it does work, and is working better as our experience increases.

The Los Angeles riots offer fresh evidence that, whether we who are *not* poor like it or not, the poor *are* going to participate in American life. The question is, how will they participate? Destructively, or constructively? The answer is obvious, and the Economic Opportunity Act provides, indeed requires, that the poor be involved in our planning for the future.

This involvement with and for the poor may open our eyes to a lot of things, correcting a lot of myths about the poor. For example, the experience of the Fund to date, and the experience in North Carolina, has responded concretely to many myths about the poor, and particularly the Negro poor.

1. It was said that the illiterate did not want to learn; but thousands have responded everywhere throughout the state to the adult basic education program. The sad feature of this program is that there is not nearly enough money to meet the demand.

2. It was said that the poor would not leave their homes, whether on an eastern farm or a mountain cove, to seek employment. But a Fund-sponsored mobility program demonstrated that the poor, even the illiterate, would move wherever opportunity in the form of employment and training was offered. And the record of adjustment to urban life and manufacturing jobs was good. Likewise the experimental manpower development program in six eastern North Carolina counties demonstrated that the poor, the unemployed, the displaced want to learn to read and write, to learn a vocation, to find employment.

3. It was said that the poor could not effectively participate on community action boards and were not interested in poverty programs. But they have demanded the right to participate, they have articulated their needs and priorities, and it has given the poor, and particularly the Negro poor, the type of confidence in the local antipoverty program without which success would not be possible.

In too many cases, however, the willingness to respond is greater than the ability to respond. If motivation can result from the realization that long-locked doors are being unlocked, that the opportunity to take part in community affairs can lead to programs that better meet the felt needs of the poor, that the community's helping hand is not linked to conditions which deny self-dignity—if such motivation can result, then more exploration must be made of the avenues by which this motivation is stimulated and assisted.

A second danger, a critical one, is that once opportunity has been promised, the gates may close again—for lack of funds, as in the adult education program, or for lack of jobs, as in all programs dealing with manpower development.

Involvement of the poor has been criticized on other grounds. Some critics have charged that it builds unhealthy social conflict into the community action process, and indeed it can result in conflict where communication is not established. But there can be constructive conflict, where those without a voice gain a voice, and destructive conflict, where those without a voice continue to be denied a voice. The techniques of involvement, of motivation, of community organization, may vary from community to community, but motivation is not likely to come in a community where opportunity to speak, to participate, to find education and employment is not forthcoming.

Although the problems of motivation and opportunity exist without regard to color, it is demonstrably greater in the Negro community, as shown in North Carolina in the community action projects in the East and Piedmont. There is a continuing need for a more open dialogue between the races in these communities— for dealing directly with the need for the education and jobs and services that can both lead out of poverty and lead to healthier community-wide relationships. The Fund was founded to deal with poverty wherever it is found, but it must also recognize the problem of equality of opportunity—in whatever sphere—for the Negro will not take part in these programs unless he has confidence that he is part of it and that the program is color blind.

E. The Problem of Time and Experience

The Fund staff has had extensive experience during the last two years with the limitations of crash planning, with administration of complex new programs by inexperienced personnel, and with lay leadership unequipped to cope with intricate problems. Time has not allowed careful planning, adequate training of personnel, or proper negotiation and coordination of related agencies at state and local levels. The system of professional education in the United States simply has not turned out people with the experience and breadth of understanding to move easily into top administrative positions in community action programs. And there is no agreement on what combinations of education and experience are best designed to equip people for these positions.

Limitations of the planning process will show up as disappointing results in programs once thought to be promising; similarly, the impact of inadequately-trained personnel will become more marked as the number and complexity of state and local programs increase.

It is highly essential that continued emphasis be placed on establishment of programs in the university system, and within the community college system, to insure better professional education, better education for sub-professional careers, and better education for citizens and administrators undertaking complicated tasks without prior experience.

F. The Problem of Public Understanding

As a general rule, the public fails to understand the problems of poverty, and understands even less the problems of dealing effectively with the causes of or solutions to poverty. Lack of understanding may be the result of lack of information, in part of bias and prejudice, or of difference of opinion in interpreting the operation of our society or how to deal effectively with acknowledged problems. Too many new problems introduced too quickly have magnified the problem, so that there tends to be more confusion as a result of the new program than when emphasis was simply on the problems alone.

IV

ROLES OF THE FUND

In seeking to define both the science and art of the possible in this context of community, and under crisis or crash conditions, the Fund has adapted its choices to a range of needs, a range of priorities, a range of conclusions. It was early clear that the simple grant-making approach would not result in bringing about the kind of change that was necessary in a community. The problems were too complex; the resources of trained manpower and of civic leadership were too scanty; the points of possible impact were too numerous.

The staff and board of directors had another problem to face. They had their own image of what the Fund was supposed to do and what it could best do. Likewise, others throughout the state had a specific image of what the Fund might do in the "war on poverty." State and local agencies looked upon the Fund as a source for financing new services but in continuation of old patterns. The new-born community action projects looked upon the Fund as a bank account for resources and money not available from Washington. Some representatives of the poor looked upon the Fund as an advocate. Educational institutions looked upon the Fund as a source for additional research. All sorts of people made it clear that they had the answers to the problems of poverty, the simple answers that could cut through the complicating and frustrating factors described above. There was even the serious proposal that the Fund use all its resources to bankroll a new industry, for only with new jobs could the problem of poverty be solved.

Although community action became a national policy in the summer of 1964, rather than a simple experimental approach, the Fund did not abandon either its own emphasis on or concern for what might be achieved in local communities. The belief continued that a central change must become a reality in the community if it is to be a lasting change.

Focus on the community as the arena for change has many advantages. First of all it is in the community that we gain an understanding of the human perspectives of poverty—the impact of the environment, of lack of education, of lack of income. Likewise, it is in the community that we see at first hand how all of the resources of the federal system are now employed—some successfully, some unsuccessfully—and we gain insights into these weaknesses—insights that need to be fed back to state and federal levels. We see the limitations of, as well as the potential for, coordination. We see the gaps in essential services, the absence of rational planning, the cross purposes with which many agencies and groups in professions work.

It is also in the community that we see the democratic system at work, sometimes succeeding, sometimes failing. It is in the community, along the slum streets and down the dusty roads of the rural areas, that we come to know the poor, to discover their attitudes toward the establishment as enemy, to discover how little middle-class America is sensitive to the dreams and the aspirations and the capabilities of those who have fewer resources but no less humanity. And it is in the local community that we see how governmental policy can be used to help, or frustrate, the poor.

Thus the Fund's focus continues to be the community as a whole, and the poor in the context of the community. This focus does not exclude Fund activities in relation to the essential roles of the state and federal government, or educational institutions, or of other statewide and national organizations. In many important respects policies and programs at these levels govern community action and response. But the emphasis, the focal point, is on the poor in the context of the community in which they live.

A. The Fund in the Community

Before the Economic Opportunity Act became a reality, the board of directors of the Fund had assured the community action programs (those first selected for Fund support) a small annual grant for a period of four years to permit each of the communities to organize, employ a competent director, and begin the overall planning process. These grants assured each community the funds to compete successfully for qualified executive staff; and because they were staffed before the Economic Opportunity Act became a reality, each of these projects was able to get a head start on other communities not similarly organized.

In addition, the Fund provides to each such program technical assistance in the mobilization of resources from all levels of government, development of proposals that require technical training not available at the community level, and pilot grants for initiating developmental programs.

As community action programs have grown rapidly, without patterns or a reservoir of trained manpower from which to draw, stresses and strains have appeared in the administrative fabric. This has necessitated special technical assistance in administrative organization, financial accountability, personnel administration, and in-service training.

From the beginning the Fund has been concerned that the poor themselves be involved in the development of community action programs. With the passage of time, and a better understanding of the problem, the Fund has concluded that one of its major objectives must be to help the poor show they can be effective not only in identifying their own needs and opportunities, but in participating in the decision-making process of the entire community. In support of this objective the Fund provides technical assistance to community action agencies in the techniques of involving the poor, in preparing board members from low-income neighborhoods for effective policy-making responsibilities, and in promoting dialogue between the traditional power structure of the community and representatives of the poor and of minority groups.

In some cases, moreover, a good and workable idea comes up for financial support of a character not available from the federal government. One community action agency covering four counties in the Appalachian mountains asked for a grant to permit it to offer incentive payments to remote mountain communities which could organize, identify local needs, and meet those needs with the aid of a little money. The initial reaction to this program is very positive.

B. Fund Programs in Support of Communities

In some cases, however, financial or technical support to community action agencies is not enough or cannot be calculated to meet priority needs.

In the summer of 1964 the Fund recognized the critical shortage of trained manpower capable of dealing at first hand with the technical problems arising in the community action agencies. As a stopgap measure, the Fund proceeded to organize and support a program for training young men and women interested in community action operations. With a small grant from the Department of Labor's Office of Manpower, Automation and Training, the Fund brought together its first group of community action technicians in August of 1964. These fifteen young men and women were drawn from the North Carolina Volunteers (an experimental program in the utilization of college student volunteers during the summer months in community action programs), Peace Corps returnees, and state government interns.

Following a period of five weeks of residential training, these young men and women were assigned for an additional three months period to community action agencies. Later they entered regular employment with these agencies.

The program was so successful that a grant was secured from the Office of Economic Opportunity to continue the program. Two more groups were trained during 1965, and the grant has been renewed to enable continuation of the program during 1966.

Section 603 of the Economic Opportunity Act[9] provided for the recruitment and training of VISTA volunteers for assignment to antipoverty programs. Since each of these volunteers had to receive advance training before assignment, the Office of Economic Opportunity had to organize crash training programs. At the request of the Office of Economic Opportunity, the Fund entered into a contract for training of the first group of thirteen VISTA volunteers recruited under the Economic Opportunity Act. The training program was successful, and after a second group, the Fund entered into a contract to train six additional· groups. Although these volunteers have been assigned all over the country, a significant number are serving in North Carolina communities today.

The Fund also took under contract the training of twenty-five community services consultants for the State Board of Welfare under a special grant from the Department of Health, Education and Welfare. These consultants were assigned to twenty-five communities for the purposes of helping coordinate the services to meet the needs of low-income people.

The combination of these training activities focused attention on the need for a training center in the state, for training at the professional, sub-professional and indigenous levels. Rather than institutionalize its training function, the Fund asked the University of North Carolina to explore the possibilities of establishing a center that could coordinate the resources of all university schools and departments to provide training at all levels in the new antipoverty programs. The University responded positively to this request, and had established a committee to explore how such a center might be established when the Office of Economic Opportunity asked that the University of North Carolina accept a demonstration grant for creation of such a center. The University is one of four in the country with such a grant. The new Center for Community Research and Services has been established at the University of North Carolina at Chapel Hill with a grant from the Office of Economic Opportunity supporting initial staff to help coordinate and develop training programs and programs of consultation. Because the University was interested in a total, balanced program which would include research and evaluation, the North Carolina Fund made a grant to the University to support the research component until additional funds for permanent support of this component can be

---

[9] 78 Stat. 530, 42 U.S.C. § 2943 (1964).

located. With establishment of the Center, the Fund hopes that it can phase out its general training functions.

One of the major problems in the "war on poverty" is the need for introducing change into professions and institutions responsible for essential services to low-income target groups. Often traditional professions regard grants from foundations as the excuse for "more of the same," and they are not willing or anxious to listen to the attitudes of the poor and to experiment with the types of changes which would better reach the poor. For this reason, it is often difficult to identify proposals from such agencies which promise true innovation. From its developmental funds the Fund is in a position to make a number of grants aimed at institutional change; and it is eager to do so.

In areas where there are no agencies presently providing essential services, or coordinating a range of related services, it is sometimes difficult to arrange for proposals for innovation. In such cases, the foundation may be faced with the decision to sponsor and administer directly a demonstration project itself. One such example is the manpower development program undertaken by the North Carolina Fund in six eastern North Carolina counties, aimed at the problem of identifying and helping to improve the employability and therefore the income of rural low-income families.

One of the techniques successfully used in this program is employment of men and women from the rural community as field workers to find and identify those heads of household qualifying for the program (by having an annual income of less than $1,200 per year or unemployment for six months or more). From the results of these exhaustive surveys by the field workers, counselors review the opportunities available in vocational training or on-the-job training for those eligible, and arrangements are made to provide the type of training which is appropriate.

While the results of the program are beginning to be impressive in terms of persons trained and placed in employment, the initial significant factor was that the field worker, a sub-professional, was having success in finding and motivating men and women of all races to seek additional opportunities. They were finding that these men and women, acquainted only with the farm, poorly educated, displaced from the farm by automation, unfamiliar with the institutional resources of American society, were anxious to receive training, to receive opportunity, and to work. The field worker has been an essential factor in helping these men and women find opportunity and take advantage of services and resources to which they were entitled but which were unavailable to them.

The results of this manpower program have been used by community action programs throughout the state to help define new ways of approaching the problem of manpower development.

From the very beginning in 1963, the Fund has been concerned with evaluating its programs. It has also been concerned with seeking out the information on which to build good programs.

What do poor people think about? What are their values, their attitudes, their aspirations? A survey of low-income families, designed to help answer these questions, is one project of the Research Department of the North Carolina Fund. The Fund initiated this survey during the summer of 1964, and a year later received further financial support for it from the Office of Economic Opportunity. The Research Triangle Institute, a non-profit research organization located near Durham, contracted to do the survey's field work, which included interviews with around 13,000 families in the eleven Fund-related communities. After the field work was completed, late in December of 1965, the Fund's research staff began data analysis, which is still in process.

This is one project of the research program, the overall purpose of which is to evaluate the effects of Fund and Fund-related activities. Such evaluation serves both to inform the funding agents of the value received for dollars spent, and to furnish guidelines for the improvement of existing and future programs.

Evaluation efforts involve two dimensions. The first dimension includes three levels of evaluation: individual projects, such as pre-school centers; each community action program in its totality; and the impact of the Fund on the state as a whole.

The second dimension includes two foci of evaluation: the program product, or impact—that is, the measurable changes which occur, as a result of community action programs, in the concomitants of poverty (low income, unemployment, inadequate housing); and the program process—the social and political aspects which influence the results of a given community action program.

One way to evaluate the program process is to analyze the relationship between a community action program and the community—including its social, political and economic components—in which the program takes place. Aided by a June 1965 OEO grant, the Research Department undertook this analysis.

In fact, the research functions of the Fund have been limited only by lack of staff and lack of financial support. Although the Fund would have preferred to have made available to each of its community action programs a full and qualified research staff, neither the manpower nor the money was there. It is hoped that the research staff of the newly established center at the University of North Carolina will be able to provide assistance to community action programs in effective evaluation of their component programs.

Finally, it became increasingly clear during 1965 that many people did not understand the antipoverty program. A successful mobilization of resources in a community to attack the problem of poverty requires widespread public support, and the Fund found itself called upon to provide aid to the community action projects in using every possible means of communication to explain what was being done under antipoverty programs and why. The initial efforts in this respect were so successful that the public information staff of the Fund has been increased, additional support is being given communities, and staff has been employed to work through civic clubs and conventions, and to use all other means to bring to the people of the state a better understanding of the purposes and objectives of the antipoverty programs.

C. Fund Activities at the State Level

It bears repeating that the Fund's emphasis and focus on the community has not been taken with blinders on. The job cannot be done at the community level alone, particularly in this era of efforts to establish "creative federalism" and to define the most effective roles for state government as well as the federal and local governments.

From its very beginning, the Fund has been closely related to the efforts of all state agencies to play a constructive role in the "war on poverty." Again, the ways in which the Fund works with state agencies depend upon needs and priorities at any given time.

For example, in the early months of the "war on poverty," the Fund was able to provide technical assistance to the state government, to educational institutions, and particularly to the state's new economic opportunity staff concerning antipoverty programs, the mobilization of resources, and new approaches to the delivery of traditional state services.

There have been grants to state agencies. At the time the Fund was established, $2,000,000 of the resources made available by the Ford Foundation were earmarked for a grant to the State Board of Education to experiment with new ways of teaching the first three grades of school. The comprehensive school improvement project has been a major effort of the State Department of Public Instruction in adjusting to new demands in school systems; and it has enabled school systems throughout the state to anticipate and prepare for the opportunities afforded under the Elementary and Secondary Education Act of 1965.[10]

One of the first acts of Governor Moore in 1965 was to establish the State Planning Task Force to help coordinate the resources available from federal programs for administration within the state. A grant was made to the State Planning Task Force to enable it to include a human resources coordinator on its staff. A similar grant went to the Task Force to help support a staff position to develop a low-income housing program within the state.

The North Carolina Fund joined with the University of North Carolina, Duke University, and the State Board of Education in support of the Learning Institute of North Carolina as a new and critical agency for administering research and demonstration programs aimed at improving the system of public education in

---

[10] 79 Stat. 27 (codified in scattered sections of 20 U.S.C.A. (Supp. 1965)).

this state. A later grant went to support Youth Educational Services, an effort by a committee group of college students to introduce effective tutoring programs in both urban and rural areas in North Carolina.

As in the case of the communities, every opportunity for innovation and change could not be handled by an existing agency. In the absence of another agency able to administer the mobility program, for example, the North Carolina Fund accepted a grant from the U.S. Department of Labor to conduct the experiment.

D. The Fund as Critic

In all of its processes of learning more about the problems of poverty in North Carolina and the complicated reasons why it is so difficult to break people out of poverty, the Fund staff and board have become aware of the critical role that certain systems—such as education, housing, and manpower development—play in determining whether opportunities can be opened to the poor. The systems of local, state and federal agencies, and of private agencies, involved in the administration of these critical services and in making them meaningful to the poor are so critical to the success of the antipoverty program that they bear separate study as systems. The Fund has established several committees composed of board members, staff members, and citizens from across the state to take a look at some of the critical systems affecting antipoverty programs and to identify the weakness in those systems that, if corrected, can help bring success to the "war on poverty."

CONCLUSION

With a little more than two years and about half of its initial development funds to go, The North Carolina Fund is engaged in a continuing examination, with board and staff members, of needs, priorities and problems affecting poverty in North Carolina. It is more than ever conscious of the possible, of investing in efforts that will bring long-range benefits to the poor and the communities in which they live. It is conscious of the advantages and limitations of the direct grant (particularly where there is no assurance of financial support once the grant has been spent), of the need to insure that persons and agencies do not come to rely on technical assistance that cannot be maintained past 1968, of the need to build in and build on new programs under institutions that have a continuing life.

Now that communities have gained experience in using the resources available under federal antipoverty programs and related "great society" legislation, the Fund need not be so concerned that these resources be properly used. The patterns of use are being established. Likewise, concern for programs of professional and subprofessional training and for continuing research and evaluation is no longer of the highest priority because of the developing programs at the university.

But persistent and major problems remain on the Fund agenda. Where priorities for continuing effort will be determined depends on board and staff action, but the area of action is relatively clear.

(1) There is the problem of finding and supporting articulate leadership from the ranks of the poor, of all races, to insure that the point of view of the poor is fairly expressed.

(2) There is the problem of how to help the poor better define their own priorities and to communicate them to key community agencies.

(3) There is the problem of whether the community action agency, aptly compared to an international treaty organization, can carry out an effective role of helping all community agencies plan, identify, and carry out programs essential to reducing or eliminating poverty and its effects.

(4) There is the problem of whether communities can develop operational planning processes that involve all related service and educational agencies, and involve a representative cross-section of the community.

(5) There is the problem of whether the poorly-educated and displaced can be provided the skills and the opportunity to become productive and more self-reliant.

(6) There is the problem of whether public education can adapt itself to the needs of children from disadvantaged homes so that, as they grow through the school system, they acquire the knowledge and capabilities that can overcome an inadequate beginning.

(7) There is the problem of overcoming the continuing effects of racial bias and prejudice in order to open educational and employment opportunities to Negroes and Indians that are responsive to their needs and aspirations.

The Fund does not have enough dollars to meet head-on any one of these problems. It must survey the possible needs and opportunities, assess the possible consequences, and act in its best judgment. The board and staff have had ample experience in adapting to a changing situation. There is no reason to believe that they cannot continue to do so. And in so doing, it may be that they will define a role for the use of philanthropic funds to help meet the changing needs of a state that will not be limited to antipoverty programs. Poverty is a current national problem, as well as a state problem. As our society grows and matures, new problems will arise. The foundation which can anticipate, define and help a state meet new challenges will have a continuing usefulness.

COORDINATION OF THE WAR ON POVERTY

After one and one-half years of operation, it is becoming increasingly clear that "total war" on poverty is an exceedingly large and complex undertaking. It is well recognized that President Johnson led the country to a remarkable national consensus on the goal of eradicating poverty. Perhaps less well seen is the significance that this national effort has in providing a unified focus for the planning, organization, and administration of social programs. Success in achieving the goal of eradicating poverty may well require a far-reaching change in public administration:

(1) Want, disease, ignorance, squalor, and idleness—to use Lord Beveridge's list of the giants responsible for poverty[1]—require a many-pronged attack. Even if the causes of poverty were fully understood, many of the tools for eradicating them are still in the design or test stage.

(2) The federal machinery for combating poverty requires teamwork among a dozen federal agencies which administer a wide variety of programs. While these many programs contribute much to the antipoverty effort, only a few are specifically and wholly directed to this objective. The funds available to the Office of Economic Opportunity (OEO) constitute only a part, and not the largest, of the federal resources for combating poverty; and, indeed, some of the largest programs are in other agencies.

(3) The pluralistic principle of our social, political, and economic organization complicates planning and action at the local level. The checks and balances of our federal system of government, with its national, state, and local levels of legislatures, legislation, and administrations, make it difficult to mobilize communities to take comprehensive action and to reach the poor in all the corners of the country. "Creative federalism" must overcome this challenge of complexity.

(4) The injections of new organizations, new approaches, and new programs since 1964 have challenged some older institutions and existing methods and have produced many conflicts.

Under these circumstances, high premium attaches to inspired insight in the allocation of resources, good organization, and efficient administration. Because scarcity of resources always prevails, effective coordination is the sine qua non of

* Assistant to the Chief of the Education, Manpower and Science Division of the Bureau of the Budget, in the Executive Office of the President.

The author acknowledges his gratitude to numerous staff members in the Office of Economic Opportunity, the Departments of Labor, Health, Education and Welfare, and in the Bureau of the Budget, as well as persons outside the Government, who contributed insights and facts for this article. However, the views expressed are those of the author and do not necessarily represent those of the Bureau of the Budget or any other agency.

[1] See WILLIAM BEVERIDGE, SOCIAL INSURANCE AND ALLIED SERVICES 6 (1942).

a successful war on poverty. Vice President Humphrey has commented strongly on
this point:

> ... I hope we can be truly non-parochial in our interagency coordination and
> cooperation. It will require a degree of interagency cooperation, a degree of func-
> tional rather than organizational concern, which has seldom, if ever, been achieved
> in domestic affairs in this country.[2]

Effective coordination is needed horizontally and vertically among federal, state,
local, and private agencies. Poor people and poor families frequently have multiple
problems. The delivery of variegated services and other assistance for a long enough
period and in concentrated enough form to break the intergenerational cycle of
poverty is at best a difficult problem. Subsequent sections examine the problem of
coordination at both the national and state-local levels from several standpoints.

The "war on poverty" is a landmark in the focusing of public concern on the
broad range of social problems and programs which affect people, and in developing
new and more effective approaches for concerting resources and action to strike at
the root causes of poverty. In considering the role of coordination in this effort, it is
useful to bear in mind that the distant goal of eliminating poverty may appear
clear, but the routes and the road maps for reaching the promised land are not.

Many of the roadways have never been traversed or even built; the signposts are
often blurred or lacking. Numerous promising routes are blocked by institutional
obstacles. Neither the longest residents of poverty-land, nor the most respected
sages of higher-income-land, can prescribe with certitude the best route. Some
claim to know shortcuts—usually labeled "jobs," "negative income tax," "representation of poor," "social security"—while others counsel carefully planned, long
term expeditions along multiple routes to develop the capacities of people, and
especially of children and youth, through human investment, and to eliminate the
culture of poverty. Many who are involved are convinced that shortages of funds
will wreck the whole effort. Planning and action are, moreover, often disrupted
by strong disagreements.

If this accurately describes the situation in poverty-land and our state of knowledge regarding the exits from it, there is much good reason for adequate provision
for search, for trial and error, for toleration of new ideas and multiple solutions.
The need for coordination must be balanced against the importance of innovation.
Coordination is not an end in itself, but only a means toward solving complex problems involving action by multiple agencies at least cost. One of the most significant
elements of the Economic Opportunity Act is its massive commitment to innovation
and the opportunity it affords for innovation. Yet the act places much weight on
coordination; and coordination cannot be disregarded, because even in a wealthy

---

[2] Remarks of Vice President Hubert H. Humphrey prepared for the Economic Opportunity Council,
March 12, 1965.

society, scarcity of resources is an ever-present, dominant constraint. Thus, without constant, effective husbanding of energies and funds, both in their allocation and their administration, it is a virtual certainty that many urgent needs in our society will continue to go unmet.

The specific objective of coordination in the "war on poverty" is to concert resources and action and to increase the speed and efficiency of response by communities, states, and the federal agencies to meeting the needs of the poor. At the local level it seeks to promote the linkage of related programs to secure concerted antipoverty action in providing services and benefits to enable the poor to obtain self-sufficiency. At the federal and state levels it seeks to elicit the cooperative, united action in allocation of resources and administration of programs which will complement local comprehensive planning and action by both public and private agencies.[3]

I

THE FEDERAL ORGANIZATION FOR COORDINATING THE "WAR ON POVERTY"

Many of the organizational problems in the major new effort against poverty were foreseen in late 1963 and early 1964 by the staff of the Council of Economic Advisers, the Bureau of the Budget, and the special task force on poverty which helped advise President Johnson in developing plans for the "war on poverty." A number of approaches to the organization of the federal effort were carefully considered. But from an early date it was clear that coordination would have a central role and that new patterns of action would have to be devised, particularly at the community level, and that this would have a corresponding effect on the mode of federal action.

In his message to the Congress on March 16, 1964, President Johnson called for a "national war on poverty." To prevent the war from becoming "a series of uncoordinated and unrelated efforts—that it [not] perish for lack of leadership and direction," the President recommended establishment of a new Office of Economic Opportunity in the Executive Office of the President. The Director of this Office was to be "directly responsible" for the new programs and was to "work with and through existing agencies of the Government."[4]

The Congress followed the President's recommendations. It enacted the Economic Opportunity Act of 1964, approved on August 20, 1964, creating the OEO[5] and providing broad authority for coordination of antipoverty programs, including authority for the Director "to call upon other Federal agencies to supply such statistical data . . . and other materials as he deems necessary to discharge his

---

[3] *Coordination in the War on Poverty*, II OFFICE OF ECONOMIC OPPORTUNITY, CONGRESSIONAL PRESENTATION 93 (1966). The succeeding sections of this article draw extensively on this document, which provides an authoritative description of coordination as envisioned by the OEO.

[4] H.R. Doc. No. 243, 88th Cong., 2d Sess. 4 (1964).

[5] Sec. 601, 78 Stat. 528, 42 U.S.C. § 2941 (1964).

responsibilities . . . and to assist the President in coordinating the antipoverty efforts of all Federal agencies . . ."[6] and for the President to

direct that particular programs and functions, including the expenditure of funds, of the Federal agencies [which are engaged in administering programs related to the purposes of the act, or which otherwise perform functions relating thereto] shall be carried out, to the extent not inconsistent with other applicable law, in conjunction with or in support of programs authorized under this Act.[7]

The most far-reaching innovation in the act was the provision in title two for "community action programs" to be conducted, administered, or coordinated through "community action agencies." The community action programs were to provide the glue for binding together fragmented programs and the resources for filling gaps in existing efforts. To strengthen the role of this new set of programs and organizations, Congress provided two sorts of preferences.

Section 211 specifies that "In determining whether to extend assistance under this Act, the Director shall, to the extent feasible, give preference to programs and projects which are components of a community action program. . . ."[8] This section applies to the nine other programs authorized by the act.

Section 612 provides that:

To the extent feasible and consistent with the provisions of law governing any Federal program and with the purposes of this Act, the head of each Federal agency administering any Federal program is directed to give preference to any application for assistance or benefits which is made pursuant to or in connection with a community action program approved pursuant to Title II of this Act.[9]

This section is designed to assure preference to community action programs from funds for other related programs administered by agencies other than OEO.

II

OVERALL COORDINATION OF THE ANTIPOVERTY EFFORT

To provide top-level interagency coordinating machinery, Congress also established an Economic Opportunity Council to "consult with and advise the Director in carrying out his functions, including the coordination of antipoverty efforts by all segments of the Federal Government."[10] The Director is Chairman of the Council, which includes the Secretaries of Defense, Interior, Agriculture, Commerce, Labor, Housing and Urban Development, and Health, Education and Welfare, the Attorney General, the Administrator of the Small Business Administration, the Chairman of the Council of Economic Advisers, the Director of Selective Service,

[6] Sec. 611(a)(1), 78 Stat. 532, 42 U.S.C. § 2961(a)(1) (1964).
[7] Sec. 611(a)(3), 78 Stat. 532, 42 U.S.C. § 2961(a)(3) (1964).
[8] Sec. 211, 78 Stat. 520, 42 U.S.C. § 2791 (1964).
[9] Sec. 612, 78 Stat. 533, 42 U.S.C. § 2962 (1964).
[10] Sec. 604(a), 78 Stat. 531, 42 U.S.C. § 2944(a) (1964).

and, by invitation, the Federal Co-Chairman, Appalachian Regional Commission, and the Director of the Bureau of the Budget.

At its first meeting, President Johnson stated that he looked to the Economic Opportunity Council "as a domestic national security council for the war on poverty."[11] He asked Vice President Humphrey to take a leading role in the "war on poverty" and in the work of the Council. The Vice President was also asked by the President to serve as honorary chairman of a twenty-man National Advisory Council provided by section 605[12] to review the operations and activities of the OEO.[13]

The Cabinet-level Economic Opportunity Council and the staff-level Interagency Working Group of the Council provide a valuable forum within the government for top-level consideration of OEO and related antipoverty programs. At its regular meetings the Council has focused on many key interdepartmental questions such as a minimum wage for poverty-related activities and problems of agricultural migrant workers. It has also covered broad questions of interagency coordination, of church-state relations, and governmental information systems.

A. The President's Paramount Role

In popular terms, the "war on poverty" is equated with the new programs under the aegis of the Office of Economic Opportunity. Although there are nine or ten OEO programs budgeted for the three fiscal years 1965-1967, for annual enacted or proposed appropriations of $ .8 billion, $1.5 billion, and $1.75 billion dollars, respectively, the total federal antipoverty effort is much broader and larger. OEO has identified some 250 other "great society" and related programs administered by at least fifteen other federal agencies—including programs for education, manpower, health, welfare, social security, housing and urban renewal, and economic development—as contributing to the antipoverty effort.

The President is the only official who has authority to direct and coordinate the manifold aspects of this government-wide federal effort. He alone can give meaning to the broad goals, exercise major initiative in presenting a broad legislative program, establish priorities for allocation of fiscal resources through proposed expenditure and revenue measures, shape the organizational alignment of the numerous cooperating and often competing agencies, and establish the broad administrative policies which provide for efficient administration. Coordination is the essence of the presidential process.

While it may usually not be visible to outside observers, the President can, and does, draw on a broad range of staff resources to help discharge his coordinative functions, including (1) his immediate White House staff; (2) the Council of Economic Advisers, which, for example, gave a strong initial impetus to the develop-

---

[11] U.S. PRESIDENTS, PUBLIC PAPERS OF THE PRESIDENTS OF THE UNITED STATES, LYNDON B. JOHNSON, 1963-1964, Bk. II, at 1657 (1965).

[12] 78 Stat. 531, as amended, 42 U.S.C.A. § 2945 (Supp. 1965).

[13] White House Press Release, Jan. 28, 1965, and 79 Stat. 973, 978.

COORDINATION OF THE WAR ON POVERTY

ment of the antipoverty effort;[14] (3) the Bureau of the Budget for advice and assistance relating to the organization and management of the executive branch, coordination of legislative proposals, program evaluation and programming of resources, and preparation and execution of the federal budget; (4) the Office of Economic Opportunity, whose Director is the President's chief assistant in the "war on poverty," and the Cabinet-level Economic Opportunity Council; and (5) the whole circle of Cabinet officers and agency heads who are responsible for carrying out the policies set by the President under laws enacted by the Congress, and whose assistance and cooperation is more often than not welded together through the units in the Executive Office—in which the Bureau of the Budget serves as a principal institutional coordinating mechanism.

B. Policy Control by the Congress

Congress determines national policy in these far-sweeping poverty programs through substantive legislation and the appropriation process. At least ten committees of the House and Senate share in the important function of developing the legislation which determines the nature, shape, and magnitude of the federal programs combating poverty; and additional committees participate in the oversight process. The House Committee on Education and Labor and the Senate Committee on Labor and Public Welfare have an especially important role because they are responsible both for the Economic Opportunity Act and for the bills on education.[15] Education has been described by the President on several occasions as the major weapon against poverty. The latter committee also handles public health bills.

The House Committee on Ways and Means and the Senate Finance Committee also have a very large role, not only because they are responsible for revenue legislation but because they have in their control social security bills covering cash aid, welfare services, and increasingly important medical care programs. Old-age, survivors and disability insurance and public assistance are today, respectively, the largest providers of federal funds to the poor. The House Committee on Interstate and Foreign Commerce handles public health legislation; and the House Committee on Veterans Affairs is responsible for veterans' bills, which provide pensions and medical benefits to needy veterans. The House Agriculture Committee and the Senate Agriculture and Forestry Committee have the principal role on legislation affecting farmers and other rural residents. Finally, the Appropriations Committees

---

[14] See PRESIDENT, ECONOMIC REPORT, 1964, at 55-84 (1964), for a clear marshalling of the facts on poverty following the President's January 1964 State of the Union message, in which he declared all out war on poverty in America.

[15] See, e.g., Hearings on Examination of the War on Poverty Program Before the Subcommittee on the War on Poverty Program of the House Committee on Education and Labor, 89th Cong., 1st Sess. 1-7 (1965) (opening statement by Chairman Adam C. Powell, criticizing umbrella agencies for hindering creative programming and involvement of the poor).

of the House and Senate exercise profound influence on the course and size of federal programs by their actions on appropriations recommended by the President.

Within all these committees there are numerous subcommittees, and additional legislation is handled by other committees.

C. Coordination Through the Allocation of Federal Resources

The setting of action goals and the allocation of federal funds to achieve them is perhaps the single most important and powerful focus for coordination of the antipoverty effort today. The effort to eradicate poverty requires multi-purpose, multi-program, long-term endeavors. Resources must be allocated with a careful balance between the short-run relief and long-term human investment programs, between income transfer programs for the aged and education, training, and health services for youth; between programs for redevelopment of physical facilities and human renewal and rehabilitation; between innovative but untried programs and established but often non-dynamic existing programs.

The budgetary process is the federal government's chief action-forcing mechanism for coordination. The budgetary review involves not only allocation of resources but scrutiny of administrative efficiency and questioning of organizational assignments.

President Johnson's budget recommendations for the fiscal year 1967 include estimated expenditures of $21 billion for federal benefits and services to the poor from administrative budget and trust funds—an increase of nearly $4 billion over 1966 and $8.6 billion over actual 1963 outlays.[16] This $21 billion is the estimated portion for the poor out of a total $45 billion in "great society" and other related programs, and it represents nearly 14.5 per cent of all cash payments to the public from administrative budget and trust fund accounts. Additional benefit will be derived by the poor from the remaining expenditures in the budget, although no one has estimated what their total share may be.

Of the total of $21 billion identified for the poor, expenditures from funds appropriated to the President for the new programs under the OEO comprise $1.6 billion, or 7.5 per cent. The Department of Health, Education and Welfare accounts for 68 per cent, including $8.6 billion from the social security and health insurance funds and an additional $5.9 billion from appropriated funds. The remaining $5 billion, or 24 per cent, is distributed among nine other agencies—the Departments of Labor, Agriculture, Housing and Urban Development, Interior, and Commerce, the Veterans Administration, the Small Business Administration, the Railroad Retirement Board, and the Appalachian Regional Commission.

The federal government's efforts to assist the poor are more clearly revealed by looking at the purposes for which the $21 billion will be expended in fiscal 1967:

---

[16] See THE BUDGET OF THE UNITED STATES GOVERNMENT, 1967, at 126 (1966). For a useful brief description of many of the programs mentioned below see SAR A. LEVITAN, PROGRAMS IN AID OF THE POOR (1965).

(1) $7.3 billion will be for old-age, survivors, and disability insurance payments by HEW, an increase from $5.3 billion in 1963 and $6.9 billion in 1966.

(2) Other cash benefit payments will total $5.4 billion in 1967, compared with $4.8 billion in 1963 and $5.4 billion in 1966. In 1967 public assistance grants to states by HEW, exclusive of medical care and services, will total $2.4 billion. Veterans Administration compensation and pension payments directly to individuals will be $2.3 billion. The remainder of $.7 billion is unemployment insurance benefits by the Labor Department and Railroad Retirement Board payments.

(3) Education and training programs will total $2.8 billion in 1967. They show the sharpest rate of increase, rising from $.2 billion in 1963 and $1.3 billion in 1966. The new Elementary and Secondary Education Act of 1965[17] accounts for $1 billion and the Economic Opportunity Act of 1964 for about $.8 billion of the total in 1967. The remainder includes the manpower development and training activities of the Department of Labor, education services to Indians by the Department of the Interior, and other HEW programs.

(4) Health benefits and services will also total $2.8 billion in 1967, compared to $1.1 billion in 1963 and $1.5 billion in 1966. The 1967 total includes $1.2 billion for the new Medicare and supplemental health programs for the aged. About $.8 billion is for medical care under public assistance, and the remainder consists of a variety of HEW, OEO, and Veterans Administration health activities.

(5) All other aids, including a large variety of services and programs for economic and community redevelopment, will account for about $3 billion of expenditures in 1967, compared with $1.4 billion in 1963 and $2.5 billion in 1966. Included in this total is nearly $.8 billion for Agriculture Department programs, of which direct food distribution and food stamp programs are the largest. Public housing, urban renewal, and other aids by the new Department of Housing and Urban Development account for $.4 billion. Welfare, employment, small business, and community and economic development programs account for much of the remainder.

About $9 billion of the total of $21 billion is for programs specifically restricted to the needy—such as the OEO programs, public assistance, Veterans Administration pensions, educational aid for children of poor families. The remainder represents other programs which aid the poor as part of their broader role.

The concept of a total "war on poverty" is still, as governmental endeavors go, a very new one. No single, agreed-upon grand strategy pervades these programs. There is not in them a neat correspondence between the single stated need of overcoming poverty and a carefully balanced and coordinated action plan. Exceedingly significant new initiatives have come out of the effort to mold a "great society." Yet many of the existing programs date back to the "new frontier," "fair deal," "new deal," and even earlier days. They are the accumulated product of hundreds of laws winnowed out of thousands of bills introduced in the Congress. Their character is

---

[17] 79 Stat. 27 (codified in scattered sections of 20 U.S.C.A. (Supp. 1965)).

often embedded solidly in laws, precedent, philosophies, and institutions which can be changed or redirected only with great effort. Coordination and interrelationship of programs were not heavily stressed when they were created. Agency and professional jealousies, often mirroring the views of supporting private groups and organizations, reinforce this compartmentalization. All but a few of the programs serve purposes broader than aid to the poor.

Thus, while the President has enunciated and the Congress has adopted a national policy "to eliminate the paradox of poverty in the midst of plenty,"[18] it is still too true, as Gunnar Myrdal observed in early 1964, that "in almost all respects— minimum wages, Social Security, agriculture, housing, etc.—American economic and social policies show a perverse tendency to favor groups that are above the level of the most needy."[19]

The strongest brand of "presidential government" can remold or give new direction to such established programs only with the greatest of difficulty and only gradually. In many instances, this can only be done if the Congress enacts legislation.

Decisions relating to commitments of federal financing resources to particular programs are made principally through the legislative and budgetary processes. The principal machinery which the President uses to achieve coordination on such decisions are the staff units through which the White House develops the administration's legislative program and the President's budget. This machinery has developed through the years to become highly responsive to the President's wishes. It is supported by a general-purpose staff in the Bureau of the Budget which serves as an institutional coordinating resource capable of reaching, on short notice, into the far corners of any agency to bring forth information and response. On the question of how much to spend for any program, and on the balance of funds for antipoverty programs against the legions of other demands on the federal budget, the decision is uniquely the President's.

The OEO role in advising the President on the allocation of resources is still emerging. OEO representatives may participate on administration task forces or work groups endeavoring to develop new program ideas. OEO develops an overall plan for combating poverty which provides a basis for considering the financial needs of OEO and some of the needs of other agencies. However, along with other agencies, the OEO presents its requests for funds to the President through the Budget Bureau. It also reports on legislation to the Budget Bureau or to the White House as do other agencies.

A measure of coordination can be achieved by filling the gaps in existing programs—either by adding new ones or by expanding old ones. The all-out "war on poverty" has been enthusiastically received by the federal establishment. Many agencies have sought and found a significant way to relate their activities to the

---

[18] Economic Opportunity Act of 1964, § 2, 78 Stat. 508, 42 U.S.C. § 2701 (1964).
[19] Myrdal, *The Matrix*, in POVERTY IN PLENTY 118, 122 (Dunne ed. 1964).

new objective. On the whole, opportunities to establish new programs or to author-
ize additional funds have evoked a particularly ready and willing response among
the agencies. They are typically dominated by established laws and purposes, and
it is much easier to add new programs than to reallocate funds. In 1965, a number
of major new programs were enacted, including the Elementary and Secondary
Education Act of 1965[20] and the Social Security Amendments of 1965,[21] which make
particularly large contributions toward the "war on poverty." Many other major
laws in the education, health, vocational rehabilitation, housing and urban development, economic development, and other fields were also enacted.

Despite the limitations of a stringent budget in a period of international uncertainty, major new legislative proposals of great importance to the "war on poverty"
are included in the President's 1966 legislative program. One of the most important
is the $2.3 billion, six-year city demonstration program which includes provision
for both urban and human renewal. Other proposals include legislation to increase
the income criterion for allocating aid under the Elementary and Secondary Education Act of 1965 from $2,000 to $3,000 per family in fiscal 1968, to raise the minimum
wage and to extend protection of the Fair Labor Standards Act[22] to over five
million more workers, to provide improvements in the unemployment compensation
system, to strengthen programs giving assistance to unemployed parents of needy
children, and to improve the nutrition of needy children.

The budgetary process also provides an important tool for redirecting programs
so that they concentrate more on helping the disadvantaged. The 1967 budget,
through proposed legislation or administrative action, reflects redirection of the
manpower development and training program to concentrate more on training the
less skilled; the school lunch and special milk program to focus more on needy
children; the public assistance program to provide more financial aid and better
medical care to families with dependent children; and the federal-state vocational
rehabilitation program to enroll more handicapped persons for receiving public
assistance.[23]

It is altogether clear, however, that the available tools for measuring the effectiveness of federal programs are not precise. Even in the OEO where a strong program
analysis staff has been assembled, programs are new and judgments regarding their
effectiveness are largely a priori. The President has directed all agencies in the
executive branch to develop and introduce a new planning-programming-budgeting
system which will "incorporate the most modern management techniques now used
in government and industry."[24] This new approach will certainly be directed
to measuring the effectiveness of programs in combating poverty.

---

[20] 79 Stat. 27 (codified in scattered sections of 20 U.S.C.A. (Supp. 1965)).
[21] 79 Stat. 286 (codified in scattered sections of 26, 42, and 45 U.S.C.A. (Supp. 1965)).
[22] 52 Stat. 1060 (1938), as amended, 29 U.S.C. §§ 201-19 (1964).
[23] THE BUDGET OF THE UNITED STATES GOVERNMENT, 1967, at 27-28 (1966).
[24] Id. at 33.

III

THE ROLE OF THE OFFICE OF ECONOMIC OPPORTUNITY

The Economic Opportunity Act of 1964, with its sweeping commitment to a social goal with very broad implications, represents a new departure in public administration. It has far-reaching significance for coordination of public and private nationwide action to achieve the major national goal of eradicating poverty. Its new features include: (1) A sweeping "clientele" approach concentrating on the then thirty-five million poor, as distinct from the typical, although not exclusive, focus of agencies and programs along "functional" lines. The new programs extend even where present agencies follow clientele lines—as does the Veterans Administration or the Department of Agriculture. (2) Strong emphasis on programs to help children and youth, bespeaking a long-term human investment approach for breaking the intergenerational cycle of poverty. (3) A heavy emphasis on direct federal aid to local communities, in contrast with the typical pattern of federal aid through the states. (4) The invention of the community action program concept to spark the creation of new institutions and to serve as an innovating and coordinating mechanism in local communities. (5) Authorization of nine other additional or "gap filling" programs. (6) The creation of the OEO with broad authority, already described in an earlier section,[25] to help the Director assist the President in the coordination of the overall federal antipoverty effort.

In many respects this was a frankly pragmatic and experimental approach to a pervasive, long-standing national problem.

A. Over-All Leadership Functions of OEO

In the leadership arena, the OEO still largely is defining its role. Although the OEO is in the Executive Office of the President, an echelon higher than the regular department, pressures have led it to lean more toward its functions as an operating agency, rather than toward those it possesses as a coordinating agency. Perhaps this is understandable in these early phases, because the "heat was on" to get the new programs "off the ground." This has, however, introduced a competitive element into a situation where OEO may endeavor to coordinate activities of other agencies, although it has also given OEO certain leverage to bring about a common alignment of agency programs.

On the broader front of planning and resource allocation, OEO has a strong staff for research plans, programs, and evaluation. In the summer of 1965, a government-wide survey was made by the OEO of programs operated by other agencies which contribute to the "war on poverty." This survey was useful as background information in the preparation of the 1967 federal budget and in the development of the OEO's own budget. But a great deal of action is still required to utilize fully

---

[25] See text accompanying notes 10-13 *supra*.

the OEO's broad authority under the preference provisions of the Economic Opportunity Act with respect to programs of other agencies. This is discussed further in a subsequent section.

B. The Operating Programs of OEO

The ten programs authorized by the Economic Opportunity Act of 1964 have involved the OEO in a wide variety of interagency and intergovernmental relations. Perhaps no other operating agency in the federal government has as numerous relationships with other federal agencies as OEO has developed in a year and a half.

About half of the new OEO programs were essentially extensions of existing federal programs, although their beneficiaries were confined to the "poor." With the concurrence of the President, six programs have been delegated by the OEO to federal agencies that administer related broader programs:

(1) The Neighborhood Youth Corps, covering both in-school and out-of-school projects, scheduled to aid some 350,000 youths in 1967, is being administered by the Manpower Administration in the Department of Labor. Some Neighborhood Youth Corps projects, however, are sponsored by local Community Action Agencies or by their delegate agencies.

(2) The Work Experience project grant program, largely paralleling the community work and training program under public assistance, and estimated to provide aid to 105,000 trainees in 1967, is administered by the Welfare Administration of HEW. It has arrangements with the Adult Basic Education program for support.

(3) The Adult Basic Education program, with an expected enrollment of 75,000 individuals in 1967, is being operated as a grant-in-aid program by the Office of Education in HEW.

(4) The two-part Rural Loan program is being administered by the Farmers Home Administration in the Department of Agriculture.

(5) The Small Business Loan program has been delegated to the Small Business Administration, although the creation of small business development centers is often tied to local community action agencies.

(6) The College Work Study program, originally delegated to HEW, has been entirely transferred to that department by the Higher Education Act of 1965.[26]

The remaining four programs are being operated directly by OEO:

(1) The Job Corps program, consisting of conservation centers for men and urban training centers for men and women, is scheduled to have 124 centers with a capacity of 45,000 by the end of fiscal 1967, and is being directly operated by OEO. Contractual agreements have been made with (a) the Department of Agriculture and the Department of the Interior for the operation of the conservation centers, (b) the Department of Labor for recruitment and placement of enrollees, and (c) the Department of Defense for handling their pay. Contracts with private

---

[26] 79 Stat. 1219, 20 U.S.C.A. §§ 1001-144 (Supp. 1965).

firms and nonprofit agencies have been made for operation of the urban training centers.

(2) VISTA is likewise being directly operated and is scheduled to utilize 4,500 volunteers by June 30, 1967.

(3) The Community Action Program, which involves the making of grants to nonprofit and public agencies, is the largest and most far-reaching direct OEO operation.

(4) The Migrant Assistance program is operated as part of the Community Action Program.

C. Emerging Mechanisms of Interagency Coordination by OEO

Although delegation has scattered the new programs under the Economic Opportunity Act, the OEO coordinating role is strongest with respect to OEO-financed programs. With respect to these programs, the OEO exercises various controls over basic policy decisions and retains full coordinating authority by such means as: exercise of the power of the purse through allocation of funds, from the single OEO appropriation, among the various programs delegated and directly operated; entering into memoranda of agreement with the other agencies to which the several programs have been delegated, and further reinforcing control through jointly-approved regulations; holding frequent, usually weekly, meetings with top officials from agencies operating such delegated programs; requiring reports on operations, on proposed use of funds, and on recommended budget requirements; using the fungible Community Action Program resources in conjunction with the various delegated programs—for example, to enrich Neighborhood Youth Corps projects, to finance Youth Opportunity Center personnel in Community Action Program projects, or to participate in multiple agency financing of projects; and utilizing on a contractual basis specialized services of other agencies—such as those of the U.S. Employment Service for Job Corps recruitment and placement of Job Corps recruits—thereby achieving closer relationships with other ongoing programs.

As might be expected, especially numerous relationships are growing up between the OEO community action programs and other agencies of government. Interagency agreements, formal and informal, on a bilateral basis between OEO and other departments and agencies are a major OEO technique for achieving coordination of planning and action at the federal level. Responsibility for initiating these interagency agreements rests with OEO's Office of Interagency Relations, a top level staff office within the Office of the Director. These agreements provide the basis for joint action, for joint funding of projects, and for maintaining effective coordination of planning and operations at the federal and local levels.

A general "umbrella" agreement between OEO and HEW has widened coordination between the two agencies. Under this agreement HEW has made available its personnel to OEO on a reimbursable basis; and OEO has funded special poverty coordinators in seven HEW regional offices, as well as in the Office of the Secretary. A joint OEO-Office of Education unit for the education of the disadvantaged—established by agreement between OEO and the U.S. Commissioner of Education—has facilitated cooperation on special education programs, such as Head Start, remedial tutorial programs, and title one of the new Elementary and Secondary Education Act of 1965.[27]

Under the "umbrella" agreement with HEW, the Public Health Service has also lent its support in the development of new Community Action Program projects —such as neighborhood health centers, the Home Health Aides program, health and dental care services in Head Start, and the expansion of medical care to the needy under the new Social Security Amendments of 1965.[28]

Other joint agreements between the constituent agencies of HEW and OEO led to the development of the Foster Grandparents program (Administration on Aging); "operation medicare alert" and a training program for Bureau of Federal Credit Unions (Social Security Administration); training of home health aides (Public Health Service); a joint rehabilitation project in California (Vocational Rehabilitation Administration); and provision of services for female applicants with dependent children wishing to enroll in the Job Corps (Welfare Administration).

Agreements with the Department of Labor have provided for coordinated action in the development and location of youth opportunity centers in conjunction with local community action programs leading to the out-stationing of youth opportunity centers personnel in many neighborhood centers; screening of the vast majority of Job Corps enrollees by state employment service agencies; reimbursements for employment service personnel stationed in community action program neighborhood centers; and funding of positions within various bureaus of the Department of Labor and within OEO.

An important multi-agency agreement on coordination of manpower programs developed by the President's Committee on Manpower sets the stage for cooperative action by the Labor Department, OEO, and HEW in thirty cities through a three-member selected cities task forces. Labor and OEO also have several jointly-funded projects, including the Star project in Mississippi aimed at 25,000 severely under-educated people, youth training projects in Watts in Los Angeles, and skill centers in New Haven.

Close cooperation between OEO and the Department of Agriculture has enabled antipoverty programs to be launched in rural America with greater speed and com-prehensiveness than would otherwise have been possible. A recent agreement with the Department of Agriculture will provide closer coordination between OEO's Rural Task Force and the Rural Community Development Service, the Federal Extension Service, the Rural Electrification Administration, and the Farmers' Home

[27] 79 Stat. 36, 20 U.S.C.A. §§ 821-27 (Supp. 1965).
[28] Sec. 121(a), 79 Stat. 343, 42 U.S.C.A. §§ 1396-96d (Supp. 1965).

Administration. The Department of Agriculture has provided valuable services in initiating Head Start and Community Action Program projects in rural areas and in recruiting for Job Corps and Neighborhood Youth Corps enrollees.

Close ties are maintained between OEO and the public housing and urban renewal activities of the new Department of Housing and Urban Development. Cooperation by Department of Justice officials has speeded the launching and development of the new Legal Services program. The Appalachian Regional Commission and OEO exchange information on project proposals and on statistics pertaining to the Appalachian region. There is a continuing relationship between OEO and the Bureau of Indian Affairs in the Department of the Interior in developing antipoverty programs on Indian reservations.

D. The Complex Skein of OEO Relationships

Perhaps no other agency in the federal government has such far-flung relationships with public and private agencies and organizations as OEO. Except for the limitation in section 205 of the Economic Opportunity Act that the community action program funds may not be used for "general aid to elementary or secondary education,"[29] OEO may finance virtually any antipoverty program, even if a similar program is being carried on by another agency. Any public agency or private nonprofit group, except a political party, may be used. Thus OEO is supporting local projects in an extremely wide variety of fields, cutting across the lines of many other federal agencies.

The historic drive to provide opportunity for the poor was planned to mobilize not only the energies of government but also of private organizations and individuals. Many thousands of people from all walks of life—businessmen, educators, labor officials, social workers, public administrators—have made themselves available for service in this effort. OEO has involved numerous advisory groups in its activities. The National Advisory Council, specifically authorized by the Economic Opportunity Act, has met four times in the past year to discuss policies, issues, and problems. Groups such as the Business Leadership Advisory Council, Labor Advisory Council, Community Representatives Advisory Council, and Public Officials Advisory Council have been established to provide OEO with expert advice and guidance. In addition, national advisory committees on Legal Services, Head Start, and the Older Poor make available a wealth of experience. Other groups, such as Women in Community Services, and the Inter-Faith Planning Committee on Poverty, also have provided much assistance and have added to the broader understanding of the "war on poverty," which in hundreds of communities is being translated into action through community action agencies involving a wide variety of interests on their governing boards.

[29] Sec. 205(b), 78 Stat. 518, 42 U.S.C. § 2785(b) (1964).

IV

Coordination of Antipoverty Efforts at Local, State,
and Regional Levels

One of the main purposes of the Economic Opportunity Act is comprehensive action and coordination of action against poverty. It emphasizes local initiative and voluntary action, buttressed by federal financial assistance covering ninety per cent, or even one hundred per cent, of project costs. A principal objective is to create opportunities for the impoverished to help themselves. Strong authority is provided for coordination, but there is also great flexibility.[30]

The major new thrust in the Economic Opportunity Act is the Community Action Program concept. The objectives of the community action programs are to call upon the huge reservoir of local initiative, to fill gaps in the spectrum of existing programs, and, above all, to provide mechanisms for coordinated local planning and action. In his first message on poverty, President Johnson stated:

> . . . through a new community action program we intend to strike at poverty at its source—in the streets of our cities and in the farms of our countryside among the very young and the impoverished old. This program asks men and women throughout the country to prepare long-range plans for the attack on poverty in their own local communities. . . .
>
> These plans will be local plans striking at the many unfilled needs which underlie poverty in each community, not just one or two. Their components and emphasis will differ as needs differ. These plans will be local plans calling upon all the resources available to the community—Federal and State, local and private, human and material . . . .[31]

Although nine other programs were also authorized, the heart of this commitment was embodied in title two of the Economic Opportunity Act which authorizes "Urban and Rural Community Action Programs" to provide stimulation, incentives, and resources to combat poverty.[32] A community action program is a program which is operated in "any urban or rural . . . area . . . including . . . a State, metropolitan area, county, city, town multicity unit, or multicounty unit"; provides "services, assistance, and other activities of sufficient scope and size to give promise of progress toward elimination of poverty or a cause or causes of poverty . . ."; is developed and administered with the "maximum feasible participation of residents of the areas and members of the groups served"; and is "conducted, administered, or coordinated by a public or private nonprofit agency . . . or a combination thereof."[33]

[30] See March, *Poverty: How Much Will the War Cost?*, 34 Social Serv. Rev. 141, 153-54 (1965).
[31] *Message from the President of the United States Relative to Poverty*, H.R. Doc. No. 243, 88th Cong., 2d Sess. 4 (1965).
[32] 78 Stat. 516, 42 U.S.C. §§ 2781-91 (1964), as amended, 42 U.S.C.A. §§ 2782, 2785, 2788, 2789 (Supp. 1965).
[33] Sec. 202, 78 Stat. 516, 42 U.S.C. § 2782 (1964), as amended, 42 U.S.C.A. § 2782 (Supp. 1965).

The first community action program grant was made in November 1964. By the end of January 1966 more than 900 grants had been made to over 1,000 of the 3,300 counties in the United States, including more than 600 active community action agencies. All of the fifty largest cities, with a population of eight million poor people, had community action agencies. By the end of fiscal 1967, it is estimated by OEO that community action agencies will be operating in more than 900 urban and rural areas, which contain over three-fourths of the thirty-two million poor people in the nation within their jurisdictional boundaries. Moreover, in fiscal 1967 the community action agencies will probably provide some service to about one-fourth of the people in their boundaries, or to one-fifth of all the poor. In addition, planning projects will be funded during 1967 in an estimated 300 additional communities. Of the $1.75 billion of appropriations recommended by the President for all OEO programs for fiscal 1967, $914 million is for community action programs, including $310 million for Head Start projects.

A. The Milieu for Community Action Programs

Poverty has many manifestations and many roots, although some roots go deeper than others. Among the thirty-four million poor in 1964, there were nearly fifteen million children and 5.4 million persons over age sixty-five. An estimated $12 billion of additional income was needed to fill the poverty income gap of all these poor.[34]

The planning and conduct of a comprehensive attack on poverty requires the mobilization in a community of an extremely broad spectrum of community agencies and resources. The human resource thrust of the "war on poverty" clearly requires participation of employment, job training, health, rehabilitation, welfare, education, and related agencies. Since environment is important, the housing, urban renewal, and other agencies charged with providing community facilities must be included. Financial and manpower resources of both local, public, and voluntary agencies must be harnessed, and must be supplemented by resources that are provided by states and, beyond them, by the federal government. Coordination, both horizontally and vertically, is imperative at the local level. However, coordination is difficult because:

(1) Available federal resources are typically provided through categorical programs. OEO in 1965 listed about 250 "programs" administered by fifteen agencies as related to the antipoverty mission.[35] Almost every program has its own organizational, special eligibility, and financial provisions.

(2) The compartmentalization of federal programs is more often than not projected into the organization of states and through them into the localities. Education,

---

[34] PRESIDENT, ECONOMIC REPORT, 1966, at 114 (1966).

[35] CATALOG OF FEDERAL PROGRAMS FOR INDIVIDUAL AND COMMUNITY IMPROVEMENT.

health, welfare, and employment agencies all have their professional and their jurisdictional boundaries, across which they work only with reluctance.

(3) Federal, as well as state, funds are often distributed by allotment formulas, based on population, incidence of disease, area, or other special factors, in order to assure "equitable" distribution. The federal budget includes about 140 grant-in-aid programs, many of which contain allotment formulas. More often than not, federal grant-in-aid funds in the vital education and health fields are allocated to the states, which in turn distribute them to the localities. Even Community Action Program funds are apportioned among the states according to a statutory formula and among counties by a flexible administrative formula. It is extremely difficult for a locality to concert available resources and muster an enlarged, coordinated effort.

(4) Local communities, especially rural or small town areas, are confronted by vast information gaps and skill shortages. They may not have the know-how or professional personnel to keep informed of the rapidly emerging possibilities for financial or technical aid under state programs and, least of all, federal programs. Furthermore, to qualify for available grants, a locality has to muster a good deal of statistical information and fill out complicated forms.

(5) Resources for local public services are not only compartmentalized, but tend to be vested in public agencies which may or may not be responsive to the poor people in the community or to coordination by a new "umbrella" agency. The OEO utilizes both public and private resources in community action programs and requires "maximum feasible participation" of residents of the areas and members of the groups served in community action agencies. Approximately seven out of ten of the community action agencies are private or mixed public-private nonprofit corporations, further complicating community relationships. Such agencies have the advantage of flexibility enjoyed by private corporations. But as "private" agencies they may often have limited capacity to raise the required local share of project costs or otherwise to engage the energies of the local public organizations.[36] However, since most of the mixed corporations are joint public-private ventures, it may work out that public resources at the local and state levels will be channeled into them readily, just as federal funds are now provided to them.

Not only is the problem of organizing in local communities complex, but to be effective the new resources of the portion of the "war on poverty" financed by the OEO must be used so as to achieve a leverage or multiplier effect—by which resources of local communities, states, and other federal agencies will be involved to the utmost.

B. Allocation of State, Local, and Private Nonprofit Resources for the Poor

The 1962 Census of Governments reported more than 91,000 units of state and local government in the United States. There is no similar comprehensive enumeration of private voluntary agencies, but it has been estimated that there are 200,000

---

[36] See, e.g., Loftus, *Oakland Is Split On Poverty Plans*, N.Y. Times, Jan. 17, 1966, p. 20, col. 1.

such organizations, plus 300,000 churches, in the United States.[37]   State and local governments and private voluntary agencies already play a major role in helping the poor.   Expenditures aiding the poor by state and local governments—according to a study for the OEO covering the years 1963-1964[38]—approached $13 billion and included: nearly $4 billion for current expenses of elementary, secondary, and vocational education or training; more than $3 billion for community facilities, such as school, medical, transportation, utility, and similar facilities; more than $2 billion for direct financial assistance through general relief, unemployment insurance, temporary disability insurance, and workmen's compensation programs; more than $2 billion for physical and mental health services; and more than $1 billion for social rehabilitation—that is, costs of operating correctional institutions and combating juvenile delinquency.

While the foregoing figures include many rough estimates, they are conservative in one major respect: They exclude state and local expenditures where the federal government provides more than fifty per cent of the program cost.   Thus, they omit about $2 billion of state and local outlays for old-age assistance, aid to the blind, aid to the permanently and totally disabled, and aid to families of dependent children.

According to the same study, private voluntary agencies spent nearly $2.5 billion to assist the poor, including more than $1 billion for educational services and nearly a half billion dollars for health services.   Thus, expenditures by state, local, and private voluntary agencies for the poor were in the neighborhood of $17 billion in 1963-1964 and will certainly have increased considerably by fiscal 1967.

The allocation of these financial resources is accomplished through an almost infinite diversity of governmental organs and private boards under widely-varying policies.   The bulk of these expenditures which assist the poor are only parts of broader programs.   Only a few, such as public assistance, are directed entirely to the needy.   In some programs, such as education, the poor may—often do—receive less than their pro rata share.   Recognition that many social and economic problems were going unmet in this highly decentralized system of pluralistic government has been one of the principal factors leading to the creation, during the past several decades, of numerous categorical federal grant-in-aid programs which seek to direct assistance according to need and financial ability, and to encourage states and localities (and, in some cases, private nonprofit agencies) to engage in activities which may otherwise not be carried on.[39]

In the face of large unmet needs, the dominant concern until the "war on

---

[37] ROBERT H. HAMLIN, VOLUNTARY HEALTH AND WELFARE AGENCIES IN THE UNITED STATES 9 (1961).

[38] Data are cited in a study by Griffenhagen-Kroger, Inc., entitled Anti-poverty Programs in the United States, prepared for the Office of Economic Opportunity in July 1965.   The data on funds in this section are from this study.

[39] See SPECIAL ANALYSES, BUDGET OF THE UNITED STATES, FISCAL YEAR 1967, particularly Special Analysis J on "Federal Aid to State and Local Governments," which estimates a total of more than $14.6 billion of such aid from budget and trust accounts for fiscal year 1967.

poverty" began had been to create and develop new programs, rather than to worry about their coordination. Thus, as pointed out earlier, local and state resources may be constricted into narrow compartments where they match existing federal programs. Most of the OEO programs also follow in this categorical pattern; but the community action programs are very broad because the spectrum of causes for poverty is broad. In view of the broad powers of OEO under this program, the challenge is clear: Will OEO be able to exercise the leverage of its flexible funds and preference provisions to contribute materially to the concerting of resources and action in the many other on-going programs?[40]

C. The OEO Building Block Approach

Although armed with substantial authority to require priorities and coordination based on comprehensive local plans, the OEO thus far has leaned heavily on a "building block" approach. The Economic Opportunity Act does not require comprehensive planning; and OEO has recognized that many communities, at the outset, were unable to initiate coordinated community action programs which would link different programs and service systems. Accordingly, communities were permitted to move forward to secure approval for "component projects" while they were engaged in program development and before they had a comprehensive community action program.[41] As of late January 1966, approximately 600 community action agencies had received funding for nearly 2,900 action components—that is, an average of about five per community action agency.[42]

This step-by-step approach under the Economic Opportunity Act has contrasted sharply with the emphasis on pre-planning that had been required for grants under the Juvenile Delinquency and Youth Offenses Control Act of 1961.[43] The comprehensive planning under that act, with its strong emphasis on evaluation, was in many ways the prototype for the community action programs, but it had been criticized as too slow. OEO is considering trial of a broader approach in the community action field in a few cities in the months to come.

Components of community action programs are typically developed by separate committees or community organizations, with little implementation of overall

---

[40] For various impressions regarding the effectiveness of coordination in the poverty program see II Office of Economic Opportunity, Congressional Presentation 93-116 (1966); U.S. Conference of Mayors, Special Report: The Office of Economic Opportunity and Local Community Action Agencies (1965); U.S. Conference of Mayors, Economic Opportunity in Cities (1966); Spivak, *Anti-Poverty Flaw*, Wall Street Journal, March 1, 1966, p. 16, col. 4; series on poverty programs entitled *The Better War* in Washington Post, Jan. 30-Feb. 13, 1966, particularly the story *"Maximum Feasible Participation" of Poor Has Not Yet Been Realized*, Feb. 4, p. 1, col. 2.

[41] Office of Economic Opportunity, Community Action Program Guide, Instructions for Applicants 22 (1965).

[42] New Haven, Connecticut, often is cited as the outstanding example of a community action program. Other cities often cited as showing good progress include Detroit, Pittsburgh, Atlanta, and Oakland, Cal. See address by Sargent Shriver to the AFL-CIO Convention, Dec. 9, 1965 (quoting United Press International survey).

[43] 75 Stat. 572, as amended, 42 U.S.C. §§ 241-48 (1964).

priorities. Under the concept of local initiative, there are practical constraints on how much guidance as to priorities OEO can provide. Instead, it has focused more on questions of representation and getting the program going.

Even so, many communities have found the requirement of preparing successive project proposals and the attendant delays to be discouraging and wasteful of time and money. In other cases, OEO has been criticized for funding activities which duplicated going projects in the community.

An adjunct of the "component project" approach has been a tendency of the community action programs to develop a conglomeration of national programs, such as Head Start, Upward Bound, Foster Grandparents, Migrants, and Legal Services. Some of these may assume the status of independent programs. OEO has encouraged adoption of its "packaged" programs such as Head Start, Legal Services, and the like.

Within the community action program area, perhaps the most unified projects have been the neighborhood centers. By the end of December 1965, sixty-nine of the approximately 600 active community action agencies had received funding for a total of 175 neighborhood centers. In many respects, the neighborhood centers represent a move toward the concept of a "one-stop" social service center. The first objective was to move the focus of community service out into the neighborhood in which the poverty-stricken people reside. The second objective was to enable those who were seeking service to make contact at one location with as many of the services that they needed as possible. The most common functions of a neighborhood center are those of outreach, advice, intake, and referral. Individuals or families seeking help are interviewed and guided to other specialized agencies which might help them, such as health clinics or welfare offices. In many instances, community welfare, employment, and health agencies have placed some of their employees in the center to render service on the spot. For example, an estimated 166 centers had Youth Opportunity Center personnel or other personnel financed by the employment service available to help needy youth.

Other federally-financed agencies have also shown a strong tendency to move their services toward outlying neighborhoods. The guidelines for youth opportunity centers provide that they will be located by the employment service in fringe areas where they can be reached by all youth, and satellite youth opportunity centers have been set up in outlying poverty areas. Similarly, the Welfare Administration has reported that of the 3,500 public welfare offices in the United States, more than 350 were decentralized to local neighborhoods.

The concept of concerting resources of local communities through physical relocation of the many public service agencies—welfare, health, rehabilitation, housing, vocational education, and employment—in one convenient location, with some common intake and referral unit, has not yet gotten very far. Families or individuals who need help often need assistance not only in establishing contact with community agencies but in working out the combinations and the sequence in which services can best aid them.

Nor has the present pattern of interagency community action, even as reinforced by OEO's broadened authority and resources, gone far enough in coordinating aid to local communities so that it would promote integration and relocation of existing and new programs in convenient one-stop locations. The concept of a "social service shopping center," housing most or all the local agencies sponsored by OEO, HEW, Labor, Housing and Urban Development, and other related agencies which finance programs that serve people, is undeveloped.

There is room for experimentation with broadening of the neighborhood center concept and with various patterns for concerting and providing a continuum of services at "one-stop" locations in communities, in neighborhoods, or even in whole urban areas. Action in this direction not only by OEO but also by other related agencies might provide speedier, more effective service to the citizens and eliminate duplicate paper work and overhead expenses.

D. Coordination Through OEO's Check Point Procedure

The OEO effort toward greater local coordination of the antipoverty projects is accomplished in two main ways: (1) by encouraging or requiring communities to develop comprehensive plans through their community action agency; and (2) by setting up requirements that there be an interaction between the community action agencies and other public community agencies, officials, and organizations in the development of community action program plans and encouraging such agencies to consult with the community action agencies on their proposed applications for assistance under other OEO, or other federal, programs. The authority of the OEO in this latter area lies largely in the preference provisions mentioned earlier. Since preference defined strictly in terms of priority access to funds may tend to lose its meaning when community action programs cover most of the poor population, the chief value of this authority may be in enabling OEO to promote more effective coordination at the local level.

The main OEO mechanism for interagency consultation at the local level is the so-called "check point procedure."[44] An applicant for a Community Action Program project grant is responsible for ascertaining the relationship of the proposed community action program project to approved and prospective projects financed under other parts of the Economic Opportunity Act (Work Experience, Work Study, Neighborhood Youth Corps, Adult Basic Education), and to other related programs, whether federally, state, or locally financed. Thus, the OEO requires that before submission of an application, the community action agency must have checked its proposals with the chief elected official of the community, and, where the subject matter is appropriate, the local director of the state employment service, the super-

---

[44] See OFFICE OF ECONOMIC OPPORTUNITY, *op. cit. supra* note 41, at 40-41.

intendent of schools, the director of the county welfare department, and other officials, such as the director of the local urban renewal, public housing, or public health agency, the local representatives of the agricultural extension service, the Farmers' Home Administration, and so on. Many community action agencies include these officials on their boards; and this is one of the most used techniques of local coordination in the poverty effort.

Conversely, arrangements have been made in the case of a few non-OEO financed programs for a "reverse check point procedure" in which agencies planning project proposals for federal aid under laws other than the Economic Opportunity Act must check with the local community action agency. At the present time, such a procedure is required only in two instances:

(1) Applications for federal assistance for education of children from low-income families under title one of the Elementary and Secondary Education Act of 1965[45] must, by law, be checked out by the local education agency with the community action agency, if there is one. Instructions by the Office of Education require that the application must be accompanied by a form indicating the position of the community action agency on the application.[46]

(2) Applications to the Department of Housing and Urban Development for neighborhood facilities grants, under section 703 of the Housing and Urban Development Act of 1965,[47] must be accompanied by a statement showing the relationship between such facility and the community action program and making reference to the specific community action program elements involved. The act authorizing this program specifies that priorities are to be given to projects which primarily benefit members of low-income families or further the objectives of the community action program.[48]

Section 101(a)(1)(A) of the Public Works and Economic Development Act of 1965[49] authorizes the Secretary of Commerce to make grants for public works and economic development under that act if they will further the objectives of the Economic Opportunity Act. A procedure is being developed to provide community action program certification on such projects.

As of early 1966, the OEO had not promulgated specific forms and provided specific working staff for assuring that the required checks are made in the local communities and that the resulting information is delivered to officials in federal

---

[45] 79 Stat. 27 (codified in scattered sections of 20 U.S.C.A. (Supp. 1965)).

[46] OFFICE OF EDUCATION, DEP'T OF HEALTH, EDUCATION & WELFARE, REVISED INSTRUCTIONS (1966), accompanying OFFICE OF EDUCATION, DEP'T OF HEALTH, EDUCATION & WELFARE, GUIDELINES: SPECIAL PROGRAMS FOR EDUCATIONALLY DEPRIVED CHILDREN (1965). See id. at 27-28 for requirements as to cooperation with community action agencies under Elementary and Secondary Education Act of 1965, § 2, 79 Stat. 30, 20 U.S.C.A. § 241e(a)(7) (Supp. 1965).

[47] 79 Stat. 491, 42 U.S.C.A. § 3103 (Supp. 1965).

[48] Ibid. See DEPARTMENT OF HOUSING & URBAN DEVELOPMENT, NEIGHBORHOOD FACILITY GRANT PROGRAM (Letter No. NF-1, 1966).

[49] 79 Stat. 552, 42 U.S.C. § 3131(a)(1)(A) (Supp. 1965).

regional offices or in Washington who pass upon the applications for OEO grants. Such specific working procedures were in the process of development. Likewise, broadening of the check point procedure to the delegated OEO-financed programs and to other federal programs was under active discussion.

E. Coordination at the State and Regional Level

Under the Economic Opportunity Act, local communities deal directly with the federal government, except in the delegated Work Experience and Adult Basic Education programs, which HEW channels through the states. This de-emphasis of the role of the states departs from the prevailing pattern in the grant-in-aid programs, in which federal aid is mainly channeled through the states.[50] The cooperation and the assistance of the fifty states is essential, however, in a country that has some 90,000 lesser governmental units. States control the distribution of billions in other federal grants and provide billions of their own to assist local communities. Thus far the state financial participation in the OEO antipoverty projects has been small.

States also have much of the technical expertise needed by local agencies, especially in rural areas. Section 209 of the Economic Opportunity Act established a basis for participation of the states in the community action programs.[51] Grants to and contracts with state agencies are authorized to enable them to provide technical assistance to communities in developing, conducting, and administering the community action programs. Through December 1965, $8.7 million dollars in technical assistance grants had been made by OEO. By late January 1966, all fifty states had established or designated offices to cooperate with OEO. A number of states had shown excellent progress by the end of fiscal 1965, according to Sargent Shriver, Director of the OEO:[52] In Georgia multi-county units blanketing the state had been formed, and almost every county had been covered by an OEO grant; in Kentucky a state-wide child care and preschool program had been set up; in Missouri the state health department had received money to establish mobile dental clinics; and in New Jersey and California, action by state coordinators had stimulated rural communities to come in for program development at rates far faster than in rural areas in other states.

According to the OEO, state technical assistance offices have contributed to many state governments a degree of coordination seldom achieved for other broad programs. Many such offices utilize interagency committees or have close relations with

---

[50] For an incisive and interesting review of the background and significance of the OEO poverty programs, especially of community action programs, for the federal system, see Davidson, *Politics, Poverty, and the New Federalism*, in W. E. UPJOHN INSTITUTE FOR EMPLOYMENT RESEARCH, DIMENSIONS OF MANPOWER POLICY, RESEARCH, AND UTILIZATION (forthcoming). Another broad-scale evaluation by the Advisory Commission on Intergovernmental Relations, of intergovernmental relations in the poverty effort, based on substantial survey data, should prove extremely useful when it is published.

[51] 78 Stat. 519, 42 U.S.C. § 2789 (1964), as amended, 42 U.S.C.A. § 2789 (Supp. 1965).

[52] Address by Sargent Shriver, 57th Annual Governors' Conference, Minneapolis, Minn., July 20, 1965.

the planning agencies of the states. In California the state technical assistance office acts as central coordinator for state participation in OEO programs, utilizing quarterly meetings of an interdepartmental council and participation by the director of the state technical assistance office in the governor's cabinet deliberations on antipoverty subjects. In Colorado the state technical assistance office coordinates the state antipoverty activities through the Coordinating Council for Economic Opportunity. In New York antipoverty state efforts are coordinated by the state technical assistance office through the cabinet-rank governor's coordinating committee, which is chaired by the Executive Assistant to the Governor and of which the director of the state technical assistance office is executive secretary.[53]

The Economic Opportunity Act provides that the governor of the state may have the opportunity to review community action program applications for his state, although the original so-called "veto" provision was modified in the 1965 amendments to give the Director of OEO authority to override the governor's disapproval on community action program projects.[54] Section 109 of the act still permits proposed Job Corps Conservation Camps and Training Centers to be vetoed by the governor[55] and section 603(b) requires the consent of the governor for VISTA volunteers.[56]

The problem of technical assistance and organization for community planning and action is difficult, both in metropolitan areas and rural areas. There is no set pattern for demarcation of planning areas, although clearly the 3,300 counties of the nation often have arbitrarily drawn boundaries and do not provide natural economic or social units for planning and action. At present, the federal government offers technical assistance directly to local communities, sometimes through the state. Community action programs may be flexibly organized. Early OEO tabulations, however, indicated that about three-fifths of the community action programs were on a county basis, one-fifth on a city basis, and one-fifth in multi-county or other units.

The planning process is an important tool of coordination. Various federal programs at the present time support or encourage "comprehensive" planning units for economic or social action:

(1) OEO is financing the formation of community action agencies which numbered more than 600 in January 1966, and are projected to exceed 900 by the end of fiscal year 1967, plus additional ones in the planning stage. The community action agencies operate in the human resources and opportunities area and are not usually oriented toward broader economic or community facilities planning.

(2) The Economic Development Administration of the Department of Commerce

---

[53] II OFFICE OF ECONOMIC OPPORTUNITY, CONGRESSIONAL PRESENTATION 93, 102-13 (1966).
[54] Economic Opportunity Amendments of 1965, § 16, 79 Stat. 975, 42 U.S.C.A. § 2789(c) (Supp. 1965).
[55] 78 Stat. 511, 42 U.S.C. § 2719 (1964).
[56] 78 Stat. 530, 42 U.S.C. § 2943(b) (1964).

has sponsored the development of more than 800 overall economic development program organizations concentrating on economic base planning.

(3) The Housing and Home Finance Agency of the Department of Housing and Urban Development is providing funds to local public bodies for comprehensive planning of public housing facilities and to some 700 public agencies for urban renewal planning, including grants to some 150 communities for the development of comprehensive community renewal programs.

(4) The Department of Agriculture has encouraged the formation of more than 2,100 rural areas development committees to prepare comprehensive rural community development plans.

(5) The Appalachia program provides for additional economic planning units in that area.

Various other agencies have community planning approaches in effect or on the drawing boards. The Department of Labor is moving ahead with plans for broadly based community programs of human resources development to reach out to individuals in groups with the highest unemployment rates. Related task forces, under the President's Manpower Committee, have been established pursuant to an interagency agreement into which the OEO and other agencies have entered. Members of the task forces have been assigned specific responsibility as "city coordinators" of manpower programs in thirty major metropolitan areas. The objective is to determine how the total departmental resources can be most effectively deployed to solve manpower problems and to speed up action. The first experimental project involving cooperation of the Department of Labor and HEW, and the Office of Economic Opportunity, was undertaken in three slum areas of Chicago in December 1965.[57] The Federal-State Employment Service System, which has nearly 2,000 offices, would play a major role in this new effort to renew manpower resources.

President Johnson has also proposed a major program for comprehensive redevelopment of slum neighborhoods through a $2.3 billion six-year "Demonstration Cities Program." It would be administered by the new Department of Housing and Urban Development and would encompass planning and action for both physical and human renewal in an effort to transform slum neighborhoods into livable communities in sixty or seventy cities.[58] Related legislative action has also been proposed to broaden the project grants under section 701 of the Housing Act of 1954,[59] to provide support for community development districts designated by the Secretary of Agriculture in rural areas, towns, and smaller centers of population. The purpose is to help support surveys of resources and needs within these districts; to provide for coordinated and comprehensive planning for all public services,

---

[57] See MANPOWER REPORT OF THE PRESIDENT, AND U.S. DEP'T OF LABOR, A REPORT ON MANPOWER REQUIREMENTS, RESOURCES, UTILIZATION, AND TRAINING 4-5, 82-83 (1966).

[58] *City Demonstration Programs*, H.R. Doc. No. 368, 89th Cong., 2d Sess. (1966).

[59] 68 Stat. 640, as amended, 40 U.S.C. § 461 (1964).

development programs, and governmental functions; and to enable a continuing liaison of the local areas with federal and state agencies.[60]

The structure of regions and distributions of regional and field offices of the various federal agencies does not provide a fully effective pattern for coordination among federal agencies in the field or for convenient, coordinated relationships with individual states. The Office of Economic Opportunity has seven regional offices, to which the processing and approval of most Community Action Program applications has been decentralized. The Department of Health, Education and Welfare has nine regional offices, some located in different cities from those with OEO offices. The Department of Labor does not have overall regional offices; its bureaus have separate regional offices. The Neighborhood Youth Corps has seven offices; the Bureau of Employment Security has eleven; the Bureau of Apprenticeship and Training has thirteen. Regional boundaries among the three agencies in some regions are not coterminous. And even where the offices are located in the same city, they are frequently not in the same building. Just as local public agencies may not stress geographical convenience of the services for citizens, so the federal agencies do not always provide coordinated and geographically juxtaposed regional offices to assist the states and local communities in their dealings with the federal government. Even on OEO-financed programs there is no common basis for decentralization. Community Action Program projects under $500,000 ($250,000 for Head Start) may now be approved in the field. Applications under the delegated Work Experience program and Neighborhood Youth Corps program are still processed in Washington.

CONCLUSION

Public and private voluntary agencies in fiscal 1967 will probably spend more than $40 billion, more than five per cent of the gross national product, to assist the poor—about equally divided between federal funds and state-local-private public and nonprofit funds. Allocation and authorization of these resources is largely through broader programs which have aid to the poor as only one of their objectives. Perhaps only one-third of all these funds will be from programs restricted to the needy. Funds are authorized and administered by a host of pluralistic institutions. Federal funds are perhaps the most subject to central, coordinated review—although OEO has not, thus far, extensively used its powerful preference provisions. At the non-federal level, plurality of purpose in organizations is dominant.

The establishment of an Office of Economic Opportunity marks a major effort to create coordinate mechanisms at the federal and at the local community levels for focusing resources and providing improved, concerted administration to eradicate poverty. The states have not been as heavily involved.

Invention of the Community Action Program concept for involvement of public and private agencies in comprehensive planning and action and for taking the

[60] *Rural Poverty Program*, H.R. Doc. No. 367, 89th Cong., 2d Sess. (1966).

initiative in combating poverty at the local level is a major, promising breakthrough. Such agencies have shown a capacity for innovation; the promise of comprehensive, coordinated action is yet largely unfulfilled. OEO is not alone, for many other efforts—most still in the beginning stages—are being made to develop comprehensive planning machinery.

At the national level, the OEO has only begun to have an impact in coordinating action. It has important assets of location in the Executive Office, strong legal sanctions for coordination, and substantial appropriations for grants covering ninety per cent or even one hundred per cent of costs for an almost unlimited spectrum of program purposes. But in a pluralistic, democratic society there are substantial obstacles to coordination. The magnitude of OEO's star in the galaxy of federal agencies is yet unmeasured.

The enactment of the Economic Opportunity Act of 1964, establishing a major national purpose of victory over poverty, provides an important prerequisite for effective coordination of efforts at the national, state, and local levels. It serves to heighten public understanding, to smooth the achievement of consensus, and to promote informal coordination. It serves to ease the coordination of planning and action against the incredibly complex, deep-rooted, multi-faceted problem which is poverty.

Overcoming the existing fragmentation of programs and compartmentalization of agencies, particularly at the local community level, serving multiple-problem clientele, in order to provide coordinated, convenient services, continues to be one of the great challenges facing American government.

THE REPRESENTATION OF THE POOR IN AMERICAN SOCIETY

A SUBJECTIVE ESTIMATE OF THE PROSPECTS OF DEMOCRACY

WILLIAM STRINGFELLOW*

After nearly ten years in which most of my practice as a lawyer has been among the indigent or those otherwise dispossessed or disowned by society, it has become impossible for me to think dispassionately or consider hypothetically or address academically the issues of the representation of the poor in politics and in the law in America. I suspect that there is, about these matters, no such thing as objectivity anyway; I know there is no option of neutrality about them. It would be pretentious for me to feign objectivity; it would amount to fraud to assert that I am neutral.

Be cautioned, therefore, that in what follows I speak as a partisan—as someone with a definite viewpoint—though, in doing so, I trust, I thereby uphold the discipline of advocacy which is the venerable societal office of the lawyer.

My viewpoint regarding the representation of the poor in society, especially in the realms of politics, legislation, administration of the law, and litigation, is, of course, informed by my own practice among the poor. No doubt every reader who is a lawyer is similarly positioned in relation to his own particular experience in practice, whatever it happens to be, whether he is specifically conscious of that or not, unless he be some mere legal mechanic who forbears to reflect as a human being upon the work he does every day.

I am a Christian, moreover, which means that the focus of my attention in work, as well as everything else, is upon *this* world and the possibility and actuality in this world of mature human life in society. Biblically and empirically, the Christian concern is characteristically mundane, not spiritual. If there be preachers who none the less deny this world and vainly talk of other worlds or after lives, if there be ministers of institutional religion who spread a word that Christianity is bothered only with personalistic salvation and not with the corporate existence of mankind— and there *are* legions of them—then they are either knaves or harlots: it is sometimes difficult to distinguish between the two. They had better read the Bible more avidly

---

* A.B. 1949, Bates College; LL.B. 1956, Harvard University. Research Fellow, 1950, London School of Economics; Member of the New York bar and the bar of the United States Supreme Court; private practice in Harlem since 1957; Partner, Ellis, Stringfellow & Patton, New York City. Author, DISSENTER IN A GREAT SOCIETY (1966), MY PEOPLE IS THE ENEMY (1964), FREE IN OBEDIENCE (1963), INSTEAD OF DEATH (1963), A PRIVATE AND PUBLIC FAITH (1962). Contributor to legal and theological journals. Visiting Lecturer at law schools in the United States and abroad. Chairman, National Conference on Christianity and Law, 1958.

and the daily newspapers more discerningly, because both of these testaments bear witness that the scene of God's presence and vitality is this history in which men now live, with all its ambiguity, alienation, strife, controversy, and scandal.

My law practice began and remains much in Harlem, where clients are Negroes or Puerto Ricans, usually uninformed about their legal rights and causes, mostly impecunious, existing commonly in abominable tenement slums, their children attending radically deprived public schools, with the highest percentile of male unemployability in the nation, frequently not registered as voters and hence without organic or effectual political power, whose main access to the rest of society is a relationship of paternalistic charity in one form or another. They are, in short, among the indigenous American urban poor—the disinherited, the unskilled, the unwanted, the neglected, the concealed and as yet mainly quiescent poor who populate the interior of every city of any significant size in the nation.

On some vague principle such as "misery loves company," I suppose, my practice has diversified beyond Harlem citizens and represents a number of other persons and factions in society that are also unpopular, or perchance just unfamiliar, to many lawyers. By that I refer to clients who are political nonconformists, various pacifists and agitators, sexual offenders of both sexes, and a somewhat bizarre assortment of other outcasts and cast-offs in society.

My practice as a lawyer originated and continues in this way, representing those who, in one sense or another, live at the extremities of society, because in law school I heard, approvingly, the dictum that everyone is entitled, regardless of race or class or politics or sex or education or other status, to representation in society in the making, administration, enforcement, litigation, and adjudication of the law.

As a citizen, as well as a lawyer, I believe most urgently that if, at any given juncture, those who exist on the borders of society, because they are poor or politically unpopular or socially discriminated against, are not represented, as a practical matter then the whole of society is jeopardized and indeed the very idea of a democratic community is aborted.

That is the substance of the point of view from which I approach the specific issues of the representation of the poor in politics and in the law.

POVERTY AND POLITICS

Poverty and race are profoundly entangled in America. That has been very evident in the past fifteen years in which the civil rights movement has achieved organic significance; but it has in fact been the case from the origins of chattel slavery four centuries ago. There are regions in the country where poverty and race are not intimately associated one with the other—for example, among some of the rural white farmers whose poverty is a consequence of agricultural mechanization or also among the poor whites in the hinterlands of Appalachia. And there have been the successions of European immigrants who have endured poverty for a generation or two in the great cities before becoming substantially assimilated into the mainstream of the economy. For all of that, poverty remains most stubborn in America where it is associated with those who are not white, notably the Ameri-can Indians and Negro citizens. Of these, emphatic attention is now given to poverty among Negroes most appropriately if only because of the multitudes of Negro citizens. If the association of poverty and race is not resolved with respect to Negroes, then it is a moral certainty that it never will be with regard to the Indians—the Indians will simply die off before they are emancipated.

For both Negro and white citizens the contiguity of poverty and race poses sensi-tive and complex issues; but that does not inhibit some insight into why so many Negroes remain poor, generation after generation, both in the deep South and in the black ghettos of the urban North.

For one thing, though property has generally ceased to be a condition of holding office or of suffrage, as a practical reality, property is much esteemed in the United States as a credential for full citizenship. Those who have property, even those who are modest wage earners, can retain lawyers; their special interests are the concerns of candidates; legislators listen to them; and those who have or control much prop-erty are very ably represented in politics and in the law. Those who are, however, unorganized, unemployed, or unemployable or only marginally employed, welfare recipients, or nominal taxpayers so far as property or income are concerned are not likely to be represented in either politics or the law. They are seldom able to locate, much less afford, counsel of their own choosing. Their interests are not taken into account in state legislatures. School boards leave their needs unheeded. Thus property, at least to the extent of having a relatively secure job, remains virtu-ally indispensable to the effective exercise of the ordinary requisites of citizenship.

Meanwhile, waiving racial discrimination per se in education and employment, as the impact of cybernation and automation accelerates, even the menial, seasonal, unskilled jobs heretofore available to many Negroes are eliminated and the legacy of prolonged deprived education becomes vested in unemployability. The prospects of full citizenship consequently diminish for ghettoized Negroes.

The esteem for property as a sanction for citizenship is most poignant, and most pathetic, in the case of Negroes because of their unique inheritance in chattel slavery. Whatever the bigotries which have assaulted other ethnic groups in this nation, whatever their tribulations and grievances, only the Negro in American history has ever been legally and socially regarded as property. Slavery in the United States represented the most radical ethic of white supremacy conceivable; and though slavery was abolished, that ethic remains deeply imbedded in the folk mentality of white Americans. Nowadays it seems to be the case that the virulent and vulgar expressions of white supremacy are waning (though if the ghetto riots continue to spread, it may turn out that the more savage forms of white supremacy have only been sublimated). In any event, the more subtle condescension which prompts white citizens to suppose that theirs is the prerogative to dispense to Negro citizens certain rights and opportunities is itself a symptom of the ethic of white supremacy from which most white Americans, I fear, have yet to be exorcised.

It is this latter consideration—this ethos of white supremacy in which so many generations of Americans, in both South and North, have been reared—which answers the redundant query of white citizens about why, since Portugese, Italians, Jews, and others immigrated to this country, endured hardships for a while but finally became assimilated, Negroes have not or cannot do the same. I suggest that immigrants could be far more readily assimilated into American society because their presence never challenged the white supremacy ethic and that, indeed, many immigrants emulated that ethic. It has been, in fact, only in the past decade or so that white supremacy has been directly threatened at all, in the maturing of the Negro revolt.

Furthermore, the assimilation of immigrants was abetted by the political system dominant in the major cities of the North in the earlier part of this century—a system which bartered services essential for assimilation of votes. For instance, when East Harlem was still an immigrant neighborhood, in the twenties and the outset of the thirties, one congressman maintained no less than sixteen offices in his district where the people could obtain free legal counsel, bargain for jobs, make complaints about housing, sanitation, fire hazards, schools, arrange for economical medical care, or bring any problem. In other words, for all their troubles, the immigrant poor were able to secure representation of a sort in politics and in the law. For all the taint of corruption and bossism of the old-time city machines, their contribution to immigrant assimilation was substantial.

The migration of Negroes in great numbers from the South to the northern cities began as this political system was starting to die, and though vestiges of it survive here and there to this day, American Negroes never really became beneficiaries of such a system, as the immigrants had. Politicians did not register Negroes as voters readily; and those Negroes who became active in politics or received some political recognition were with few exceptions accommodated to the white political establishment—"Uncle Toms" useful for ceremonial functions. That has remained true in the northern black ghettoes until the present decade.

To some extent, the Negro churches that followed the migration from the South, or that were spawned inside the ghettoes because white churches in the North did not welcome Negroes, substituted in providing services similar to those which the politicians had furnished immigrants; but this only emphasized the exclusion of Negroes from the rest of society. At the same time, in the aftermath of the depression the vast expansion of private and public welfare agencies and programs took place. If anything, this also became evidence of the resistance in the white establishment and white society generally to integration of Negro citizens in education, employment, housing, and politics. The social work bureaucracy became perhaps a more benevolent paternalism than that represented by the old-line political machines; but it became a more blatant paternalism, too. It has been able to provide for the subsistence of the ghetto Negroes in rent subsidies and allotments for food and clothes and medical care, but it has offered no remedies to poverty. No doubt charity is to be preferred to starvation or unattended illness; but neither private nor public welfare in the last thirty years has created exits from the ghettoes for urban Negroes in any significant numbers. Welfare has been addressed to meeting dire emergencies, to merely maintaining existence in a minimal way in the slums, but has opened few doors that lead out of the slums; it has not had the technical capability of furnishing the Negro poor with education and sophisticated occupational skills marketable in society outside the ghettoes. Welfare has been a means, in other words, of underwriting and institutionalizing urban poverty associated specifically with de facto segregation in the North. And, because it has not had the element of reciprocity characteristic of the earlier political barter of services for votes, it has had the effect of retarding the assimilation of Negro citizens, of re-inforcing their imprisonment in ghetto neighborhoods, and of inadvertently feeding prejudicial stereotypes, popular among citizens who are prosperous and white, that Negroes are indolent, generically inferior, or content to live in the slums with their own kind.

The war on poverty has the potential of changing all this if the congressional mandate for representation of the poor in antipoverty programs were to be followed. That could be a beginning to the far broader representation in politics and in the law which is essential to breaking the deadlock of poverty and race that has come to pass in the Negro migration to the northern cities. It could be the means of exposing a whole array of issues that have been pretty much ignored up to now but which are part of the everyday aggravations of ghetto existence. For example, the design and routing of public transportation in many cities fails to provide economical and convenient access for ghetto residents to other regions of the community, though that is indispensable to integration in education and employment and consumer activities. In some jurisdictions, notably New York City, rent control statutes which originated in the Second World War, and are supposedly safeguards for the poor, have become so archaic in the present circumstances that they actually have caused rents on slum dwellings to reach astronomical figures. If the poor were to emerge as a political voice in their own right, such laws might be reformed, and remedies might be found for the failure of urban renewal programs to hinder the spread of slums or the deepening congestion of ghetto areas, the absence of viable sanctions against landlords, and the inability or unwillingness of municipal authorities to enforce health, sanitation, fire and building codes. The stamping out of usury, the upgrading of schools and the integration of city schools by the abandonment of the fiction of "the neighborhood school," the increase of apprenticeship and other on-the-job training programs in business and industry, the opening of the construction and building trades to Negro union membership, the provision for free higher education for qualified Negro students, the availability of credit for small business ventures, home mortgages, and consumer purchasing—all of these things become possibilities only if the ghetto poor are represented politically and in the making and administration of the law. The legislative authorization for participation of the poor in the design and execution of antipoverty programs—if implemented—could begin to move America toward the renovation of society sorely needed if the black ghettoes are to be eliminated.

With few exceptions—Philadelphia appears to be one, San Francisco is at least struggling to become one—this mandate of the war on poverty is *not*, however, being implemented. This war has been a bonanza for the social work bureaucracy, of course, creating new jobs for these professionals and permitting an expansion of traditional welfare programs, but the promise of the war on poverty will be surely frustrated if it ends up as merely a further extension of the welfare concept. Even more ominous are the indications that the incumbent political authorities in the major cities have seized upon the war on poverty as a means to enhance and entrench their own power. In one midwestern city, in less than eighteen months, about 8,000 new patronage jobs have been manufactured by funnelling antipoverty funds through the local political machine. At least two high officials in the Washington administration of the war on poverty—Adam Yarmolinsky and William Haddad— have been required to resign because of pressures from congressmen and local politicians provoked by the efforts of these men to honor the mandate for representation of the poor. One of the pioneer antipoverty programs—Mobilization for Youth—has been emasculated by the elimination of its "community action programs," which involved the participation of the poor, by a savage attack upon the agency by the then head of New York's antipoverty program, Paul Screvane, who later in 1965 aspired to become mayor of the city.

It takes no genius to discern what the politicians fear. If the representation mandate were implemented with vigor, the poor would acquire experience in community affairs and there would likely emerge from that a political consciousness and political organizations not beholden to the incumbent officeholders and party leaders. If the poor were represented, they might become a new and coherent political force in the cities; and, out of the most elementary instincts of self-preservation, the last thing the incumbents wish to see is a new political alignment in their jurisdictions. There is a certain poetic irony in the recalcitrance of politicians toward the participation of the poor in antipoverty efforts: they are now visited with the consequences of their own indifference and neglect, and that of their predecessors, for the acceptance and assimilation of Negroes migrating from the South to the northern cities.

I am well aware that arguments can be mustered against the participation of the poor in the war on poverty. The antipoverty programs should be administered by experts. Fine, but in many jurisdictions the bona fide experts have already been shunted to the sidelines—as Dr. Kenneth Clark, the distinguished Negro social psychologist, was by New York politicos in the HARYOU-ACT program. Moreover, just such experts—Saul Alinsky in the Woodlawn ghetto in Chicago is an example—originated and advocated the involvement of the poor. If the poor do have a voice, they may waste public monies. Perhaps, but that is already being accomplished wherever the effort is usurped as patronage. The poor have little or no experience in community organizations and projects. True, but how else shall the poor acquire experience? There is disorder and violence in the ghettoes. Indeed there is; and one of the proximate causes of that unrest is the failure of this society to afford representation in politics and law for generations. If the poor are activated it might lead to radical social change. Precisely, it might even overthrow the ethic of white supremacy, a change long overdue in America.

If the poor were represented, there would be hope for the vindication of democracy in this country.

THE POOR AND THE LAW

The issues raised by the representation mandate in the war on poverty cannot be comprehended or evaluated apart from the context of the experiences of the people over the long period in which so many urban Negroes have been confined to the ghettoes.

Their exposure to the law in these circumstances has hardly been one which would cultivate respect for law and order or be persuasive about the likelihood for them of equal protection under the law.

Now and then there is some notorious and specifically provocative case, as where an off-duty white police officer shot and killed a fifteen-year-old Negro school boy in the presence of scores of other school children in the prelude to the Harlem riots of 1964. It is too easy, however, to attribute the cynicism and animosity of the ghetto residents toward the law to such relatively occasional incidents. It is, rather, I suggest, the reality that each dramatic incident such as this summons to the recollection of virtually all ghetto folk their own grievances and complaints against the law. It is as if each caustic happening triggers the memory of a multitude of comparatively trivial cases. I have in mind the cases typical of my own practice: a tenant is unable to obtain heat or light or water from a slum landlord and finds that the courts assess, if anything, only nominal fines if the tenant prevails, while the condition continues uncorrected; a boy is stopped on the street and detained and searched without explanation by the police; a parent whose children are in constant peril from the rats which infest the tenement discovers that the building inspectors are being bribed to ignore the condition; an addict is repeatedly arrested under the presumption that he possesses drugs for illegal transfer, while the pusher from whom he gets his stuff operates openly and is never touched by the narcotics squad;

a marriage fails but the costs of obtaining a legal separation or divorce place such remedies out of reach; a family is capriciously evicted from public housing without explanation or hearing. Every famous case recalls all the numberless, anonymous, and apparently minor matters, through many generations, in which those who are poor and those who are black in the great cities have suffered indignity, discrimination, importunity, and persecution in one way or another under the auspices of the law. Thus the only image of the law which is credible to the ghetto poor is of the law as a symbol of their rejection by society.

Is there a breakdown of law and order in the inner city? Is there crime in the subways and violence in the streets? Are the police sometimes assaulted when they make arrests? Are there riots in Watts and Rochester and Cleveland and skirmishes in Springfield and Roxbury and Buffalo? Will the next season be long and hot and volatile and bloody? Answer all such questions in the affirmative— but then ask *why?*

The answer to *that* is that the accumulation of grievances against the law, and against how the law has been made and administered and enforced for so long, has become more than can any longer be humanly endured. Besides, what is to be lost? The worst that can happen is that one would be killed—and one who is a ghetto person in America is already as good as dead.

That is the mood that is now overtaking both the civil rights movement and the war on poverty. And if this sounds bitter or extreme to those outside the ghetto regions, let me assure them that it is mild and understated in the hearing of the ghetto captives. The truth is that the internal state of the ghettoes is fundamentally chaotic and imminently threatens to descend into anarchy.

As such a fatal unrest festers in the hearts of ghetto citizens, so far as I can discern, the intransigence of established society outside hardens, and the public authorities seem beset with what can only be described as incipient hysteria. The politicians and law enforcers have become so accustomed to inertia toward the situation in the ghettoes that on the day—today—when the issues of the ghettoes can no longer be ignored or rationalized, their instinct is to stomp out any trouble by naked violence.

That was the case in the 1964 Harlem riots. The authorization was issued, when the early incidents happened, for the police to fire their weapons to disperse those congregating on the streets. The initial resort was the most extreme that could be undertaken. Not fire hoses, not mounted police, not tear gas, but, first of all, guns to subdue the rioters. That came as no surprise to anybody in Harlem. After all, there, as in all black ghettoes of the North, the police have long since functioned basically as an occupation army: It is not just that a place like Harlem is heavily policed, though it is; it is more that every corner is guarded, that every movement is under surveillance, that a stranger entering the ghetto is emphatically advised to turn back, that those indigenous to the neighborhood are often detained and interrogated about their business—it is that sort of thing, which has been going on for a long time now, which makes Harlem, and its counterparts in other cities, occupied territory.

I am not alleging, notice, that all policemen are racists, or brutal, or either like or approve what they are ordered to do. I have observed some policemen in Harlem who would no doubt have achieved great distinction in the S.S. Corps; but I am not persuaded that they are typical. I have also known some officers who were knowledgeable and sensitive, though I am not convinced they are typical either. I am saying that most policemen are workingmen, who want to keep their jobs and perhaps win promotions and who obey their orders—and that the mentality which governs the assignment and conduct of the police in the ghettoes is one which manifestly regards the crises of race and poverty as essentially military problems. Hence the determining operational factors are to confine the residents of the ghetto and keep them quiet, to prevent them from leaving the area unless they are going to work, to break up and disperse them if many gather in the same locality, to keep everybody moving, to be sure all are aware of the police presence on the scene by conspicuous deployment of patrols and paddy wagons, and, if, after such "preventive" measures fail (as I believe they inevitably will), riot erupts, at all costs to localize the violence inside the ghetto so as to most efficiently suppress it.

The crises in poverty and race in the urban ghettoes will never be resolved by ever more anxious resort to force and ever greater escalations of police power. Did Watts, with its appalling fatalities, or the other sixteen riots of 1964 and 1965 teach the nation nothing? Shall the militia be summoned for permanent duty in the ghettoes? That is what is coming; that is what is morally certain unless the legitimate discontent of the ghetto people is answered in fundamental redress, rather than futile reliance upon the superiority in firepower of the police against rioters.

If that comes, the fundamental structure of this society as a democracy will be subverted.

I do not imply, by calling attention to the change in the function of the police to a military role in the ghettoes, that the police are worthy of all the blame for the present hostility between the law and ghetto poor. It is, rather, that the prolonged failure to provide representation in the law for the rights, complaints, and causes of these poor is now brought to focus in this way. After all, legal education, while insistent that law students cram accounting, has not been zealous in its concern for either social justice in the law or social conscience in the profession at the level of the ordinary issues of ghetto existence. And right now, as some ideas are circulated and some effort launched to provide representation for the indigent in the neighborhoods where they live, strenuous opposition from within the bar seeks to block these ventures. In New Haven a whole year was lost before a neighborhood legal program could really begin to function because of such opposition among local attorneys. In one Ohio city, it took a major riot to convince leaders of the profession and of the law school that representation of the poor before the law, specifically in those redundant and apparently trivial matters which heretofore have usually been unrepresented in any way, was an urgent responsibility of lawyers.

The default of the legal profession, of legal education, and of those charged with the enforcement and administration of the law with respect to the ghetto poor jeopardizes the whole of society, not only the poor. If equality before the law is not functional—that is, readily accessible and viable in remedies for a ghetto citizen's complaint or assertion of right—then it is a fiction, even for those who are represented before the law as a matter of privilege or purchase.

CONCLUSION

So I conclude where I began: The representation of the poor in politics and in the law measures the maturity and health of society. By that assessment, contemporary America is profoundly decadent; but at least the juncture of poverty and race in the urban ghettoes has exposed the issue. Whether the nation has the moral stamina to act for its own survival as a democracy is a matter still pathetically in doubt.

CIVIL RIGHTS GROUPS—THEIR IMPACT UPON THE WAR ON POVERTY

JOHN H. WHEELER*

Whether we view the twentieth century's Civil Rights Movement in the United States as an inherent and vibrant force, necessary for survival of the Free Society, or whether we view it as an effort to close the gap between our practices and the Republic's written goals, little doubt remains that, in terms of today's all-out effort to provide the means by which every American will bear a full share of responsibility for the nation's stability, the goals of the Office of Economic Opportunity (OEO) cannot escape similarity to the aims and objectives of present-day Civil Rights organizations. To the same extent, the paths leading to equal opportunity and to proper motivation of the disadvantaged shall continue in most instances to be identical or parallel for both groups.

I

THE FIRST PHASE OF CIVIL RIGHTS ACTIVITY

Between 1928 and 1954, Civil Rights groups in the United States supported a steady flow of litigation seeking to establish complete freedom of movement in the society for every citizen regardless of his race. It was during this period that, little by little, a long line of decisions by the United States Supreme Court removed an endless number and variety of legal barriers which in former years had accounted for: (1) restricted access to public accommodations used in interstate commerce; (2) racial discrimination at all levels of publicly-supported education; (3) enforcement of racially restrictive covenants in conveyances of real property; (4) exclusion of Negroes from participation in the state primaries of political parties; (5) unequal administration of justice; and (6) many other forms of racial discrimination stemming from "state action" or acts of the federal government and/or its administrative personnel. During the same period, Philip Randolph's march on Washington in 1941 was sufficiently convincing to cause President Franklin D. Roosevelt to issue Presidential Order No. 8802, creating the President's Committee on Fair Employment Practices.[1] Roosevelt's FEPC marked the beginning of a series of orders issued in later years by Presidents Truman, Eisenhower, and Kennedy and designed to provide equal opportunity in employment, in housing and in the armed forces. Establishment of this combination of judicial decree and executive action has been described frequently as the *initial phase* of the Civil Rights Movement during the

* A.B. 1929, Morehouse College; LL.B. 1947, North Carolina College. President, Mechanics and Farmers Bank, Durham, N.C.
[1] 6 Fed. Reg. 3109 (1941).

twentieth century. It has also been described as the process of getting down in "black and white" on the printed page, the basis for a clear declaration of public policy which guarantees an equal opportunity for every American to seek and to achieve a full measure of success in keeping with his talents and his capacity for growth.

II

A SECOND PHASE

A "second phase" of the movement—characterized by direct action beginning with the lunch counter "sit-ins" in February 1960, and climaxed by the massive march on Washington in August 1963—may be regarded in retrospect as the period which prepared the climate of public opinion for acceptance of a large volume of definitive action taken in a relatively short period by the Congress.

III

A PERIOD OF IMPLEMENTATION

Indeed, the recent passage of significant pieces of legislation supporting (1) the decisions of the Supreme Court and (2) the strong civil rights stand of the executive branch of the government, are ample evidence that the nation has reached a strong and clear consensus regarding the urgent need for eliminating the pockets of poverty and disadvantage which undermine the moral and economic strength of society. It is, therefore, no accident that the President and the Congress, working closely one with the other, have been able to achieve the passage of the Manpower Development and Training Act of 1962;[2] the Vocational Education Act of 1963;[3] the Civil Rights Act of 1964;[4] the Economic Opportunity Act of 1964;[5] the Elementary and Secondary Education Act of 1965;[6] the Appalachian Regional Development Act (1965);[7] the Higher Education Facilities Act of 1965;[8] the Voting Rights Act of 1965;[9] and the Housing and Urban Development Act of 1965.[10] Passage of the foregoing bills reflects widespread recognition of the increasingly critical manner in which rapid social and economic change inflicts casualties upon families and individuals who are unable, without specific aid, to survive sudden shifts in patterns of housing, education and employment.

It is in the "third phase" or "period of implementation" that the objectives and

---

[2] 76 Stat. 23, as amended, 42 U.S.C. §§ 2571-620 (1964).
[3] 77 Stat. 403, as amended, 20 U.S.C. §§ 15aa, bb, aaa, 35-35n (1964).
[4] 78 Stat. 241, 42 U.S.C. § 2000a (1964).
[5] 78 Stat. 508, 42 U.S.C. §§ 2701-981 (1964).
[6] 79 Stat. 27 (codified in scattered sections of 20 U.S.C.A. (Supp. 1965)).
[7] 79 Stat. 5, 40 U.S.C.A. App. A (Supp. 1965).
[8] 79 Stat. 1219, 20 U.S.C.A. §§ 1001-144 (Supp. 1965).
[9] 79 Stat. 437, 42 U.S.C.A. §§ 1971, 1973-73p (Supp. 1965).
[10] 79 Stat. 451 (codified in scattered sections of 12, 42 U.S.C.A. (Supp. 1965)).

modus operandi of the antipoverty program and of Civil Rights groups appear to follow parallel or identical lines. Long before passage of the Economic Opportunity Act, *ad hoc* local groups, with or without help from established Civil Rights groups, were operating their own Head Start and tutoring programs. Many of these efforts came into being as soon as Negro pupils were able to obtain transfers from racially segregated schools to predominantly white elementary and high schools. Before being funded in 1965 by OEO, the Opportunity Industrial Corporation (headed by Leon Sullivan, a militant Negro minister) was doing an outstanding job of adult education, retraining, and job placement in poverty-stricken areas of Philadelphia. Two years ago, this project's waiting list of approximately 10,000 Negroes and whites was in striking contrast to the lack of local interest being shown in a similar program sponsored by the Philadelphia public schools—which, in spite of adequate financing, a skilled staff, and modern training equipment, appeared to have comparatively little empathy with the problems of the disadvantaged.

Other examples of Civil Rights antipoverty activity prior to passage of the Economic Opportunity Act are numerous. The NAACP has, for years, been engaged in the protection of disadvantaged persons from economic pressure—even to the extent of finding adequate financing for sharecroppers and small landowners who have suffered reprisals for trying to register and vote or for seeking to obtain better job opportunities for those who have been caught in the cycle of poverty. The National Urban League has been engaged in successful pilot programs in mobility and retraining through its National Commerce and Industry Council and its "skills bank." And the Southern Regional Council has since 1945 concerned itself with a variety of projects occasioned by the collapse of cotton tenancy and the mechanization of southern farms, which resulted in mass migration of Negro farm workers to urban areas of the South, North, and West. Following the 1954 Supreme Court decision in *Brown v. Board of Education*,[11] the Council offered its counseling service to southern school boards and superintendents. This service helped smooth the transition to court-enforced school integration; and even today the Council's services have been invaluable in helping public officials and school personnel perform the task of proper planning, within the OEO guidelines, for projects such as Day Care, Head Start, and the Neighborhood Youth Corps.

IV

OEO VERSUS "ESTABLISHED CUSTOM"

It should not be surprising to note the extent to which some governors, mayors, and big city politicians have begun to exhibit varying degrees of hostility to the Johnson administration's "War on Poverty." The U.S. Employment Service, the public schools, public welfare services, vocational training, and other programs funded

[11] 349 U.S. 294 (1955).

in whole or in part by grants from the federal government, have, in the past, been operated by each state according to its own political objectives and local custom. In many instances, provisions of the Civil Rights Act of 1964 and the new guidelines issued with reference to OEO's community action projects and certain auxiliary programs administered by the U.S. Department of Labor, the U.S. Office of Education, the Small Business Administration, the Farmers Home Administration, and other federal agencies are in direct conflict with established policies of existing state agencies operating at the local level. Some communities have long-standing commitments to local industry to maintain a large supply of surplus, unskilled labor. Others are committed to the maintenance of employment preferences which discriminate on the basis of race or class. Still others are responsive to the special demands of the Klan, the White Citizens Councils, and other special groups, or to labor unions which discriminate in their hiring and apprenticeship programs.

In spite of rising adverse pressures upon the antipoverty program by established public agencies and special interests, the impact of Civil Rights groups looms as the strongest and most positive support for the effort to eliminate poverty and disadvantage from the American way of life. The positive impact of the Civil Rights Movement is reflected in the *OEO Community Action Guidelines*, which set forth a strong policy of nondiscrimination—clearly reflecting the intent of Congress as to the letter and spirit of the law. But for the Civil Rights Movement and its forceful, persistent pressures on the federal government, the Economic Opportunity Act of 1964 would undoubtedly have followed the traditional pattern of federal legislation and programs. The concepts of *maximum feasible participation* and *involvement of the poor* are attributable, at least in part, to the "Movement." The phrases themselves imply the involvement of every element in the community; and, even if the poverty program were to follow the traditional pattern of other federal programs in the South, application of the "maximum feasible participation" rule would guarantee representation from minority groups and from the poor.

In too many instances, there has been conflict between *what* the letter of the law requires and the manner of implementation, administration, and interpretation of the law at the local level. This distinction has created many problems in the South, because some communities interpret maximum feasible participation to mean the following: (a) "white folks only" (some communities have flatly rejected Negro participation and are not funded); (b) carefully selected "safe" Negroes (primarily school principals or teachers); (c) poor people should be restricted to service in advisory capacities; (d) poor people should not select the representatives from the target areas; (e) blue ribbon whites should decide what's best for the poor people; and (f) members of Civil Rights organizations have no place on the community action agency. Even here, however, the impact of the Civil Rights Movement has been strongly felt; through protests and local interpretation of the Economic Opportunity Act itself, the Civil Rights Movement has demonstrated to local communities the intended meaning of the term "maximum feasible participation."

The impact of the Civil Rights Movement is also reflected in the organizational structure of OEO, which requires the employment of a staff person with direct responsibility for implementation of the Civil Rights provisions of the act. The Director of OEO has a Special Assistant for Civil Rights. Now that OEO has become more decentralized, a Special Assistant for Civil Rights is also on the staff of each regional office; and no programs are approved for funding without an examination of civil rights compliance by this special assistant. Such a staff person —with approval and denial authority as to the nondiscriminatory aspect of a given program—is, indeed, a novelty in federal programs.

It is also clear that except for the cooperation of Civil Rights organizations many communities would not today be funded. In fact, OEO has, in most instances, viewed the participation of Civil Rights organizations in community action programs as indispensable to the funding of local projects. Thus, local politicians and community leaders, heretofore never associated with Civil Rights leaders, have sought them out and asked for their cooperation.

Many communities in the South have never experienced the phenomenon of Negroes and whites talking together about any problem of the community, but poverty program requirements have created biracial organizations in many communities for the first time. Many other progressive changes will no doubt result from biracial discussions of community problems.

Equal employment opportunity in poverty programs, to the extent that it has occurred, is another result of the impact of Civil Rights groups, which have insisted that their support was conditioned upon the employment of qualified Negro personnel. Some communities have stepped up desegregation efforts in order to qualify for poverty funds. This is especially true of the public schools, whose boards have become fearful they will not get Head Start funds unless students and teaching personnel are integrated. The same is true of certain community organizations which have sought to conduct component projects. Before applying to OEO, they have hired Negroes in responsible positions.

The requirements for "maximum feasible participation" and "involvement of the poor" seemed to have met strong resistance from public officials and established public agencies in all parts of the country. This is particularly true in the eleven southern states, where nearly one out of every two persons lives in poverty and where almost one-half of the 11,300,000 families are classified as "poor." In this region 78.8 per cent of the Negro families are living in poverty as compared with 35.9 per cent of the white families. Forty-four per cent of the poverty in the United States is found in the South, while only one-eighth of the families living in the Northeast and one-seventh of those in the West are poverty-stricken.

It is interesting to note, however, that the prospect of new federal payrolls in poor counties of the South can produce sharp changes in local custom and traditional attitudes of race. In Coahoma County, Mississippi, the South East Recreation Association—a New Jersey corporation sponsored by an interracial group of citizens, including Baseball Hall of Fame's Jackie Robinson—applied to OEO for a grant of $271,000 with which to operate a Head Start program. Immediately thereafter, the Coahoma County Board of Supervisors attempted to pre-empt this application by organizing a community action agency, with a board composed of eight Negroes and eight whites, most of whom were employed by the county school system. In the process of selecting members for the board of directors, it was proposed that neither Sam Luckett, local attorney for the school board and for the White Citizens Council of Clarksdale, nor Aaron Henry, president of the Mississippi Conference Branch of the NAACP, should serve on the board. However, to the surprise of county officials, seven of the eight Negro appointees refused to serve unless Aaron Henry was elected to membership. Thereupon, Governor Paul Johnson sent a personal representative to a Clarksdale meeting between OEO officials and four of the town's leading businessmen. After considerable discussion, it was agreed that Aaron Henry would have to be appointed to membership; and, at the Governor's insistence, it was agreed that Sam Luckett should also be elected to membership. Although the Coahoma County project's board resisted the Governor's recommendation that Luckett and Henry be elected to membership, it finally agreed to elect both of them. The Coahoma County story is typical of many instances throughout the South where strong Civil Rights activity in the community has accounted for the funding of projects which would have suffered certain defeat under ordinary circumstances. Apparently the results stemming from Coahoma's $242,000 Head Start program conducted during the summer of 1965 have been pleasing to the Governor of the state and to a number of young liberals in the Mississippi legislature who have gained a new understanding of the economic and social progress which can be derived from an all-out assault on poverty.

V

RIVAL GROUPS

Although some opponents of the Civil Rights Movement in America have begun to predict the rise of a less militant brand of Negro leadership from the ranks of staff personnel and professionals employed in the "war on poverty," any general clash between Negroes with a Civil Rights background and Negro poverty workers appears unlikely in the foreseeable future. First of all, the successful programs which hire Negroes "across the board" in the full range of salary classifications could not do so without strong Civil Rights support and prodding. Secondly, concerted efforts of some members of Congress to eliminate persons with Civil Rights sympathies or backgrounds from employment by the Washington office of OEO have met with negligible, if any, success.

VI

WATTS

Frequently the question has been raised as to whether a concentrated attack upon conditions of poverty could have prevented the devastating riots which have swept the Watts section of Los Angeles twice within recent months. Based upon results obtained in other parts of the country, it appears that an adequately-financed community action program, properly staffed and operated within OEO guidelines, could have done much to change the feeling of hopelessness and despair which triggered the riots. This, however, is not as easy as it sounds in view of the complicated political battle over control of the community action program which had been planned for Los Angeles. To be successful in any given community, the program must be administered by an interracial staff with a firm commitment to the objectives of the war on poverty, and who are supported by a strong board of directors composed of an adequate proportion of persons holding positions of leadership among minorities and among the poor. Many mayors of our leading cities have objected to the election of Negro board members with Civil Rights experience. They have also protested OEO's requirement that representatives of the poor shall be involved as board members in the shaping of policy.

Frustrating and hostile attitudes on the part of officials, labor unions, and major industries in the Los Angeles area have all but discouraged many groups who have tried to accelerate programs of retraining, apprenticeship and on-the-job training since last summer's disturbances. Recently one major industry in the area is said to have imported approximately 1,500 unskilled white workers from the east coast of the United States while refusing to take applications from persons living in Watts. Unless checked by a firm stand on the part of the administration, pressures from entrenched political forces, from industry, and from established public agencies are capable of nullifying the best efforts of OEO to provide an effective program in Los Angeles or any other American city. This probably accounts for the fact that the majority of the cities whose programs are having a measure of success are those in which the Civil Rights leadership either has taken the initiative in establishing the local community action program or has kept a close watch for the resurgence of traditional procedures which, in large part, are responsible for the conditions of disadvantage which make the war on poverty an important item on our agenda for survival.

MANPOWER AND TRAINING PROBLEMS IN COMBATING POVERTY

MITCHELL I. GINSBERG* AND BERNARD SHIFFMAN†

Poverty in the United States has been the target of successive efforts to contain it, to mitigate its effects, and finally to eradicate it. In this country the first efforts were conducted under the auspices of religious organizations which used "charity" and volunteers and the philanthropic largesse of families of substance to help "the deserving poor." In the early 1900s, the combination of social reformers, educators, and enlightened religious and lay leaders responding to mass emigration, individual exploitation, and inadequate social conditions gave impetus to the social welfare approach to poverty. During this period, private social instruments of all kinds were developed to serve the poor and mitigate their condition. For example, voluntary agencies like legal aid clinics, settlement houses, orphanages, homes for the aged, citizenship and adult education programs, mutual benefit societies and labor unions were initiated and provided many with the drive required to move out of the poverty culture.

In addition, as the economy of the United States fluctuated and threw hard-working people out of the working class and into economic poverty, public agencies developed in the areas of housing, welfare, education, employment and health. These tried to lessen the shock of dependency and to develop those services which would soften the impact of recurring depressions or hard times. During this period, the social welfare field gave birth to the social work profession which either by design or by default was assigned major responsibility for caring for the social and economic failures in our American open society.

The convergence of the "Civil Rights" movement with the growing inability of the developed institutions to deal with social problems and their causes—for example, increasing juvenile and adult delinquency, illegitimacy, school drop-outs, unemployment especially in the Negro minority, growth of slums, and so on—gave rise to another approach to the long battle on poverty. This response came mainly from the government and led to substantial public funds being made available to initiate a new attempt to combat and control poverty. It is not at all clear what the net results will be, and the Viet Nam war may seriously cripple the attempt; but out of what has been done up to now have emerged several concepts or principles which are important in understanding the nature of the poverty effort and the implications for manpower and training. These concepts are:

* Commissioner of Welfare, New York City Department of Welfare.
† Director, Program Development and Training, Community Progress, Inc., New Haven, Conn.

(a) Economic poverty is no longer tolerable in the United States since we have an economy which can produce all the materials and services our population needs. It is no longer a production problem, but a moral problem—which if we solve in favor of eliminating poverty becomes a problem of distribution.

(b) Further economic growth in the United States will not automatically raise the living standards of "the poor." Special aid is necessary to bring the economic and socially alienated into the mainstream of American life. As a matter of fact, there is evidence to suggest that in our times the poor are getting relatively poorer.

(c) Poverty is a complex syndrome and requires a complex solution. No single discipline or service can make a real impact. If real changes are going to be accomplished, the United States is going to have to make available material and manpower resources in unprecedented amounts and in new forms. Manpower requirements will be a problem for all professions and services.

(d) In as simple terms as possible, many of our institutions and services, public and private, designed to serve people and especially "the poor" are largely irrelevant and do not in fact help the poor. All too often the courts and the law are stacked against the poor; the educational system organized to defeat the children from low-income, ghettoized communities; public and voluntary welfare structured so as to institutionalize poverty on both the material and psychological level; health services of such limited availability that the poor are often half sick and in complete despair. To some, these phenomena are a conspiracy of the "ins" against the "outs." To others, this condition is the result of living with an accumulation of conventional wisdom and a failure to up-date our values and goals with the reality in the rural and urban areas of our communities. Regardless of which rationale one favors, it is obvious that the institutions will have to change and the personnel involved will need to be redirected and reoriented.

(e) Social change cannot be effective unless there is complete involvement of those whose condition is to be changed. In many community development programs, it has become abundantly clear that people who live in the community must be involved in agreeing to participate in the planning, execution and evaluation of the programs. Politicians and experts from any of the designated fields can help but cannot alone effect social change. People who are of the poverty culture therefore must be involved in planning, in executing and in evaluating and modifying the services which they are to use—especially since no operating profession knows what it takes to destroy the poverty syndrome.

As a matter of fact, the manpower needs created by any serious attempt to reverse the poverty cycle are so immense that many of the personnel required

to staff the changed institutions will have to be drawn from the poor themselves. They and large numbers of semi-professionals will then need to
work in conjunction with the short supply of professionals in such fields as
law, education, health, employment, and social welfare.

Accepting these concepts as valid and related to the current battle on poverty,
we would like to suggest a number of points which we believe are relevant to those
concerned with staffing the antipoverty programs. At this point we shall briefly list
them and then attempt to develop them somewhat more fully later on.

1. Citizen or professional groups which continue the debate on whether there
is a choice of use of professionals or nonprofessionals are avoiding the real issues.
Among these are: What is the nature of the program which a specific community
needs? What is the technical nature of the work to be done? What parts of the
work are nontechnical and unskilled and can be done by a less well trained person?
Who can do the specific work best—*i.e.*, if a relatively untrained neighbor because
of his contacts can help his neighbor in reading, shouldn't he do this under the
supervision of a trained teacher? Or if lawyers could help more people if they were
assisted by legal aides or investigators who could prepare and gather information—
why not?

In view of the shortage of personnel in all of the helping professions, it is
essential that all disciplines re-examine the tasks contained in their services and
separate out the duties that can be performed by the less well trained. In some
instances there is evidence that there are tasks which can be done more effectively
by the untrained neighborhood worker. The homemaker aide and the health aide
are only two of the perhaps fifty aide jobs which have been identified; and there
is ample evidence to illustrate how well an aide who comes from the community
can reach out, communicate, explain a service, and recruit candidates for a service
or provide the initial service himself. There are no shortages in the services
needed and in the personnel required. The problem is to respond to the needs by
recruiting, training, and making use of personnel in such large numbers and in ways
substantially different than have been true up to now. The human service fields have
never been tooled up or manned by more than a skeleton staff. In these fields we
must demonstrate the capacity to adapt to new employment needs and perhaps help
solve some of the perplexing personnel problems.

2. The needs of the people to be served by the poverty programs are so diverse
and the programs themselves so complex that there simply is no one group of
experts qualified to assume leadership. Likewise, there appears to be no one profession with unique competence nor any one discipline or training program that can
legitimately stake out any exclusive rights. Because of our failure to find individuals
with unique and specific expertise, the "game" is wide open to almost any citizen,
group, profession or discipline. Any accumulated experience in work in undeveloped

countries, in labor unions, in the church, in factories, in social welfare, in law, journalism, politics, and so on, may be appropriate to equip a person for a strategic role in a community action program. The field is indeed so wide open and so unconfined by professional lines that in the existing vacuum a new organization called the National Association for Community Development has been organized and now includes a substantial number of workers involved in the antipoverty program.

3. The introduction of personnel with a variety of backgrounds, experience and training has major implications for the established professions and for the professional associations. Much will depend on the response of such groups as the American Bar Association, the American Medical Association, the National Association of Social Workers, the National Education Association, the American Public Welfare Association, the American Nurses Association and, indeed, of a number of training institutions, unions, business groups, and the like. Will they see the new influx as a challenge and threat to their own hard-won roles, and will they define it as an assault on standards and quality of services? Or will they, on the other hand, be ready to provide the sanction and support for establishing these new service jobs on a basis which provides respect and dignity to the new working force which must be employed if any significant part of the job is to be done? If they do respond in this fashion, it may well turn out to be a major accomplishment of the war on poverty that it was able to confront the professions and their associations, the training institutions, the labor unions and employer groups with the need to re-examine their biases and regulations and to change them in order to face up to a more realistic approach to today's needs. In turn, we would expect these new workers to recognize that more experienced, professionally skilled and trained staff in education, employment, health, social work, and similar fields, are required both for rendering specialized services and to prepare, supervise, and direct the large numbers of people who will have been employed without benefit of formal training.

In our discussion of manpower needs related to poverty, we are focusing on the community action programs which to us are crucial and represent potentially the most meaningful approach in the antipoverty campaign. Of course, all the other programs and projects do have many significant manpower and training needs and add to the problem of shortage.

Any serious attempt to arrive at a definitive estimate of the total number of personnel likely to be required by the various poverty programs is so complicated and time-consuming as to raise the question whether it is productive. Even if such a figure could be arrived at, it would only be a partial story as there are also numerous demands for similar personnel in many other programs not part of the official poverty efforts. Despite these difficulties, the Office of Economic Opportunity and other organizations and groups are making some studies in order to project both short range and long range manpower needs. Most of these projections are not yet available and those that are known vary considerably. For example, we have seen estimates of manpower need that range from an additional 400,000 to two million workers. One rule of thumb that has been suggested is that there is a need for one worker for about every forty poor persons, and that would mean that a poverty population of about 40,000,000 would require a working force of an additional 1,000,000 people to staff the poverty programs.

Dr. Leon Gilgoff, Director of the Information Center, Office of Economic Opportunity, said that "the Community Action Program's fiscal year 1965-66 staffing estimates call for about 390 positions (of which 265 are professional) in OEO's seven regional offices with a salary range of about $5,000 to $17,000." Dr. Gilgoff emphasizes the importance of these positions and then goes on to say that,

> . . . to fill these sensitive positions CAP is recruiting "Generalists," flexible individuals with diverse academic and occupational backgrounds with special emphasis on superior academic achievement, outstanding work performance, previous involvement in social action or community service projects and intelligent awareness of political, economic and social trends.[1]

Dr. Gilgoff further states that "the requirements for the estimated 150 professional positions in the central office of the Community Action Program are similar with a little more emphasis on administrative and management experience and specialized experience in such disciplines as education, manpower, health, community service . . . ."[2]

In the same letter, the Director of OEO's Information Center points out that,

> The number and types of positions to be filled in local community action programs are difficult to determine. In fiscal 1965 approximately 800 CAP grants were approved. In the first five months of fiscal 1966, approximately 650 CAP grants have been approved. In 1965 a total of 405 Community Action Agencies have been funded. The staffing needs of these many grantees are numerous and diverse, ranging in scope from directors of local community action agencies to researchers and neighborhood workers.[3]

Whatever the ultimate estimate of personnel needs turns out to be, it is clear that the comprehensive service programs envisioned will require large numbers of personnel from fields long plagued by personnel shortages. Indeed, one might be easily tempted to give up when one thinks of adding poverty personnel needs to the major shortages of personnel in the more traditionally delivered services in education, health, social welfare, urban renewal and housing, employment, adult and youth programs, correctional agencies, legal services, and libraries and museums. If an additional criterion of "staff who are knowledgeable or experienced in working with the poor" is added, the manpower problem could well defeat the antipoverty program even if the other problems did not.

---

[1] Letter from Leon Gilgoff, Director, Information Center, Office of Economic Opportunity, to Mitchell I. Ginsberg, Jan. 4, 1966.
[2] *Ibid.*
[3] *Ibid.*

What seems crystal clear is that there is no hope for doing anything significant about these personnel problems unless we can break down the tasks required into appropriate sub-roles and functions so that there can be much greater and more imaginative use of other than professionally trained staff. Without recognition and acceptance of this fundamental fact there simply is no possibility now or in the conceivable future of meeting manpower needs in any of the so-called human service professions. In our formulation of the differentiated use of manpower, we would suggest a model that includes the professional, the semi-professional and the non-professional or aide. We recognize that there is a problem of titles, and we know of none that have gained anything approaching a consensus. In the category of non-professional or aide we are including but not limiting it to the much discussed indigenous worker and the poor, although these differ in some important ways and are not mutually exclusive. The volunteer presents still other problems and perhaps ought to be put in a special category although he is often lumped in with the non-professional and the aide. Later on we will be discussing some of the issues involved in the very difficult tasks of defining specific roles and functions, developing a sound plan for the differentiated use of staff, and organizing appropriate training programs for each of these groups. Meanwhile, let us suggest some of the components and corresponding personnel needs that we see in community action programs that hopefully could be used in both rural and urban areas and that could be enlarged or reduced according to the specific nature and size of the community to be served.

All community action programs require an executive director, whatever the title, to direct the program, whether it be on a local, regional or state-wide basis and whether it be urban or rural. Such positions, particularly on the local level, have been among the most difficult to fill with persons of real competence. The responsibilities involved require versatile, flexible generalists with an ability to work with and make use of the political system. Such executives must have demonstrated a concern for and activity in social betterment. The capacity for problem-solving and the ability to administer an untidy organization are skills which they must have or must acquire. Empathy for the protection of civil rights and minority needs coupled with the knowledge and skill needed to be effective in working with such major institutions as those in education, health and welfare, are almost prerequisites for an effective community action leader.

Assuming that there will be continued emphasis on the poverty program despite the international situation, it is reasonable to estimate that there may well be 1,000-15,000 community action program directors needed by the end of 1966 with the future figure likely to be close to that of the total number of urban and rural units in the country. This is an expanding field both in size and in types of responsibilities, and this type of position may ultimately become something like a deputy mayor in charge of citizen participation and services. The idealistic nature of the work, the excitement and opportunities both for service and for personal advancement, and the salaries and status connected with these positions, do attract a great many candidates, but finding those with real competence is considerably more difficult. There are no specific credentials or formalized training for these positions. Likewise, there is no one profession or occupation which has any exclusive claim, and many of the current directors come from politics, law, labor unions, social welfare and journalism. Salaries in general range from $10,000 to $30,000 a year.

In order for the director to use his time most effectively in problem-solving, in effecting organizational change and in developing meaningful relations with the many individuals and groups involved, he must have significant administrative and program support. This makes necessary a deputy or deputies who ideally complement the qualities which the director himself possesses. One such deputy is needed to assist in the housekeeping, business operations and budgeting generated by a large organization handling funds, employing personnel, entering contracts and using properties. Related to these responsibilities is the need for comprehending the appropriate federal, state and city legislation and preparing the projects for funding bodies, and the deputy or controller must maintain liaison with the various funding groups and their staffs. By and large, it is the business world which is one of the major developing grounds for deputies who can administer and carry on these business functions.

Another type of deputy is necessary to serve as an extension of the executive in the program area. Here the tasks are primarily to initiate, organize, direct and assess and evaluate a whole series of programs and projects. The ability to work with staff who come from a wide variety of professions and occupations is a highly important criterion for effective functioning. Up to now these program deputies have been drawn from many fields including law, social welfare, education, journalism and public administration.

As antipoverty teams multiply and programs move to the action stage, there will be an increased demand for both types of deputies. Salaries for such positions range from $7,000 to $20,000, depending on the size of the operation, prevailing salaries in a specific geographic area, degree of responsibility and previous background and experience. At the moment, it is anticipated that there is a need for up to 2,500 such deputies. These positions are attractive and widely sought after. In appointing such deputies many community action programs have also been keeping in mind such realistic criteria as politics, racial balance and the competition of community sub-groups to have their "interests and rights" protected. Use of such criteria does not rule out competence, but unfortunately it does not guarantee it either.

While every member of the antipoverty team should be sensitive to civil rights, cultural factors and minority group problems, the employment of an intergroup relations specialist is often essential especially in larger communities. In some areas such a staff member is shared with the city's equal opportunity or civil rights office.

The specific team which any community would put together after establishing this basic unit depends on the size and nature of the community to be served and its relationship to the governing political unit, the urban renewal organization, the health services, the legal and police systems, and so forth. Clearly the community action program should not duplicate the systems through which a community provides essential services to its citizens. There are a number of important program areas which need to be included in any community action program. This does not mean that every community action program must have a staff member for each of these areas, but what is suggested is that the staff unit in aggregate should have some competence in these types of programs.

Among the programs or services which seem absolutely essential are those related to education, employment and training, neighborhood services and community organization activities. Depending on the community, social service and health consultants or specialists will be just about as essential or at least next in line. In addition, as the local community program moves toward developing a coordinated comprehensive approach, including the support of services required to help people take advantage of the newly created opportunities, there is need for the community social lawyer, the housing expediter or specialist, the consumer education specialist, and the small business administrator. In programs of any significant size other supporting staff such as training or staff development specialists and persons carrying on action and evaluative research are essential. The conservative estimate is that there is now, or soon will be, the need for up to 15,000 such specialists or consultants.

Up to this point, we have been slowly developing the skeleton backbone of the local community or rural action program. As suggested earlier, the staff blend required to attack poverty is a mixture of technical and experience competence—the professionally trained technician, the college or high school graduate who wishes to participate in important work either as a VISTA volunteer, college work-study student or semi-professional, and the large group of aides who are looking for entry jobs in service to their community and who need to earn their way back to self-respect and independence. The community action programs can only succeed if they are successful in employing the mixture of professionals, semi-professionals and non-professionals or aides in the appropriate amounts so that there is adequate support to each participant as he moves out into the community to carry out his appropriate helping role. Thirty thousand semi-professionals could be utilized if there is a normal growth in financing. Also a minimum of 75,000 to 100,000 aides could easily be employed by the 1,500 community action programs which we have projected for the year 1966. Both of these last two estimates could be multiplied by ten if funds were available.

Particularly with respect to the use of the non-professional, the opportunities seem unlimited. We will have more to say about this later on, but meanwhile a sample listing of some of the jobs identified for non-professional workers in the community action programs may give some idea of the potential. Such a list would include:

Recreation Aides or Leaders

Teacher Aides

Child Care Aides (Day Care & Nursery School)

Home Management Aides; Homemaker Aides

Guidance Counselor Aides

Neighborhood Aides (Connector or Link)

Lunchroom Aides

  Work Crew Foremen, Supervisors or Leaders

Administrative Educational Aides

Health Aides

Legal Aides or Lawyer's Representatives

Camp Counselor Aides

Migrant Worker Aides

Field Sanitation Aides

Home Economist Aides

Parent Worker Aides

Interviewers

Home Visitors

Casework Aides

Transportation Aides

Project Leaders

Assistant Program Developers

Vocational Counselor Aides

Employment Aides

Research Aides

Psychiatric Aides

Nurse's Aides

Family Advisors

School Library Aides

Youth Workers Aides

Craft Instructors

Assistant Librarians

Health Instructor's Aides

Field Researchers

Neighborhood Coordinators

Clerical Aides

Neighborhood Organizers

Study Hall Aides

Administrative Aides

Consumer Education Aides

Cook Aides

Bus Matrons

Sanitarium Aides

Tutors

Teacher Assistants

Training Director Aides

Maintenance Aides

Pre-school Leaders or Aides

These aides, if used appropriately on duties they can perform and supported by supervision and relevant training, can enrich the professions and accomplish the tasks instead of watering down the contribution of the profession with which the aides are identified.

To conclude this section on existing and potential needs for personnel, it might be well to comment briefly on Community Progress, Inc., a community action project in New Haven. New Haven, a medium-sized New England city of 158,000, probably is illustrative of one attempt at a comprehensive approach to poverty. After beginning its program in 1962 with approximately twelve people,

by 1965 its staff numbered about 275 individuals. The Executive Director, Mitchell
Sviridoff, in an off-the-cuff interview, stated that New Haven was meeting about
one-third of the need. To do the total job, the community action project itself would
need approximately 600 staff members. It should be noted that in New Haven while
the new instrument was being developed to supplement on-going agencies and
services, the existing systems—education, welfare, health, employment, recreation,
group work—were adding another 200 personnel.

Given the above rough estimates of manpower needs it is clear that there can be
no solution without the working out of a division of roles and a categorization of
tasks that will make possible much more use of the non-professional. It is not
suggested that the use of the non-professional is a new development stemming from
the poverty program. In some fields they have long been used, but it does seem
fair to say that in most such situations it has been out of necessity rather than
choice. It is all to the good that in recent years there has been an increasing number
of experiments and demonstrations in the use of non-professionals. While no one
experiment can be considered an unqualified success, some including the Social
Work Assistant Project, developed in the Veterans Administration under Delwin
M. Anderson and Jean M. Dockhorn,[4] seem to be having interesting results.
As these experiments are continued and expanded, the end result must be a
diagnosis of community and human needs and the differentiation of helping tasks
so that the appropriate degree of skill is mobilized for the present problem. This
means trying to make sure that professionals are not "under-helping" or "over-
helping." In all the service fields too many professionals are spending too much
time on too many tasks that simply do not require manpower so highly skilled,
expensive and scarce. Non-professionals must be used not only because of shortages but even more because they can make a positive contribution and because it is
a waste of time, money and human resources to use highly trained personnel for
tasks that do not require such skills and training.

An essential corollary to any successful differentiation of professional, semi-
professional and non-professional tasks and functions, is the development of specific
training for each of these categories. Just as it has been suggested that there is no
one profession that can provide all the manpower with the unique competence to
carry out all the responsibilities involved in working in poverty programs, so there
is no one discipline or training program that can legitimately stake out any exclusive rights.

When one thinks back to the difficult and demanding tasks facing the top level
professionals, it is clear that it is the rather rare and unusual individual who can
come even close to having all the necessary skills and knowledge to fill these top
positions. As has been pointed out, the number of such positions is undoubtedly in-

[4] Anderson & Dockhorn, *Differential Use of Staff: An Exploration With Job-Trained Personnel*,
National Ass'n of Social Workers, Personnel Information, Nov. 1965, p. 1, at 42-43.

creasing much faster than the supply of such gifted individuals, and the problem of bringing supply and demand closer together will become an increasingly serious one. Clearly, the need is for some kind of training program for such people, although we have already indicated our belief that there is no one existing training program that can do the job. What apparently has to be done is to recognize that inevitably much of the training will have to take place on the job, but that this needs to be supplemented by some high-level, short-term orientation and training programs developed and carried out on an inter-disciplinary basis. There has been some experience in bringing together relatively small numbers of local top personnel for limited periods to review common concerns and problems, and to suggest possible approaches. It does seem likely that similar programs for OEO Community Action national and regional staffs might also have some real value. In the Poverty Program, as in all others, there is some danger that the assumption may take root that because someone is on the job, he knows all there is to know and that training, including keeping up with current developments and thinking, is strictly for someone else. Indeed, this is an occupational danger which threatens all professional and top level personnel. In addition to these high level generalists and their deputies or assistants, there is the need for highly qualified professionals to carry out a variety of program responsibilities. It is essential to recognize that the key positions in health, education, welfare, employment and the other program areas do require a high level of professional competence. This is a fact that too often tends to get overlooked or even denied. There seems to be a growing trend within poverty programs to play down the role of the professional and often to eliminate it. In many cases there seems to be a feeling and attitude that the professional is somehow responsible for everything that goes wrong. Indeed, much of the current literature and not a few of our most eloquent speakers, including many a professional, seem to suggest that poverty itself is caused by these professionals, and getting rid of them would somehow solve the problem. This is not at all to suggest that there are not serious limitations in the ways many professionals have been functioning; but the need is to see what can be done to strengthen their performance and make them effective, not to eliminate them. The war on poverty is indeed too important to be left in the hands of the professionals, but it is most unlikely that it can be won without them. As we have said before, the task is to redefine those parts of the job that require the special competence of the professional. In many situations these functions are likely to include substantial components of supervision, consultation, program analysis, and planning. This does not for a moment mean that no professionals are to be involved in direct service, but it does suggest that much of the direct service may be carried out effectively by a team of personnel including but by no means limited to the professional. Acceptance of this would mean that some direct services to individuals and groups in all professional fields would be given by the professional, and some by the semi-professional and aide under supervision, and that the division would be made on some logical basis related to people's needs.

If the above approach were followed, it would have direct implications for the training of these professionals. Preparation for direct service, whether in education, welfare, or other fields, would by no means be eliminated, but would have to share time and curriculum space with preparation for supervision, consultation, planning, program analysis, and the like. We recognize that major aspects of these skills can best come from experience and more advanced training either on a part time or full time basis, but we believe that more can and should be done in the basic training programs of each of the professions. Of course, current educational curricula are crowded and it is difficult to find room for substantial amounts of additional content and knowlege, but how much curriculum space would be available if the various professional schools really took a hard look at their programs and decided that tradition was not sufficient justification to continue much of what is now being taught. This is no new thought to any group of reasonably knowledgeable professionals, and it is just as true in our own area of social work education as we firmly believe it to be in the other professions. Our tendency to prepare for today's and tomorrow's battles with yesterday's weapons is not the result of any plot or even of ignorance or lack of knowledge. Rather, it stems primarily from resistance to change, a propensity unfortunately at least as common in the professions and in educational programs as in other institutions and agencies of our society.

Along with preparation for these additional responsibilities as part of professional training must come more emphasis for helping more professionals to work with low-income people. Again, we do not suggest that this relative lack of emphasis has come about mainly by conscious design, but whatever the reasons, much of professional education, regardless of discipline, has simply not done enough to prepare its graduate to work with the poor. It is not that we accept what seems to be a developing mystique about what it requires to work with the poor, or that we think there are any great mysteries as to how one works with them. Most of the skills and many of the key areas of knowledge now included in professional training apply to the poor as well as to anybody else. What is essential is to adapt them to the needs and life styles of the poor, to make more of an effort to understand them and their ways of life, and to help develop attitudes that will help insure that the poor get at least an even break in securing the attention and services of the most, rather than the least, qualified professionals.

In our discussion of differentiating tasks and roles, we have suggested that there is a need for another level of worker whom we have called the semi-professional. This type of position is by no means a new one although this particular title is rarely used. Actually, in the social welfare field the semi-professional is the largest single group and filled most of the approximately 115,000 positions available in 1960. Only twenty per cent of such positions at that time were held by individuals with social work degrees from accredited schools of social work. One large segment of this semi-professional group is made up of young adults who are looking to "field test" their ideas and aspirations and to begin to make long range vocational decisions. Many of them see what they are doing as temporary until they can decide whether to go on to professional training or to move into another field. Still another large group is made up of middle-aged adults who in one way or another have established themselves in the field without any intention of seeking full professional status. All too often such semi-professionals are lumped together with professionals and given job assignments that do not take into account levels of skill and previous preparation.

This situation, although highlighted in social welfare, is by no means confined to it. In almost all fields, people with less than full professional qualifications are being employed either because the professional is not available or because he has too many things to do. Both of these reasons are understandable, but to us do not constitute a sound basis for having the semi-professional take over the professional role. Rather, what is needed is to factor out the tasks in terms of complexity and required levels of skill. On this basis it can then be determined what functions require one type of worker and which can make use of another. The two workers then are not seen as interchangeable but rather complement one another in getting the total task done. The semi-professional is seen as part of a team headed by the professional who generally serves as the supervisor of the other team members.

If one accepts the above formulation, then it follows that the training of the semi-professional should be related to but different from that of the professional. It should be geared to the type and complexity of the tasks and functions he will be carrying out. It should cover some of the same areas as professional training, but these can be done in less depth. It does not have to include the same breadth and range of knowledge and skill that are or should be included in professional training. The length of time spent in such training should be substantially less than that for the professional. Just how much less will vary, depending on the field and the nature of job assignments, but generally speaking six months to a year would seem to be enough and, in some cases, it can perhaps be done in less time. The training program should contain both theoretical and practice material and should include some practice or field experience. One of the major by-products of such training can be the possible impact on professional preparation. We believe that training for semi- and non-professional roles is bound to result in a recasting of professional training so as to put more emphasis on preparation for those tasks and functions that the professional is or should be uniquely qualified to carry out. We suspect that such a formulation will lead to the elimination of many areas of knowledge now considered sacred and the substitution of others much more related to current and future needs.

A crucial third member of the manpower team that we have suggested is the non-professional or aide, in which category we have included the poor and the indigenous worker despite the fact that they may differ in some rather substantial ways. As has been indicated, this category covers a wide range of positions and responsibilities, but in our formulation these would be less complex and would require a lower level of skills than the other two. Here again, we do not see the non-professional as interchangeable with either of the other two categories; but again being different does not mean that it has less value and importance.

One of the more interesting phenomena of the emphasis on poverty and the development of antipoverty programs has been the discovery, or rediscovery as some would define it, that there is a place for poor people to work in many of these programs and projects. Although differences tend to develop rather quickly when one tries to get specific as to just how they are to be used and what types of responsibilities they are to carry, few voices are being raised against the principle of such employment. In fact, employment of the poor is coming to be seen by many as the favored approach to "maximum feasible participation." Many individuals and groups most opposed to what they consider over-emphasis on having the poor in policy making and board positions maintain very strongly that employment is the most meaningful form of involvement and that this is the way "maximum feasible participation" should be achieved. On the other hand, those who urge continued and expanded involvement of the poor in key policy-making roles are also in agreement on the desirability of employment, but see it as in addition to rather than instead of. With all the emphasis on the employment of the poor in poverty jobs there is a danger that the extent of such employment may be higher exaggerated. Whatever facts are available seem to indicate that up to now the total number employed, especially on full time jobs, is quite low. However, it does seem true that, at least for the time being, poverty programs themselves have provided more jobs for the poor than they have been able to create in other sectors of the economy.

Of all the voices raised in support of the employment of the poor and the indigenous in poverty and related programs, among the most persistent and forceful have been those of Frank Riessman and his colleagues. In frequent articles and speeches they have urged that there is need for literally millions of non-professionals (a term they use for the poor and indigenous worker). In fact, in their recent book, Pearl and Riessman argue that the needs of what they call the "helping services" are so great that they say "the central thesis of this book is that in an affluent automated society the number of persons needed to perform such tasks equals the number of persons for whom there are no other jobs."[5] A review of this book, of the HARYOU proposal,[6] and of a number of other articles, indicates that there are many advantages usually suggested for this large scale employment of the poor and indigenous workers in a wide variety of human service tasks. Among the advantages frequently advanced are:

---

[5] ARTHUR PEARL & FRANK RIESSMAN, NEW CAREERS FOR THE POOR 6 (1965).
[6] HARLEM YOUTH OPPORTUNITIES UNLIMITED, INC., YOUTH IN THE GHETTO 607 (1964).

1. Such employment provides a very meaningful and appropriate form of participation which has almost universal acceptance.
2. Employment of the poor provides paying jobs. It helps reduce unemployment, provides a sense of satisfaction to the people involved, and cuts down on welfare costs. It makes it possible for poor people to earn money.
3. Bringing in the poor as workers will help reduce some of the serious and almost hopeless personnel shortages in all human service fields.
4. Employment of non-professionals in these ways can lead to badly needed clarification of what the real professional tasks are and what functions really do require professional skill and knowledge. In turn, this can serve to revitalize and strengthen professional education.
5. The use of poor and indigenous personnel in non-professional roles will tend to reduce the rigidity of the professions.
6. In addition to all the above, such use of the poor and the indigenous will provide better service to people. It is suggested that because they have the "know-how" and the "style" that comes from similar life experiences to those with whom they work, they can do things the professional cannot do and they can also provide the "bridge" between the professional and the poor.

Even if one does not subscribe fully to all of these contentions, it does seem clear that there are many advantages to the use of the poor and the indigenous as non-professionals. Once there is genuine acceptance of this idea and a willingness to be flexible as to how they are to be used, we are confident that they can take on many more tasks than have been assumed. Along with the significant contributions they can make to services, it it all to the good that they will get legitimate jobs for which they will receive pay. In addition to these major advantages, we are impressed with the contributions non-professionals can make to help meet the personnel shortages in the human service fields.

In our judgment, it is long overdue for these shortages to be faced up to with some degree of reality. It is not only that these major shortages exist now, but they will certainly get much worse if the approach continues to be "business as usual." Whatever the profession, these shortages cannot be met by simply recruiting more students, expanding or setting up new schools, providing more fellowships, raising professional pay, and the like. We are all in favor of these steps and believe they should be pushed vigorously; at the same time, we ought to recognize that they are not enough. By and large, the professions are competing mainly for the same people, and the supply is and will continue to be inadequate to meet the demand. We simply must find, train, employ and then develop career lines for non-professionals to take over many of the tasks that we have sometimes too casually defined as professional. Even if by some process not known to us, it were possible to find and prepare a large number of professionals to take on these tasks, we do not believe it could be justified as sound policy. As has been said earlier in this paper, too many of these functions are not really professional in nature and do not require professional skills. Professionals in all fields have known and talked about this among themselves for a long time. It simply makes no sense to use scarce, relatively costly and highly trained personnel to do so many tasks that others who very much need employment can do in satisfactory and less costly fashion. At the same time, such a process would free the professional to take on the duties that do require professional skill and competence, and that now are not done at all, or at least do not get the professional time and attention they need.

The case for a greatly expanded use of the non-professional, particularly the poor and indigenous, is overwhelming; but it also has to be understood that it is not a panacea. Unless there is recognition of the potential pitfalls and problems, the result will inevitably be frustration and unhappiness for all—the professional, the non-professional and, most important, the people receiving the service. Just as it is true that non-professionals can take on many more tasks than has generally been accepted, so it is equally felt that there are some that they cannot do. We cannot stress too strongly the conviction that professionals and non-professionals are not interchangeable. Each functions best when his tasks are clearly defined and differentiated. Non-professionals must be given appropriate orientation and training, and continuing staff development is essential. Also, they will need supervision and supportive help from the professional. One has to be aware that there is no guarantee that workers coming from the ranks of the poor will necessarily be especially understanding and accepting of those service recipients whose backgrounds are similar to their own. In fact, a tendency to be punitive and demanding towards those from whose ranks the worker has been recruited is not at all uncommon nor, unfortunately, is it unusual for the non-professional to out-professionalize the professional in the worst sense of the term. Just as we believe that being poor should never disqualify one from being considered for any type of responsibility, equally does it have to be recognized that poverty does not automatically qualify anyone, nor is it a guarantee of effective functioning.

The fact that the use of non-professionals opens up work opportunities to people who need employment very badly is indeed a plus, but here, too, there is need for caution. We do not believe these jobs will solve the unemployment problem in this country, and for anyone to act on this assumption and thus see this as a substitute for the major steps necessary to create more jobs in the general economy could indeed be disastrous.

Another problem that is only now beginning to receive some discussion is the danger that most of the non-professional jobs may turn out to be dead end. What will happen after the non-professional learns how to do his job effectively, has made a meaningful contribution, and wants to move ahead? This will by no means be true of all, and many can continue to function for long periods in the initial roles, provided they are given appropriate salary increments and other personnel benefits; but some will understandably look to move up the scale. Will there be opportunities for this? Failure to provide such opportunities can be frustrating and self-defeating and lead to an understandable feeling of hopelessness and bitterness. Certainly there ought to be a chance with increased skill and knowledge from experience and training to move ahead within the category in which one is placed. Thus, the aide or non-professional becomes a senior aide, or whatever the title may be, with increased responsibilities and salary. But what about moving from one category to another? How does the aide or non-professional become a semi-professional, and is there a route open to full professional status? The fact that many will not want to look for these possibilities does not eliminate the problem. For instance, how does a practical nurse become a registered nurse, a teaching aide a teacher, the welfare assistant a professional social worker, or one might even ask, the legal aide a lawyer, or the medical aide a doctor. It will not be enough to suggest that such people take the regular paths to professional status. Most of them won't have the formal qualifications or the time or the resources. What is essential is to find alternate routes with proper safeguards for those individuals with appropriate potential and capacities for professional functioning. Failure to develop such routes can be a seriously limiting factor to the use of non-professional personnel and can make something of a mockery of the much-discussed career concept.

Perhaps even more disastrous could be a continuation and acceleration of what appears to be a trend to convert the appropriate and badly needed emphasis on the use of non-professionals into a broadside and all out attack on professionals and professionalism. Of course there are problems in the ways some professionals function in their training, in their at times excessively purist notions of professionalism, in their rigidities, conservatism, and so forth. But of what individuals and groups can this not be said, and what justification is there for some of the sweeping generalizations about all professionals? Does the fact that some or many professionals have some or many of these limitations to greater or lesser degree mean that professionals as a group are to be disqualified from work with people? Being professional does not guarantee successful functioning, but we believe that being exposed to a disciplined body of knowledge and being subject to a code of ethics do provide some safeguards. The limitations one finds in professionals are not inherent in the professional role. Rather, they may be in the training, in the individual's capacities, in the way he is being used, and so on. While we have tried to make it patently clear that there is need for greatly expanded use of non-professionals, this is not because we believe professionals are not qualified. Generally speaking, it is our conviction, especially in the human services, that the good professional can do the job and, in most cases, do it better than anyone else. It is because we think he does have a high level of competence and preparation that we want him to stick to those tasks that require his skills and not be diverted to those functions which are a waste of him and can be carried out in satisfactory fashion by others.

Essential to any realistic conception of the use of the non-professional personnel is the development and implementation of a carefully-thought-through and continuous training program. In that sense, non-professionals of any category and professionals are very much alike; neither will be able to do the job without effective training. In fact, without adequate training the non-professional is likely to be a liability rather than an asset, and the agency or institution, and particularly the people to be served, would be better off without him.

Once the conception of the necessity for training is accepted, all sorts of questions arise about when, what type, how long, what kinds of curricula and under whose auspices. Pearl and Riessman[7] and MacLennan[8] make a strong case that training must not be considered a prerequisite for employment and that the training should take place after the job is secured. In the words of Dr. MacLennan:

> It is necessary to reverse current procedures and to make education and training an integral part of the job rather than conceive of employment as dependent on prior education and training. Thus, entry jobs become essentially one aspect of training for employment. . . . If training is to be meaningful, particularly to socially deprived youths, jobs have to be provided and work experience, training and education carried on concurrently so that work is considered one aspect of training.

This timing of training and making it part of the job are especially significant when we are considering using the poor and the indigenous in the non-professional roles. While there are individual exceptions, there is evidence to indicate how difficult it is to motivate them to involve themselves in the training unless they have already secured the job. Even when it is part of employment they tend to be impatient with the training aspects and want to "get on with the job." If the jobs are not provided in advance, there is also the danger that individuals taking the training in good faith may end up without a job—with all the frustrations and disappointments that this entails. Also, tying training to the job permits training to be made much more specific and concrete—qualities which are especially important in preparing non-professional personnel. In some situations it may not be possible to relate job and training in this way; but if this is so, it will still be highly important that commitments be made to a job provided the training period is completed satisfactorily. Basically, this is the approach followed by the Peace Corps and VISTA, although the trainees involved in these programs generally do not fall into the poor and indigenous groups. However, the trainees do know that they will get an assignment if they complete the training successfully. Also, our direct ex-

---

[7] PEARL & RIESSMAN, *op. cit. supra* note 5, at 3-4.

[8] MacLennan, *Training for New Careers,* in NEW CAREERS: WAYS OUT OF POVERTY FOR DISADVANTAGED YOUTH 109-10 (Center for Community Studies, Howard University, 1965).

perience with the Peace Corps and VISTA has convinced us that trainees are likely to do better in training when they have some reasonably specific ideas about the kinds of responsibilities they will be taking on after graduation. In the Peace Corps and VISTA training programs with which we have been associated or which we have observed, actual field work in community agencies has been an essential element in order to build in at least some simulated aspects of the job and to make the preparation as concrete and realistic as possible.

The issue of length of training is tied up with a whole series of factors such as nature of the job, type of training, and previous background of the trainee. There is certainly no one magic period, but again the Peace Corps and VISTA experience and other programs point to a period of between six weeks and three months. There are projects where the time has been less than that and some of them seem to have worked well, but we suspect that in those cases the trainees may have brought certain experiences and skills with them. When suggesting six weeks to three months, we are assuming that this is a combination of training and work or, as indicated above, that the training includes a very substantial component of field work, practice teaching, practical nursing, and so forth.

It appears to us that some combination of field work or guided job experience, both under supervision, along with some small group discussion opportunities, lectures or talks geared to the experience and background of the participants and the use of such devices as role playing are likely to be most helpful in training. A good deal of emphasis on "how to do it" seems essential although this, too, varies somewhat with the previous experience, education and sophistication of those involved in the training. Where one is carrying on a program for low-income people with limited educational backgrounds, it is important to be as detailed and specific as possible without taking anything for granted, although any indication of condescension is and ought to be disastrous. In Peace Corps and VISTA programs, where many of the trainees are likely to be college graduates, some more theoretical material can be introduced; but here too there is likely to be a demand for relating this to what is to be the job and for more emphasis on how and what to do.

In organizing and carrying out Peace Corps training programs for Colombia and Venezuela, the following objectives were suggested:

1. To have some impact on the trainees' philosophy and value systems about working with people.
2. To expose them to problems and sights with which they were unfamiliar.
3. To give them a beginning understanding of the complexity of the tasks involved in working with people.
4. To help them make a limited start in developing beginning skills in one or more areas.[9]

---

[9] Ginsberg, *Short-Term Training for the Peace Corps*, Social Work, Jan. 1964, p. 62, at 68.

These appear to be important if limited objectives; and there is, of course, no guarantee that they can be achieved. On the whole, they seem applicable also to the training of low-income people for work in poverty and related programs, although unfortunately one does not have to worry in the same way about exposing them to the sights, sounds and smells of poverty. However, such low-income people can be helped to understand better what poverty does to people and how they react to it. Depending on the nature of the job to be carried out, help with specific skills is essential. The homemaker may not need any help with homemaking skills, but she may well need some assistance in how to teach her skills to someone else. The fact that she has been doing these things all her life may make it even harder for her to understand that others have difficulties with them, and indeed the fact that she is doing what comes naturally may make it all the more complicated for her to explain what she is trying to accomplish. The potential recreation worker has to know about games, the health aide about health problems, and so on down the line, regardless of the field. Many low-income people being prepared for non-professional roles may need help with basic education such as reading, writing, and arithmetic, and may need considerable assistance with what might be called the culture of work —what is involved in looking for, obtaining, and keeping a job.

Pearl and Riessman likewise suggest some other specific areas that have to be emphasized in training the poor. These include:

1. The problem of confidentiality—non-professionals, especially from low-income groups, on the one hand, do not always see the need for such confidentiality and, on the other, are sometimes hesitant to share pertinent information with the agency.
2. The problem of being able to accept and make use of authority.
3. The tendency to over-identify with the agency and "look down" upon the poor with whom he is working.
4. Extreme swings from overoptimism to overpessimism which, on the one hand, may lead to expecting too much and, on the other, to getting discouraged too quickly.
5. Working out roles and relationships with the professionals.[10]

Whether we are talking about Peace Corps and VISTA trainees or low-income and indigenous people, some pattern of initial and on-going training or staff development is essential. Whatever the variations from group to group and project to project, there are attitudes, values, areas of knowledge and skills that have to be included. Training is never an end in itself and much that has to be learned will be gained on the job and from experience; but the non-professional develops and functions best when what he learns on the job is linked up and supported by a

---

[10] PEARL & RIESSMAN, op. cit. supra note 5, at 158-63.

meaningful and realistic program of on-going staff development. This is especially true when, as we have suggested, the beginning job is not an end in itself, but hopefully a step toward a more meaningful and satisfying career.

Several times reference has been made to the serious personnel shortages in the human service fields. Although everybody agrees that this is a major problem, there are different points of view as to its extent. We will focus on social work as the field we know best, but the picture here appears applicable across the board to all the service fields.

Although social work has been giving increasing attention to manpower needs and what can be done about them, nobody really knows just what is needed. In a speech at the Annual Meeting of the Council on Social Work Education in 1965, Wilbur Cohen, Undersecretary of Health, Education and Welfare, said:

> It is a startling fact that nobody today can state with confidence how many social workers we need to staff the programs we have but the facts and estimates at our disposal paint a pretty woeful picture. If it is true, as we were told in 1963, that in recent years some 10,000 to 12,000 paid social work positions remain vacant for lack of qualified social workers to fill them, and another 12,000 to 15,000 new recruits are needed each year to replace workers leaving the field and to staff new and expanding services, and that our social work schools each year graduate fewer than 3,000 workers, we have a major crisis on the road ahead. Estimates of current and projected social work manpower needed to staff the public assistance and child welfare services alone exceed the total estimated output of trained workers between now and 1970.[11]

It must also be kept in mind that these estimates for public assistance and child welfare cover only the projected need for professional social workers—the same estimate projects a need of twice as many more workers with less than full professional training.

Many other estimates of manpower needs are also available but in no significant way do they conflict with Secretary Cohen's figures. Miss Mary Baker, Director of Personnel Service, Family Service Association of America, in the *Encyclopedia of Social Work* states that "It is clear that even tripling or quadrupling . . . the number of professional social workers in the next ten years cannot meet the needs of this developing field."[12] This is true even though in the past ten years the schools of social work in the United States and Canada have had an annual increase in enrollment ranging between three and twelve per cent and there is every indication that the increase will continue and perhaps accelerate. All those who have looked into this question agree with Arnulf Pins, Associate Director, Council on Social Work Education, that:

---

[11] Cohen, *The Role of the Federal Government in the Expansion of Social Work Education*, in SOCIAL WORK EDUCATION AND SOCIAL WELFARE MANPOWER: PRESENT REALITIES AND FUTURE IMPERATIVES 57 (Council on Social Work Education, No. 65-13-41, 1965).

[12] Baker, *Personnel in Social Work*, 15 NATIONAL ASS'N OF SOCIAL WORK, ENCYCLOPEDIA OF SOCIAL WORK 532, 538 (1965).

The existing and growing needs for professional personnel in social welfare and the need for better qualified personnel demands active promotion of increased quality and expansion in social work education. To do so will necessitate increasing the capacity of existing schools, establishing new schools and considering and testing new patterns and methods in social work education.[13]

To these recommendations is often added the suggestion that there be a similar expansion of social work education on the undergraduate level to provide another group of personnel for social welfare positions.

In 1963, Secretary Cohen set up a Health, Education and Welfare Task Force on Social Work, Manpower, and Education, and in the speech mentioned above called for action toward a Social Work Manpower and Training Act in his words, "comparable in scope and objectives in social work personnel to the Health Professions Education Assistance Act in the medical field. The aim would be to secure general program support in social work education."[14] If all the above were achieved—a somewhat formidable task—it would help but by no means solve the problem. To quote Miss Baker again, "Relatively little has been done, though much theoretical attention has recently been given, to defining different functions for the professional social worker and for the worker without professional education who can be trained to do jobs that do not require a professional worker."[15] Miss Baker emphasizes the urgency of "the deployment of the total personnel in social work for the most effective use of their varying qualifications of education and experience."[16]

Along with the concern about manpower shortages and needs has been increasing uneasiness about the level and quality of the social worker's performance and especially the appropriateness of his training. Criticism of current training is widespread and comes from both within and without the profession. While the motivation behind some of the more violent attacks does seem questionable and some of the critics appear to us not to know what they are talking about, there are serious questions that social work education and the social work profession have to face. It is no secret that there is widespread concern about both the numbers and quality of social work faculty, and despite some growth in doctoral programs, there appears to be no reasonable solution in sight. Supervised field work placement is seen as an essential and major component of social work education, but there is probably not a school of social work in the country that is even reasonably satisfied with the number and quality of field work placements and with the level of field instruction

Along with these questions are other widespread doubts about the adequacy of the social work curriculum especially in view of the development of the poverty and

---

[13] Pins, *The Number, Size and Output of Programs of Schools of Social Work and the Need for Professional Manpower: Implications for Expansion of Graduate Social Work Education*, in SOCIAL WORK EDUCATION AND SOCIAL WELFARE MANPOWER: PRESENT REALITIES AND FUTURE IMPERATIVES 39 (Council on Social Work Education, No. 65-13-41, 1965).

[14] Cohen, *supra* note 11, at 69.

[15] Baker, *supra* note 12, at 539.

[16] *Ibid.*

other new types of programs. Even though some progress is being made, there is insufficient attention being given to social and cultural factors and, perhaps even more important, to helping students make use of this material in their practice.

In addition, most people close to social work education and practice would agree that insufficient attention has been given to adapting training to prepare students for work with low-income individuals and families. As we have indicated, we believe this involves a change in emphasis and attitude rather than any fundamental reorganization of the curriculum. Expanded use of certain types of field work placements, substitution of records and illustrative material dealing with low-income people, and more emphasis on teaching the life styles and culture of the poor would make considerable difference. We are not suggesting that these changes will necessarily come easily; but it is not fundamental lack of knowledge that stands in the way.

And has not social work, like many other professions, carried the whole business of specialization to excess? People's needs rarely break down into such neat categories. While there is a great deal of talk about generic training, until very recently not much has actually been done. There are now a few interesting experiments in relating or even integrating two or even three major social work methods, and it seems inevitable that this trend will continue and be expanded. Of course, these changes in field work instruction will have to be paralleled by similar developments in class teaching. It is easier to urge this than to accomplish it, but the need seems to be obvious. A variety of agencies, both governmental and voluntary, the National Association of Social Workers, the Council on Social Work Education and a number of schools of social work are considering or testing out approaches in this area. One other development that we think offers promise and may make some interesting changes if it works out is the development by the Columbia University School of Social Work and a few other schools of teaching or training centers based on the medical model, where the school actually operates the service program in order to try to introduce a number of service and training innovations.

One other aspect relating to training must be mentioned. As has been said several times, the introduction of significantly larger numbers of non-professionals inevitably will require professionals to be involved more in supervision, consultation, program analysis, and the like. If this is to be the pattern, as we are urging, then these areas will have to be covered, at least to some extent, in social work educational programs. This further substantiates what has been suggested before—the development of new models of workers, whether professional or non-professional, inevitably means changes in the training for each of these categories.

As part of a review of manpower and training one ought to look briefly at the question of the relationship of the professions to the poverty programs, including the issue of the use of non-professional personnel. We have already touched on this issue but here again, would like to focus on social work—both because of knowledge and our belief that it is reasonably typical of all the others.

It does seem fair to say that the reaction of the social work profession and the poverty programs to each other is very mixed and difficult to categorize. The profession has been widely attacked both for its supposed reluctance to participate in these programs and, perhaps even more, for its alleged inability to make a meaningful contribution. It is often suggested that welfare in general and social work in particular have had their chance, have messed things up and are simply not relevant to meeting the needs of the poor. In a widely discussed speech given at the National Conference on Social Welfare in May 1965, Sargent Shriver sharply criticized welfare and the profession as not having met their responsibilities to the poor and warned that they would inevitably be by-passed unless there were significant changes in their philosophy and approach. While the speech did seem to upset a substantial number of those present and those who heard about it, the reality is that much the same points and in stronger terms have been made by many in the profession itself. Thus, Professor Richard Cloward and others have time and again attacked the profession's "flight from the poor" and have emphasized what they consider the profession's turning away from its historic mission by what they consider to be an inappropriate and self-defeating concentration on the most narrow and rigid aspects of professionalism. Terms such as "social welfare colonialism" and the "social work establishment" are very much in current usage and relate to what are considered the profession's failure to respond to the needs of the poor. Articles and speeches on this theme appear regularly in the profession's and related publications and in all sorts of conferences and meetings. Not at all atypical is the point of view of Professors S. M. Miller and Martin Rein that "certain social service professionals would rather protect their power positions and control of funds and preserve the importance of their skills—however outdated—rather than undertake a program of change however promising for all concerned."[17]

In turn, many social workers and leaders in the welfare profession have attacked the poverty programs on a variety of grounds. Among their major criticisms which represent different points of view and thus are not necessarily consistent with one another are:

1. The programs reflect nothing new and they are simply pale copies of what has been done for many years.
2. They represent a gimmick rather than a carefully thought through approach to helping the poor.
3. They are mainly for publicity and political purposes.

[17] See Shostak, *The Poverty of Welfare in America*, in NEW PERSPECTIVES ON POVERTY 94, at 103 n.19 (Shostak & Gomberg ed. 1965), citing S. M. Miller, Stupidity and Power: Two Competing Modes of Explanation (an unpublished paper, privately distributed), and Rein, *The Social Service Crisis*, Transaction, May 1964, pp. 5-7.

4. They are by-passing the existing agencies and setting up an unnecessary competing and highly expensive duplication of what is already available.

5. They are receiving and will receive an undue share of existing and potential funds, a result of which will be to waste a lot of money and to starve out those programs which have already proved their value.

6. By paying excessive salaries and by unfair recruitment tactics, they are taking badly needed personnel away from existing programs.

And finally

7. They are really not designed to achieve anything worthwhile and they simply represent a diversion away from focusing on real needs and meaningful change. The net result will not help the poor at all and may even make their lot worse by creating the delusion that something is really being done.

In addition, and probably for a variety of reasons, many professionals have been and are very skeptical about the major emphasis being placed on the use of non-professionals, particularly the poor and the indigenous. Doubts are widely expressed that these non-professionals can really accomplish anything worthwhile, and there is concern that the results may simply be a poorer level of service. Another point often made which may not be completely consistent with the preceding one is that non-professionals and volunteers have been used in the field for many years; and so what's all the current excitement about. While there is no doubt as to the sincerity and conviction of many who express the above points of view, it also seems clear that some of the responses are defensive reactions springing from the widespread and, as we believe, at times much too sweeping attacks on the profession and on welfare generally. At the same time, it seems to us equally true that some of the profession's responses and its attack on the poverty programs and their use of non-professionals have also been somewhat extreme and hysterical in tone, and do arise, at least partially, from perhaps excessive concern with professional status and how its own standing in the community will be affected. We believe, and to some extent it may be wishful thinking, that the profession and the poverty programs are beginning to make some effort to work out these difficulties. Certainly there is an increasing involvement of social workers and social agencies in the poverty effort, although some may see this as a not unmixed blessing. The National Association of Social Workers has had a special committee on poverty which has met with Mr. Shriver and some of his top aides to think through how the profession can be more helpful and what its role should be. Mr. Shriver himself, in a recent and very well received speech to the American Public Welfare Association, spoke very positively of welfare's contribution to the poor and called for mutual help and support in the future. Certainly poverty and the poverty program are very fashionable with social work and related groups. It is far and away the number one topic in conferences and meetings and ranks equally high as a subject for papers and articles.

For better or worse, and in our judgment it is for the better, the social work profession and the whole poverty effort are likely to move closer together, although at best the relationship will be an uneasy and uneven one. As has been suggested, the realities of the personnel situation are likely to force the social work profession to experiment more with the use of non-professionals entirely aside from the push of the poverty program. Also, even if there are substantial differences of opinion about the "flight from the poor," both as to whether it has really happened and whether the profession ever was much involved with this group, all the discussion has helped to focus the profession's attention on the needs of this group and the necessity for an appropriate response. It is likewise interesting that in recent weeks, as the international situation has brought about talk of cutting back or even eliminating the poverty program, there seems to be a growing tendency on the part of the social work profession to rise to its defense. This does not mean, nor should it, that the profession will put aside its right and duty to criticize, but it may be that the criticism will be somewhat more constructive. It also does seem likely, and we believe it will be helpful, that there will continue to be substantial concern expressed about the program's not going far enough and not doing enough to bring about badly needed and fundamental social change.

The most effective use of the non-professionals, particularly as they are drawn from the poor and the indigenous, will continue to be a problem. Reality will demand their use; but reality also requires that their jobs be clearly defined, that career opportunities be specific, that initial training and on-going staff development be more clearly formulated and improved, and that supervision be strengthened. We must recognize that these jobs require a combination of idealism and skill—that good intentions are important but insufficient, and that competence remains an essential factor.

We would like to repeat what has been said several times before. Our discussion of the profession and its relation to the poverty program has concentrated, for what we consider good and sufficient reasons, on social work and social welfare; but this is illustrative only. With what we believe are minor modifications any of the other human service professions and fields could have been substituted.

One of the most frequently expressed concerns about manpower and the poverty program is that these workers will be involved in politics and these jobs will be used as a source of patronage. There is no question that much of the political leadership does see these programs as a potential source of political power and leadership. One needs only to look at the responses of the mayors and of other local and state political leaders to see the pressure exerted, particularly in many of the larger urban communities, to make sure that the programs are centered in the mayor or local executive's office. Only recently the mayors have again demanded that all local programs be processed through the central community action organization, and it is not cynical to suggest that they feel it would be easier to exercise control over one organization than over many. It is also true that there has been widespread publicity about alleged mismanagement, poor administration and dishonesty in programs in several of the large urban communities, and an assumption often made is that this comes about because of political interference and involvement.

Along with everybody else, we are opposed to mismanagement and dishonesty and to the appointment of unqualified political appointees on a patronage basis. At the same time, we consider it to be naïve, unrealistic, and probably self-defeating to talk about insulating these programs from politics. Indeed to suggest that poverty programs be kept completely separate from politics is probably a contradiction in terms. Programs such as these have been traditionally involved in the political structure of our country; and in a democratic system that is probably just as well. Many of the poverty programs are political in nature and are likely to affect political power and influence. Actually, not too many people seem to be troubled about this issue in general. Rather, it is more a question of whose power and influence will be affected, and which politicians will benefit and suffer as a result of these programs and of the ways in which people are involved. Aside from questions of political losses and gains, there are significant differences in point of view among many of the professionals about the relationships of these programs to the power structure; and these differences are reflected in the way programs have been developed in a number of communities. There is a point of view that suggests that these programs can be effective *only* to the degree that they are identified with the community political structure, and that this is the only way that meaningful change can come about. As evidence, they point to what has happened in a number of communities where the programs are not so connected.

On the other hand, the contrasting point of view is that the programs will be destroyed *to the degree* that they become identified with the political leadership. The proponents of this view argue that no real meaningful action will be permitted, that the interests of poor people do not coincide with those in control of the political structure, and that no city hall or other governmental unit is going to finance its own destruction. They point also to the danger that in programs under city sponsorship and leadership the representatives of the poor may too often be co-opted and bought off.

Whatever the merits of these points of view—and we think both of the suggested approaches should be experimented with—we would strongly urge some sense of perspective about these issues. It must be recognized that many of these programs are large in size, highly experimental, and are moving in relatively uncharted directions. Also, many of them have to be put together in a hurry and have had to call on inexperienced and untrained personnel. Mistakes are inevitable, particularly when one remembers how complex, complicated and enormous are the needs of the people whom they are trying to serve. There must be some margin for error, just as there is in the nation's space efforts and in some other major national programs both past and present. We must maintain our right to criticize and do everything to avoid and certainly not repeat mistakes; but we must also recognize that there will be waste and failures, that at best progress will come slowly, and that success is by no means certain and in any case will not come easily. Those who would use these limitations or others to destroy these programs might do well to keep in mind the consequences. The poor and their needs are still with us and we cannot expect them to be patient forever.

CONTROLLING THE BUREAUCRACY OF THE ANTIPOVERTY PROGRAM

VICTOR G. ROSENBLUM*

Roscoe Pound's view of law as an instrument for satisfaction of social wants retains significance as both a rallying ground and problem maze for today's reformers:

> I am content to think of law as a social institution to satisfy social wants—the claims and demands and expectations involved in the existence of civilized society—by giving effect to as much as we may with the least sacrifice, so far as such wants may be satisfied or such claims given effect by an ordering of human conduct through politically organized society. For present purposes I am content to see in legal history the record of a continually wider recognizing and satisfying of human wants or claims or desires through social control; a more embracing and more effective securing of social interests; a continually more complete and effective elimination of waste and precluding of friction in human enjoyment of the goods of existence—in short, a continually more efficacious social engineering.[1]

As rallying ground, Pound's "contentment" calls attention to law as satisfier of social wants more than of individual wills. As problem maze, it demands choice from among competing claims, demands, and expectations without offering certainty of outcome. What programs, procedures, or controls give "effect to as much as we may with the least sacrifice"? What are the ascertainable relationships between degree of sacrifice and degree of want satisfaction? Since all social wants cannot be satisfied simultaneously, what criteria shall be invoked to determine the rank ordering of priorities?

We know that stratification occurs in every social structure, that some roles receive different rewards or sanctions from others. What are our standards for such differential distributions? Are they apportioned according to need, power, values, interests, community censensus, majority opinion, constitutional mandate, or some combination of these? Only recently have we begun realistically and systematically to face such problems, let alone find national agreement on them. At the same time, the majesty of aspiration that underlies the war on poverty requires that action be taken and choices made, even if the data for evaluation and prediction are still amorphous.

Dissensus over some details of allocation and administration of hundreds of

* A.B. 1945, LL.B. 1948, Columbia University; Ph.D. 1953, University of California at Berkeley. Professor of Political Science and Law, Northwestern University; Director of the Russell Sage Program in Law and the Social Sciences at Northwestern University; Editor-in-Chief, *Administrative Law Review*. Author, LAW AS A POLITICAL INSTRUMENT (1955); Co-author, THE USES OF POWER (1962). Contributor of articles to professional journals.

[1] ROSCOE POUND, AN INTRODUCTION TO THE PHILOSOPHY OF LAW 47 (1922).

millions of dollars by myriad bureaucratic structures to enhance individual and community welfare is inevitable. The purpose of the present article is not to delineate or take sides in the emergent conflicts, but to examine the institutions and methods that have been proposed to keep the expanding power apparatus that copes with poverty accountable both to the individuals with whom it deals directly and to the public generally. As a representative of one of the community action programs has pointed out, ". . . the range of publicly provided resources has become so extensive that the poor in this society can only survive if they learn how to maneuver successfully within the bureaucracies that control these resources."[2]

What are the instruments of accountability, redress, revision, and reform?[3] Are appeals to the courts more or less available and effective than appeals to one's congressman, precinct captain, or interest group? Let us examine a number of devices —some of them proposed importations and others currently in use. In the category of importations are the French Conseil d'État, the British Citizens' Advice Bureaus, and, glossiest of all, the Swedish Ombudsman.

THE CONSEIL D'ÉTAT

The Conseil d'État, a "reliable and virile guardian of individual rights,"[4] offers

---

[2] Mogulof, *Involving Low-Income Neighborhoods in Antidelinquency Programs*, Social Work, Oct. 1965, p. 51.

[3] Two recent but unconnected works are valuable in developing criteria for accountability. Charles Reich of Yale Law School has summarized basic standards for decision making that have come through experience and legal development to represent a fundamental conception of fairness; and David Apter of the University of California has applied his expertise on the politics of emerging societies to postulate conditions for the emergence of democratic society. Reich sets forth eight standards of fairness:

"(1) The rules which are to furnish the standard of decision should be clearly formulated in advance of any action; (2) the rules should be available to the public; (3) every action should begin with actual notice of the proposed action and a full statement of the basis for it; (4) the relevant facts should be determined in a proceeding at which the person or company affected can know the evidence and have an opportunity to rebut it; factual findings should not be based on hearsay or secret evidence known only to the agency; (5) the person or company should have the right to be represented by counsel; (6) there should be a distinct separation between those officials who investigate and initiate action and those who find the facts and make the decision; the latter officials should be subject to different authority than the former and free of any of the atmosphere in which the action was begun; (7) the decision, once made, should be accompanied by findings and reasons; (8) there should be opportunity for review of the decision within the agency, and, ultimately, in the courts."

Reich, *Individual Rights and Social Welfare: The Emerging Legal Issues*, 75 YALE L.J. 1245, 1252 (1965). Apter believes that the conditions under which the transition to and functioning of democracy become possible are:

1. "Privacy must be a consummatory value." He sees the desire for privacy in modernizing and industrializing societies as a reaction to the growing visibility of life in schools, factories, and other public places. 2. "Authority problems must be transformed into equity problems." Modernization and industrialization can reach the point where inequality and other problems of distributive justice threaten the continuity of authority. When this occurs, mechanisms for establishing equity are necessary as a basis for solidarity. 3. "Information must be available from a variety of sources including free public communication media, opposition parties, and the like." 4. The means of maintaining equity, accountability, and practical realism are "the constant translation of value conflict into interest conflict," conciliar control over the executive, formalized opposition, and popular sovereignty expressed through universal suffrage and periodic elections. DAVID APTER, THE POLITICS OF MODERNIZATION 455-56 (1965).

[4] HENRY J. ABRAHAM, THE JUDICIAL PROCESS 241 (1962).

a simple and inexpensive procedure for obtaining review of administrative action, in which the government itself takes the responsibility for investigating the facts and the law pertinent to the complainant's petition. After the plaintiff makes a summary statement of the facts and the relief sought, his request may lead either to proceedings to annul the administrative act in question through invocation of the ultra vires or abuse of power principles, or to proceedings requiring payment of money damages or other affirmative action. The complainant may choose to be represented by counsel; but he need not, and in many instances does not, retain counsel.

An especially appealing feature of the Conseil d'État is that it places on the government both liability for fault and liability for creation of unjustifiable risk as well. Thus, redress is available not only against improper administrative action but also against nominally legal action by an agency that operates unequally and unjustly on a citizen in practice. The government bears the cost of equalizing the burdens without necessity for passage of a private bill by the legislature. This has led analysts like Professor Abraham to observe that ". . . in effect, the *droit administratif* is developing in the direction of absolute liability to ensure equitable sharing among all citizens of the burden of government action."[5]

Another reason for enthusiasm over the Conseil d'État's role is its recognition of administrative law as a broad-based discipline encouraging systematic analysis within a unified framework of key public law problems.[6] It facilitates the perception of issues of administrative law in such emergent areas as government contracts and responsibilities and immunities of government officials. Professor W. Friedmann has hailed the development of administrative courts alongside the common law courts as a necessary recognition of the duality of the legal system in order to develop "a healthy balance between the needs of administration in the modern welfare state and the essential rights of the citizen."[7]

Even if one discounts such academic enthusiasm, the trends and refinements in administrative court systems in countries like France and Germany have been impressive. Administrative disputes are submitted in the first instance to tribunals separated from the administrators who have been challenged. Appeals can be taken on fact and law, and the final decisions of the Conseil d'État in France or the Bundesverwaltungsgericht in Germany assure a combination of professional judicial impartiality with administrative expertise.[8] One problem area of the administrative courts, however, concerns enforceability and efficacy of court rulings. Professor Weil of the University of Paris has reminded us recently that the admin-

---

[5] *Ibid.*

[6] See generally CHARLES J. HAMSON, EXECUTIVE DISCRETION AND JUDICIAL CONTROL (1954); BERNARD SCHWARTZ, FRENCH ADMINISTRATIVE LAW AND THE COMMON LAW WORLD (1954); CHARLES E. FREEDMAN, THE CONSEIL D'ÉTAT IN MODERN FRANCE (1961); MARCEL WALINE, DROIT ADMINISTRATIF (1957).

[7] W. FRIEDMANN, LAW IN A CHANGING SOCIETY 413 (1959).

[8] For a comparison of prevailing Anglo-Saxon and European systems for review of administrative behavior, see *id.* at 402-13.

istrative court judge can annul an illegal decision or order payment of compensation "but he goes no further." In annulling the dismissal of a civil servant, for example, the judge will not order reinstatement, and in annulling a permit refusal, the judge will not force the administrator to grant the permit.[9] Professor Weil is not enthusiastic about the likelihood of progress in enhancing compliance with judgments. He deems it advisable "to bring pressure to bear on the actual procedure of reaching decisions in the Administration."[10]

CITIZENS' ADVICE BUREAUS

The Citizens' Advice Bureaus (CAB) facilitate accountability through information about the bureaucracy rather than through subjecting it to review. The CABs are not courts or sanctioning agencies of the government; they constitute, rather, an "objective, friendly, and well-informed advisory and information service to the ordinary citizen."[11] Established in England in 1939 as a result of a conference on disruption of family life held by the British National Council of Social Service, the CABs are located in settlement houses, churches, libraries, and casework agencies, and are manned by professional social workers as well as by volunteer help. More than 400 offices located throughout England, Scotland, and Wales advise the general public on how they can best use government welfare services. They also explain the functions and operations of government agencies and acquaint the citizen with his rights so that he can stand up against wrongful government action. Mobile CABs, financed by the Carnegie United Kingdom Trust, visit small towns on market days in order to assist rural populations.

Although CABs are developed on a local basis and are connected only loosely with the central organization, basic policy in providing service is governed by the national CAB council. Publications like the Citizens' Advice Notes Service and the Monthly Information Service Circulars describe local resources and annotate administrative practices. The CABs exercise watchdog functions by giving visibility to hardships and unfair dealings stemming from agency determinations.

Although few CABs retain lawyers to give legal advice directly through the bureaus, their investigations and reports have been instrumental in the revision and bettering of Britain's legal aid program. The charge for filing an application for legal aid is often waived when CABs refer the case. The CABs are credited also with an active role in the confrontation of consumer problems and the drafting of legislation to control high-pressure selling.[11] The fact that the CABs answer more

---

[9] Weil, *The Strength and Weakness of French Administrative Law*, 1965 CAMB. L.J. 242.

[10] *Id.* at 259.

[11] Zucker, *Citizens' Advice Bureaus: The British Way*, Social Work, Oct. 1965, p. 85.

[12] Mildred Zucker, executive director of the James Weldon Johnson Community Center in New York, presented a paper on "Citizens' Advice Bureaus" at the Conference on the Extension of Legal Services to the Poor, in November 1964. See PROCEEDINGS OF THE CONFERENCE ON THE EXTENSION OF LEGAL SERVICES TO THE POOR 111-21 (1965). In updated form, her paper appears in Social Work, Oct. 1965, p. 85. See also NATIONAL COUNCIL OF SOCIAL SERVICE, CITIZENS' ADVICE BUREAUS IN THE CONTEMPORARY

than a million inquiries annually does not measure the quality of their work, but it does indicate widespread use of and confidence in the services they render. The British CABs have also received the compliment of emulation in such countries as Australia, Kenya, and Israel.

The Ombudsman

Of all the devices available to citizens for redress of grievances against the bureaucracy, the Swedish Justitieombudsman is perhaps the most colorful and has, in any event, received the most attention recently.[13] Established by the Swedish Constitution of 1809 as Parliament's overseer of administrative behavior, the Ombudsman's sole job is to protect the people from infringement of their rights by proceeding against "those who in the execution of their official duties, have, through partiality, favoritism or other causes, committed any unlawful act or neglected to perform their official duties properly."[14] The Ombudsman is elected by a committee of forty-eight members of Parliament—twenty-four from each house—

SCENE, 1959-61, A Report for the National Citizens' Advice Bureau (1962); John Whyatt, The Citizen and the Administration: The Redress of Grievances (1961); and National Council of Social Service, Report of the National CAB Committee 1962-1964 (London, 1964).

[13] An excellent collection of essays has been compiled and edited by Professor Donald Rowat of the University of Toronto and published by the University of Toronto Press: The Ombudsman Citizen's Defender (Rowat ed. 1965). Law reviews and political science journals have featured the Ombudsman abundantly. Destined to become the major article on the subject is Walter Gellhorn's *The Swedish Ombudsman*, 75 Yale L.J. 1 (1965). Professor Gellhorn's worldwide examinations of procedures for settling disagreements with government officials will be published in a Harvard University Press volume in 1966. Other major articles already published by him, which will comprise the substance of this volume, include: *The Norwegian Ombudsman*, 18 Stan. L. Rev. 293 (1966); *Finland's Official Watchman*, 114 U. Pa. L. Rev. 327 (1966); *The Ombudsman in New Zealand*, 53 Calif. L. Rev. 1155 (1965); *Citizens' Grievances Against Administrative Agencies—the Yugoslav Approach*, 64 Mich. L. Rev. 385 (1966); and *Settling Disagreements With Officials in Japan*, 79 Harv. L. Rev. 685 (1966). Professors Henry Abraham and Kenneth Davis were early supporters of the importation of the office of Ombudsman into the United States. In *Ombudsman in America: Officers to Criticize Administrative Action*, 109 U. Pa. L. Rev. 1057 (1961), Professor Davis endorsed the Ombudsman as an institution that might provide an additional check on the excesses of administrative power. His article was destined to be read primarily by lawyers, whereas Professor Abraham's *A People's Watchdog Against Abuse of Power*, 20 Pub. Admin. Rev. 152 (1960) was directed toward political scientists and administrators. Abraham saw establishment of the office of Ombudsman as engendering hope of "trust and good will that are so desperately needed today" in relationships between the governed and the governors.

Other informative analyses and commentaries on the Ombudsman include: Aikman, *The New Zealand Ombudsman*, 42 Can. B. Rev. 399 (1964); Anderman, *The Swedish Justitieombudsman*, 11 Am. J. Comp. L. 225 (1962); Blom-Cooper, *An Ombudsman in Britain*, 1960 Public Law 145; Christenson, *The Danish Ombudsman*, 109 U. Pa. L. Rev. 1100 (1961); Hurwitz, *The Danish Parliamentary Commissioner for Civil and Military Government Administration*, 1958 Public Law 235; Hurwitz, *Denmark's Ombudsman: The Parliamentary Commissioner for Civil and Military Government Administration*, 1961 Wis. L. Rev. 169; Jägerskiöld, *The Swedish Ombudsman*, 109 U. Pa. L. Rev. 1077 (1961); Jain, *Ombudsman in New Zealand*, 5 J. Indian L. Inst. 307 (1963); Pederson, *The Danish Parliamentary Commissioner in Action*, 1959 Public Law 115; Powles, *The Citizen's Rights Against the Modern State, and Its Responsibilities to Him*, 13 Int'l & Comp. L.Q. 761 (1964); Reuss, *An "Ombudsman" for America*, N.Y. Times, Sept. 13, 1964 (Magazine); Reuss & Anderson, *The Ombudsman: Tribune of the People*, Annals, Jan. 1966, p. 44; William A. Robson, The Governors and the Governed 22-31 (1964); Rosenthal, *The Ombudsman—Swedish "Grievance Man,"* 24 Pub. Admin. Rev. 226 (1964); Rowat, *Ombudsman for North America*, 24 Pub. Admin. Rev. 230 (1964).

[14] Swedish Const. art. 96.

to a four-year term. He can be and usually is re-elected, though custom limits him to three terms. Maximum care is taken to insulate the Ombudsman from partisan political pressures. He has no responsibility whatever to the executive and reports only to Parliament. While his annual reports are made to and reviewed by the First Law Committee of Parliament, there are not even remote indications that the Committee in particular or Parliament in general has ever sought to influence negotiations, inquiries, or prosecutions he has undertaken.[15]

One of the most appealing aspects of the Ombudsman's role is its aura of unlimited access. Anyone, any time, can complain to him, and he can proceed against any public official except the Cabinet ministers or the King in council in correcting alleged injustices. There is no requirement of exhaustion of administrative remedies before the Ombudsman's aid is invoked.

Gellhorn's research shows that citizens' complaints account for more than eighty-five per cent of the Ombudsman's docketed cases, with newspaper stories and office inspection on his own initiative accounting for the remainder.[16] While the complaints include a normal quota of "crank" letters that should be quickly discarded, many of these are examined carefully and given at least preliminary investigation so that the complainant will not feel rebuffed. The work of the Ombudsman's office is highly personalized. He reads the incoming complaints as they arrive and decides whether to request the official body involved to forward the applicable files to him. He conducts directly even informal conversations with officials, relegating only paper work to his staff. He and his staff appear to operate speedily and efficiently. Gellhorn reports, for example, that more than eighty per cent of the cases are disposed of within six months after docketing.

The Ombudsman's powers as an investigator are virtually unlimited. He has access to all official files and records, can interrogate any public official, and can—though hardly ever does—observe the deliberations of all courts and government agencies. He may choose to prosecute for violations or give "reminders" to errant bureaucrats. That only thirty-two punitive proceedings were instituted from 1960 through 1964, whereas there were 1,220 reprimands and suggestions issued during the same period, shows a preference for reform through admonition. The admonitions are accompanied by reasoned opinions designed to educate the wrongdoer and to provide guidelines and resolve doubts for all officials in similar circumstances.

The power to prosecute or to admonish is not, of course, the same as the power to reverse decisions. The Ombudsman cannot order a decision changed or require formally the reopening or reconsideration of a judgment. The possibility that he may commence proceedings that can lead to rebuke, fine, or even removal from office, however, offers a strong incentive to officials to respond to the Ombudsman's recommendations or reminders by correcting the particular injustice or breach of duty.

The institutions and areas covered by the Ombudsman's docket are impressively broad. They include alleged violations by judges, public prosecutors, police, prison administrators, hospital officials, school administrators, and tax authorities. Gellhorn has found that the administration of social insurance and other welfare state programs has not been a dominant element of the Ombudsman's caseload.

Of the complaints received, roughly ten per cent have been found to be justified by the time investigation has been completed. Of 1,410 docketed cases in 1964, for example, 722 were dismissed after inquiry, 381 were dismissed without inquiry, 283 elicited "admonitions or other remarks" by the Ombudsman, and only two were prosecuted.[17]

The range and scope of the Ombudsman's inquiries are immensely helpful in keeping officials aware of their public accountability. His function as a "supervisory shadow" influences present official behavior, even though the probability of actual inspection by him is remote.

An important factor in the Ombudsman's role is the relationship of the press to his office. He has been traditionally a strong proponent of the newspapers' "right to know"; and the press serves as occasional critic, frequent source, and constant publicizer of the Ombudsman's findings. The Ombudsman's relatively small budget makes his impact on administration all the more remarkable. The entire operation, occupying half of the third floor of a small building in downtown Stockholm and staffed with three secretaries and from six to nine lawyers, is maintained at a cost roughly equivalent to $120,000 a year. The Ombudsman's own salary is the same as that of a Swedish supreme court justice.

From a functional standpoint, the Ombudsman—at relatively low cost to the taxpayers—educates the citizenry and the bureaucracy about the processes of government. While placating the aggrieved citizen through speedy and thorough attention to the injustice alleged, the Ombudsman's carefully reasoned opinion is more likely to support than to reprimand the government official or agency involved. In the small proportion of cases in which wrongdoing is found, the Ombudsman's opinion and judgment help to formulate appropriate standards for administrators in many areas. The Ombudsman provides what a British observer views as the needed machinery "to handle complaints about the *manner* of the exercise of power by officials, to take them out of the political area and to investigate them dispassionately, without too much trouble or fuss."[18] By expressing his opinions clearly and persuasively in a context that holds the promise of follow-up, he induces courts and administrators voluntarily to follow his recommendations. While his interpretations may certainly be rejected, "a certain presumption exists that these interpretations

---

[17] *Id*. at 18.

[18] HENRY W. R. WADE, TOWARDS ADMINISTRATIVE JUSTICE 101 (1963). (Emphasis in original.)

are correct. The annual reports of the Ombudsman are carefully studied as evidence of the law."[19]

Another significant function of the Ombudsman is his performance as "the generalist in a specialized world." Whether dealing at a typical time with an allegedly negligent chairman of the housing council, the chairman of a child welfare council charged with committing improperly a father who had been lax in contributing to his children's support, a public prosecutor for failing to inform the court that a state's witness had to his knowledge committed perjury, or an errant official of the National Board of Civil Aviation for accepting a free ride from an airline whose application for license renewal was pending with the Board, the Ombudsman's concern is less with the differential powers and needs of the governing structures involved than with the broadly applicable criteria of fair and equitable administration. Perhaps the most important achievement of the Ombudsman's office, according to one of its occupants, is that "its very existence prevents any number of faults and abuses of power."[20]

The combination of low cost and high popularity has accounted for adoption of the office of Ombudsman as a device for controlling the bureaucracy in Finland, Denmark, Norway, and, just recently, in New Zealand. The office is certainly not a captive of any particular form or structure of government. While Sweden and Finland have administrative courts in addition to the office of Ombudsman, Denmark and Norway do not. The fear that the Ombudsman idea would not work in common law countries is refuted by the initial achievement of the office in New Zealand. Professor Rowat evaluates the Ombudsman as "an important new addition to the armoury of democratic government" and predicts that the office or its equivalent "will become a standard part of the machinery of government throughout the democratic world."[21] Less sanguine but perhaps more realistic may be Professor Gellhorn's appraisal:

> For one who thinks in American terms, the Ombudsman system seems a useful device for occasionally achieving interstitial reforms, for somewhat countering the impersonality, the insensitivity, the automaticity of bureaucratic methods, and for discouraging official arrogance. To rely on one man alone—or even on a few men—to dispense administrative wisdom in all fields, to provide social perspectives, to bind up personal wounds, and to guard the nation's civil liberties seems, on the other hand, an old-fashioned way of coping with the twentieth century.[22]

That the office of Ombudsman alone cannot cope with all the problems of the administrative state is hardly an adequate reason for arguing against its establishment as a supplement to other devices. There are factors, however, that could impair its utility for us. Perhaps the most serious is the fact that, no matter how

---

[19] Jägerskiöld, *supra* note 13, at 1092-93.
[20] The New Yorker, Feb. 13, 1965, p. 140. Mr. Alfred Bexelius was Sweden's 31st Ombudsman.
[21] ROWAT, *op. cit. supra* note 13, at 292.
[22] Gellhorn, *The Swedish Ombudsman*, 75 YALE L.J. 1, 58 (1965).

independent by tradition he appears to be, the Ombudsman is part of the establishment. The very element of nonpartisanship that surrounds his selection may be an assurance of relative innocuousness in the execution of his functions. His critique of petty or wayward individual bureaucrats could screen, however inadvertently, more significant failures on the part of the bureaucracy and establish the illusion for a lulled populace that all is well because the Ombudsman is on patrol. Without detracting from the high standards of public service in Scandinavian countries, it might be observed that the fiscal resources of the Ombudsman's office are so modest as to inhibit investigations that would discover and disclose major instances of incompetence or corruption. A single congressional investigation in the United States generally costs more than does the operation of the Ombudsman's office in Sweden for an entire year.[23]

Another limitation inherent in the office of Ombudsman, at least so far as the war on poverty is concerned, is that it ignores the desirability of participation by the people themselves in the processes of revision and reform. The relationship between Ombudsman and complainant is hierarchical, the Ombudsman exercising benevolence and discretionary intervention associated with eras of the "pukka Sahib" and "white man's burden." For our society, at least, institutional accountability, no matter how grudging, is preferable to institutional immunity, no matter how benevolent. Participation in the process of democracy, no matter how crass or grating, is preferable to alienation, no matter how genteel. Participation, to be meaningful, requires more than faith in officials or in the opinions of independent critics or watchmen of officials. Without minimal measures of accountability between citizens and officials, what passes for participation is in reality meretricious ritual.

To what extent do existing institutions in the United States for controlling the bureaucracy serve merely ritualistic functions? And to what extent do they in actuality or potentiality provide effective access to challenge, revision, and reform?

JUDICIAL REVIEW

The basic appeal of judicial review as a means of controlling the bureaucracy is its combination of confrontation of officials by complainants and the capacity to order immediate halts to impending actions or to apply spurs to lethargic or reluctant bureaucrats. There are no devices more effective than the injunction and the writ of habeas corpus to counter governmental terrorism; and resort to mandamus can help to achieve responsible performance by administrators of official functions they would otherwise ignore or discard. The sine qua non of judicial review is not a third party's benevolence, as it must be in the case of the Ombudsman. In a court

---

[23] For a case study of such a congressional investigation, see Rosenblum, *The FCC and Miami's Channel 10*, in THE USES OF POWER 173, 192-219 (Westin ed. 1962).

action, petitioner files his complaint as of right and the alleged offender must answer.

The problem of judicial review as a check on the bureaucracy is not found in its underlying theory, its objectives, or even its emergent doctrines; rather its problem is the practicality of access as complicated by the gaps and overlaps in judicial organization. On the whole, judicial review has produced procedurally tenable and substantively equitable standards for evaluating administrative action. The dangers inherent in early decisions—like *Schechter Poultry*,[24] *Panama Refining*,[25] *Crowell v. Benson*,[26] and the first two *Morgan* cases[27]—that might have immobilized creativity or stifled imagination have been minimized in recent years. The courts have consistently shown their respect for administrative expertise, flexibility, and representation of the public interest. On the other hand, without embracing doctrinal formalism, the courts have often required administrative accountability. Such concepts as primary jurisdiction have been allowed neither to substitute judicial preferences for those of administrators nor make administrative action unreviewable. Through decisions like *Isbrandtsen*,[28] the courts enhance agency expertise in marshalling facts and organizing them into meaningful patterns, while reserving to the judges the ultimate determination of questions of law.

There are notes of realism in recent perceptions of and admonitions to administrators by the judges. The significance attached to the state of an agency's backlog of cases in the *"Catco"* decision[29] and the admonition to the Federal Power Commission in the *Hunt* case[30] to study and perhaps emulate the National Labor Relations Board's procedures to help clear docket congestion are indicators of judicial understanding of the nuances of the administrative process. This is not to say, of course, that judicial review has ever been or is now the *deus ex machina* of our governmental system. Problems connected with standing to sue, indispensable parties, and unreviewable action have by no means been resolved,[31] but administrative accountability without impairment of administrative flexibility has certainly been encouraged by the courts. A prototype of judicial decisions in this realm has been the *Vitarelli* case[32] in which the Justices of the Supreme Court agreed unanimously that executive agencies must be rigorously held to the standards by which

---

[24] Schechter Poultry Corp. v. United States, 295 U.S. 494 (1935).

[25] Panama Ref. Co. v. Ryan, 293 U.S. 388 (1935).

[26] 285 U.S. 22 (1932).

[27] Morgan v. United States, 298 U.S. 468 (1936); Morgan v. United States, 304 U.S. 1 (1938).

[28] Federal Maritime Board v. Isbrandtsen Co., 356 U.S. 481 (1957).

[29] Atlantic Ref. Co. v. Public Serv. Comm'n of New York, 360 U.S. 378 (1959).

[30] Federal Power Comm'n v. Hunt, 376 U.S. 515, at 527 (1964).

[31] Davis treats the problems comprehensively in chapters 22 and 28 of his *Administrative Law Treatises*. For a detailed analysis of the strengths and weaknesses of the judiciary in coping with arbitrary agencies, see Berger, *Administrative Arbitrariness and Judicial Review*, 65 Colum. L. Rev. 55 (1965). See also Byse, *Proposed Reforms in Federal "Nonstatutory" Judicial Review: Sovereign Immunity, Indispensable Parties, Mandamus*, 75 Harv. L. Rev. 1479 (1962).

[32] Vitarelli v. Seaton, 359 U.S. 535 (1959).

they profess their actions to be judged. Under this ruling, any agency remains free, consistent with the statutes governing it, to establish its own modus operandi but is required to follow it, once established, unless and until new procedures are adopted formally and prospectively. Justice Harlan's view seems especially apt. He observed that in proceedings

> in which the ordinary rules of evidence do not apply, in which matters involving the disclosure of confidential information are withheld, and where it must be recognized that counsel is under practical constraints in the making of objections and in the tactical handling of his case which would not obtain in a cause being tried in a court of law before trained judges, scrupulous observance of departmental procedural safeguards is clearly of particular importance.[33]

These procedural guidelines for administrative action have, of course, had greater applicability to the work of the long-established agencies than to agencies concerned with implementing the poverty program. There is no reason, however, to oppose the application of these requirements to the work of the Office of Economic Opportunity, federal welfare agencies, and local and regional offices administering phases of the poverty program.

A key illustration of this potentiality was the California Supreme Court's landmark decision last year ruling that the Constitution's equal protection clause forbade the transfer to relatives of a mentally ill person the financial burden of care in a state institution.[34] The California Department of Mental Hygiene had sued the estate of the child of a mentally ill mother to recover the cost of the mother's maintenance in a state hospital. The court ruled that, since the administration of laws providing treatment for the mentally ill is an appropriate state function, "a statute obviously violates the equal protection clause if it selects one particular class of person for a species of taxation and no rational basis supports such classification."[35] As tenBroek has observed,

> the principal cause of dependency is not individual but social, a need for protection arising from the complexities of modern society and the imperfections of a rapidly advancing economy. Since a major cause of poverty is social, over which the individual has no control, relief is a proper charge against the total economy.[36]

Even limited to state constitutional grounds, the *Kirchner* decision embodies a significant doctrinal innovation and plants seeds for further reconceptualization of welfare administration practices.

---

[33] *Id.* at 540.

[34] Department of Mental Hygiene v. Kirchner, 60 Cal. 2d 716, 36 Cal. Rptr. 488, 388 P.2d 720, *cert. granted*, 379 U.S. 811 (1964). The U.S. Supreme Court remanded the case to the California Supreme Court for determination of whether the California court had relied on the federal or state equal protection clauses. 380 U.S. 194 (1965). The California court subsequently ruled that it had relied on the state ground. 62 Cal. 2d 586, 43 Cal. Rptr. 329, 400 P.2d 321 (1965).

[35] *Id.* at 722, 36 Cal. Rptr. at 492, 388 P.2d at 724.

[36] tenBroek, *California's Dual System of Family Law: Its Origin, Development, and Present Status*: III, 17 STAN. L. REV. 614, 642 (1965). See also *id.*, pts. I and II, 16 STAN. L. REV. 257, 900 (1964).

Vital though its functions may be, the judiciary still lacks the accessibility needed to assure equal justice under law for all. Viewed essentially as institutions through which the elite may resolve their conflicts with the bureaucracy or with one another, our courts have not until recently begun to serve as dispensers of justice to all the people. For the poor, courts have been too often the instruments through which aggressive creditors or vindictive police might demonstrate their power. The functions of courts as sources of redress of grievances of the poor were negligible, since so few could afford the fees of access to the mechanism. Even when the financial factor of access could be overcome with the help of legal aid offices or other devices, inadequate facilities, archaic rules, and problems of jurisdictional division among local courts have often necessitated prolonged litigation before a meaningful remedy could result. Typical of applicable criticisms were recent remarks of the chief justice of the Superior Court of Massachusetts castigating the denial of fundamental rights to persons "because of a shortage of judges, inadequate facilities, a lack of supporting personnel, and the failure of the bar and the legislature to promulgate modern rules of practice and procedure."[37] Judge Tauro lamented the fact that state and local courts have the responsibility for their successful operation but not always the authority to carry out desirable programs. "In truth, the superior court is almost totally dependent on the legislature for its needs. . . . The result is that many problems that could be nipped in the bud go unchecked until such time as the legislature can be convinced that remedial action is necessary."[38]

As Purcell and Specht have pointed out in a recent issue of *Social Work*, redress sought by the poor can also be impeded by the division of authority among public agencies to which recourse must be had before suit can be brought. Even a grievance as specific as one relating to water supply may be subdivided so as to fall under several different jurisdictions. In New York until recently, they maintained, complaints about no water had to be referred to the Health Department; complaints about not enough water, to the Department of Water Supply; water overflowing from the apartment above, to the Police Department; and water seepage in the cellar, to the Sanitation Department.[39]

Delaying, stalling, dodging, and buck-passing have emerged under such circumstances as the deeds, if not the goals, of the society. Courts then serve as sanctifiers and institutionalizers of procrastination and perpetuators of the status quo, rather than as sources of accommodation to social need and as guardians of human dignity. Discovery of the feasibility of judicial reform has not been accompanied by its spontaneous generation. But this does not belie the fact that judicial review *can* protect, defend, and redress in behalf of the individual, while keeping a watchful —not necessarily jaundiced—eye on the bureaucracy.

[37] Tauro, *Courts and Their Relationship to the Average Citizen*, 49 J. Am. Jud. Soc'y 58 (1965).
[38] *Ibid.*
[39] Purcell & Specht, *The House on Sixth Street*, Social Work, Oct. 1965, p. 69, at 72.

CONGRESSIONAL SUPERVISION

Extolling the virtues of Congress is hardly likely to replace baseball as the national pastime. More likely to meet public and academic approbation is the snide or sardonic critique of the legislature's defects. The complaints are legion and timeless, including

> . . . the labyrinthine convolutions of the legislative process itself, where what comes out has no predictable relationship to what went in; the ironies and occasional absurdities of the seniority system; the virtually unassailable power positions which committee chairmen enjoy; the brokerage and horse trading which the Congressional leaders must employ to get anything positive done; the shabby moral tone which emanates from the Capitol.[40]

Despite such redolent allegations about congressional infirmities, a stark and classic truth remains: in Senator Henry Jackson's words, "at the very heart of the American system of government . . . is the principle and practice of Congressional review—the duty of the legislature to cross examine the powerful."[41] Recognizing that Congress must strengthen its machinery for auditing through the committee system the actual accomplishments of executive programs, Jackson insists that the machinery must not substitute some outside individual or institution for the supervisory role of the congressman. He finds "no satisfactory substitute for members of Congress, particularly those on the key committees, personally involving themselves in the day-in and day-out pick and shovel work."[42]

The objective, if not always the product, of such direct and personal involvement is, as a noted political scientist contends, to carry the process of representation over into the bureaucracy. "And it may well be that the most abiding role of Congress in the years to come will be its *service as a place where the needs of the bureaucracy are continually being balanced against the prevailing special interests in the community.*"[43] Because Congress controls the purse strings and forms the ultimate contours of legislation, the bureaucrat must take seriously every communication from or with a senator or representative. The oldtimers who serve traditionally as chairmen of the committees in charge of substantive legislation or appropriations for government departments frequently consider the agency officials either "birds of passage" or "their own servants."[44] This congressional control over awards and sanctions for officialdom can have chaotic effects on the bureaucracy in extreme form,

---

[40] Burnham, *Has Congress a Future?*, 197 THE NATION 546 (1963), reprinted in CONGRESSIONAL REFORM 19-21 (Clark ed. 1965).

[41] Jackson, *Executives, Experts and National Security*, in STAFF OF SUBCOMM. ON NAT'L SECURITY AND INTERNATIONAL OPERATIONS OF THE SENATE COMM. ON GOVERNMENT OPERATIONS, 89TH CONG., 1ST SESS., CONDUCT OF NATIONAL SECURITY POLICY: SELECTED READINGS 76, 81 (Comm. Print 1965). For analysis of the problems Congress faces when executive privilege is invoked, see Berger, *Executive Privilege v. Congresssional Inquiry* (pts. 1-2), 12 U.C.L.A.L. REV. 1044, 1288 (1965).

[42] Jackson, *supra* note 41.

[43] Lowi, *Preface*, LEGISLATIVE POLITICS U.S.A. at xix (Lowi ed. 1962). (Emphasis in original.)

[44] *Id.* at xviii.

since it divides the loyalties of administrators between the executive and the legislature. Nothing inherent in the system requires that matters reach the extremity, however. The trading pattern that is inherent in the system—involving the congressional committee, the administrative agency, the executive, and one or more clientele groups—helps to channel or institutionalize the conflicts and assure maximum visibility of issues and policy choices for ultimate ratification by the public.

The "pick and shovel" work of Congress in supervising the operations of the bureaucracy of the poverty program has been broad and detailed. Subcommittees on the poverty program have kept officials of the Office of Economic Opportunity, as well as their regional and local associates, under persistent scrutiny and challenge through public hearings, private confrontations, and assorted jabs and jibes. That individual congressmen may sharpen political axes of their own through such practices must not obscure the fact that congressional hearings and investigations have provided a powerful impetus for accountability on the part of administrators.

Consider, for example, the work of the House Subcommittee on the War on Poverty. In the spring of 1965, after four of its task forces had examined the administration of the poverty program in eleven cities, the chairman charged at the outset of the hearings in Washington on the program that political machines in many communities had organized "giant fiestas of patronage" in order, among other goals, "to feed their political hacks at the trough of mediocrity." He particularly criticized the Office of Economic Opportunity for "administrative overcentralization to the exclusion of independent groups" and for "obvious failure to carry out a most important objective: that of involving the poor in the war on poverty."[45]

The transcripts of the hearings, although frequently verbose and repetitive, are noteworthy for their airing of immediate public problems in an environment of courtesy, challenge, and exhaustiveness. These excerpts from the questioning of Dr. Deton Brooks, who heads the program in Chicago, and of the Reverend Lynward Stevenson, President of The Woodlawn Organization and a strong critic of Dr. Brooks' administration of the poverty program, offer typical illustrations of the use of the congressional investigation to develop significant data and to bring conflicts into the open, channel them into peaceful avenues, and hold open the possibility of redress:

CONGRESSMAN CAREY OF NEW YORK. Dr. Brooks, would you answer a few brief questions on the type of projects you contemplate in Chicago? Are you establishing a credit union service?

Mr. BROOKS. It has not been funded yet but we contemplate it.

Mr. CAREY. We found this to be quite popular and somewhat effective here in the District.

Mr. BROOKS. It is almost necessary, that is right.

---

[45] Hearings on Examination of the War on Poverty Programs Before the Subcommittee on the War on Poverty Program of the House Committee on Education and Labor, 89th Cong., 1st Sess. 2 (1965).

Mr. CAREY. Secondly, do you intend to provide legal service, such as has not been available before?

Mr. BROOKS. Yes. We already have a proposal before the Office of Economic Opportunity for the Legal Aid Bureau of Chicago to provide those legal services in the urban progress centers.

Mr. CAREY. You are going to use the Legal Aid Bureau?

Mr. BROOKS. That is correct. No. 1, it takes all influence out. It would be a relationship of client and attorney. In other words, once we get them funded they can handle that client just as if he were any other client. The one problem, and I understand that it has been worked out now, was a problem on the national level concerning American Bar Association policy.

However, at our local level we had no problem. Our Legal Aid Bureau in Chicago has been working in cooperation with the Chicago Bar Association over a long period of years. They have the competence and the technique. We certainly want them to handle these services for us.

Mr. CAREY. Of course, they are handling these things now where criminal defense is involved. But beyond that, landlord and tenant, in fact the broad span of legal representation, exclusive of domestic relations, will you engage in all these things?

Mr. BROOKS. Yes. Let me point this out, that if there is a relationship of a tenant to a person, to an individual person, in any way, that person deserves his day in court regardless. . . .

I was asked one day by a civil rights group what would happen if a landlord came and the tenant hit him in the mouth because their relationship had been so bad.

I said, we would give him legal aid because he deserves his day in court.

Mr. CAREY. Doctor, are you closely coordinated in your planning function with your department of public assistance or whatever counterpart you have, welfare department? Where is your cross-over or liaison there?

Mr. BROOKS. On every level. The Department of Public Aid has been a part of our total committee since its inception. No. 2, the Department of Public Aid in certain programs is taking responsibility for the training of all kinds of people, for instance in the homemakers' program.

No. 3, at the local level, at the urban progress center level, they have a liaison in every urban progress center that we have open. . . .

Mr. CAREY. Have you any way in your planning, or do you intend in your planning, to gauge the success and effect of poverty activities by seeing the resultant effect upon your welfare roles and the number of people on assistance?

Mr. BROOKS. This would be one way. That will not be the only way, but this ought to be one measure that we should look at carefully.

Mr. CAREY. It is a highly important measure, because we sold this theory to the Congress on the theory we were going to phase out the dole and everything else, in order to make taxpayers out of tax-eaters. . . .

We have an expression that was originated by a great public utility in New York, the Con-Edison Co., and all over our city are signs "Dig we must," and I think the slogan of our task forces must be to "Dig we must."

We must go to the roots of the program and see how the legislation is working in the minds of the poor. . . .[46]

_____
[46] *Id.* at 343-45.

The House Committee's probe of "the minds of the poor" produced some ve-
hement condemnations of the program's administration. Reverend Lynward
Stevenson's accusations against the Chicago Committee on Urban Opportunity were
a typical case in point:

> Mr. STEVENSON . . . [T]he Woodlawn Organization has been conducting
> a Manpower Development and Training Act job-training program for the hard-
> core unemployed since July 1964. This program was funded directly to the
> people by the U.S. Department of Labor, the Office of Manpower, Automation,
> and Training.
>
> We do not have any so-called social engineers on our staff. We have people
> in the community—poor people—who are the counselors, who know and feel with
> the people and stand side by side the unemployed no matter what the situation
> is. . . .
>
> The result is this: Our dropouts are a mere 20 per cent of the number en-
> rolled. Ninety-eight per cent of our graduates have been hired for jobs. This
> is what the poor can do for themselves, given the chance, and we will continue to
> do this. This is self-determination. . . .
>
> Since October 1964 we have been held at bay. Public criticism of the director
> of the Chicago Committee on Urban Opportunity for his reluctance to deal with
> the TWO has only resulted in defensive action on his part by holding a number
> of phony conferences with TWO, which began nowhere and ended nowhere. . . .
>
> We are not children that must be planned for. We are not primitive savages
> that must be civilized by so-called civilized colonialists. Our retraining program
> stands as a beacon light to community organizations all over the country showing
> the way to what can be done by the poor themselves.
>
> And yet, we have been meeting over and over with Deton Brooks, the director
> of Chicago Committee on Urban Opportunity, and all we have gotten is drivel.
> We have asked Deton Brooks for funds for a day care center and a medical
> care center, but he cannot talk sense. He speaks meaningless sociological drivel
> designed not to lift people but to keep them dependent.[47]

The conflicts between the Chicago Committee on Urban Opportunity and The
Woodlawn Organization have by no means been resolved, but the visibility and
confrontation afforded by the congressional hearing have reinforced the likelihood of
settlement through peaceful political action.[48] Thus, the significance of these and

---

[47] *Id.* at 346-47, 359.

[48] The capacity of Congress to keep tabs on the bureaucracy of the poverty program and to provide
outlets and channels for community dissensus has been demonstrated also by the Senate Subcommittee on
Poverty. During its June 1965 hearings, for example, the Senate Subcommittee contributed with
political finesse to the subsequent elimination of Sargent Shriver's dual roles and made officials of the
OEO re-examine some policies in response to critics who had castigated the administrators of the
program for alleged exclusion of the poor.

"Senator JAVITS. May I ask one question: I wondered if you could tell us how you are dividing
    your time now between the Office of Economic Opportunity and the Peace Corps?
Mr. SHRIVER. You know the gossip, Senator, that I am in both places at the same time.
Senator JAVITS. Are you?
Mr. SHRIVER. Actually there is a lot more truth to it than there is joke to it. I frequently
    talk to men who are working with one operation or the other. They don't know in fact
    whether I am in one building or the other. Whether I am physically in one building I think

other illustrations of congressional supervision of the bureaucracy lies in the provision of effective opportunity for participation in and redress through the processes of government. Congress's financial resources and capacity for swift political action provide instruments for controlling the bureaucracy that are far more consistent with the nuances and complexities of twentieth-century government than Ombudsmen or administrative courts can provide.

In so far as the specifics of the Economic Opportunity Act are concerned, it is important to note that revisions in the statute have resulted from the hearings. Title two, dealing with the community action programs, for example, has been amended to require reasonable access by the public to information about programs

---

is not as important as to whether or not I am available adequately to the people who are working in the organization. They have been very kind so far. Nobody has said that I was unavailable. In fact, I think perhaps it is just the reverse. I am too available.
Senator JAVITS. You have no program as to division of time?
Mr. SHRIVER. Program division?
Senator JAVITS. Yes.
Mr. SHRIVER. No; I work all the time on both of them."
Hearings on Expanding the War on Poverty, Before the Select Subcommittee of the Senate Committee on Labor and Public Welfare, 89th Cong., 1st Sess. 123 (1965).
Dr. Reginald Hawkins of Charlotte, N.C. made a number of statements critical of the operation of the community action program in the South generally, and the Charlotte program in particular. Dr. Hawkins charged among other things that:
"Very few Negroes in the South have confidence in this war on poverty as it is presently constituted, staffed, and operated at the State and local levels. They see all the top paying jobs in administration going to white people who already had high-paying jobs. They also see the same people in leadership roles from the same old social departments and agencies that have kept them poor and dependent in the past."
Hearings, supra, at 239.
The OEO was confronted with the charge and reacted promptly in a memo to the Congressional Committee:
"We believe this statement should be considered in light of the following:
1. Every community action program in the South is either run by an organization with a biracial governing board, or has organized or is organizing a biracial policy committee program and responsibility.
2. Scores of key staff positions on local community action agencies in the South are filled by Negroes. The following are illustrative:
The deputy director of the Nashville, Tenn., program.
The organizer of the neighborhood services in Knoxville, Tenn.
The head of the Clarksdale, Miss., Head Start Program.
The associate director of the Savannah, Ga., Chatham County program.
The coassociate director of the Atlanta-Fulton County program.
The assistant director of the Dade County, Fla., program.
The associate director of the Jacksonville, Fla., program.
The coassistant director of the Winston-Salem, N.C., program.
The assistant director of the Durham, N.C., program.
The assistant director of the Corinth, Miss., program.
3. Predominantly Negro institutions such as Mary Holmes Jr. College, Paine College, Tuskegee Institute and Alabama A. & M. are playing important roles in the program.
4. Without question, the Negro in the South is participating more extensively and more intensively in their program than he has in any other whether under Federal, State, or local auspices."
Hearings, supra, at 241.

204 LAW AND CONTEMPORARY PROBLEMS

and policy, including reasonable opportunity for public hearings and access to books and records of agencies administering the programs.[49]

Congressional vanity and banality may, of course, triumph over nobler motives, but our system of checks and balances, by countervailing the ambitions and powers of one branch with the ambitions and powers of the others, limits even those congressmen prone to blatant demagoguery in efforts to control the largesse of government.

PERSPECTIVES ON THE PROBLEM OF CONTROL

Determination of preferences or priorities from among the devices for controlling the bureaucracy depends in considerable part upon our objectives and aspirations. Are we seeking merely the substantive manifestations of deeds of justice or do we aspire as well toward an administrative process that maximizes participation and the stake of every individual in the mechanisms of government? If we focus on deeds of justice alone, then selection and enhancement of the Ombudsman's role offer suitable means for assuring good deeds. But if participation in the processes of government is important as well, then emphasis must be placed on the controls that heighten participation.

What significance do we attach to political participation, with all its caviling and inefficiency, as a vital component of democracy? There can be little doubt that the Economic Opportunity Act was designed to strengthen, supplement, and coordinate opportunities for participation as well as for education, training, and employment.[50] There is some disagreement among scholars, however, over whether we should be content to keep a substantial segment of the population in a state of political inertia and vacuity. Froman's research in voting behavior in congressional elections, for example, shows that the greater the percentage of non-white population, the smaller the voting turnout; and the smaller the percentage of owner-occupied dwelling units, the smaller the voting turnout.[51] Berelson, Lazarsfeld, and McPhee in their study of voting have maintained that such examples of political apathy promote the likelihood of political stability. According to their view, the larger the number of intense losers in a political contest, the greater the possibility that the losers can be mobilized into *ad hoc* undemocratic groups. Perhaps we have to accept the view that economically poorer, less educated people in the United States are less likely to participate and more likely to have authoritarian values than those from the better educated middle and upper classes.[52]

---

[49] Economic Opportunity Amendments of 1965, § 11(5), 79 Stat. 974, 42 U.S.C.A. § 2782(5) (Supp. 1965). See House Comm. on Educ. & Labor, *Economic Opportunity Amendments of 1965*, H.R. Rep. No. 428, 89th Cong., 1st Sess. 7-11 (1965).

[50] 78 Stat. 508, 42 U.S.C. §§ 2701-981 (1964). The community action programs authorized by title II, part A, are explicitly designed "to provide stimulation and incentive for urban and rural communities to mobilize their resources to combat poverty . . . ." 78 Stat. 516, 42 U.S.C. §§ 2781-82 (1964). See generally Cahn & Cahn, *The War on Poverty: A Civilian Perspective*, 72 YALE L.J. 1317 (1964).

[51] LEWIS A. FROMAN, CONGRESSMEN AND THEIR CONSTITUENCIES 37 (1963).

[52] BERNARD R. BERELSON, VOTING ch. 14 (1964); SEYMOUR M. LIPSET, POLITICAL MAN 32 (1960).

Data like these lead such students of political behavior as Lester Milbrath to "doubt that the society as a whole would benefit if intense interest and active involvement in politics became widespread throughout the population."[53]   On the other hand, Milbrath recognizes, along with Almond and Verba, that it is valuable to admonish citizens to become active in politics because "the belief in the influence potential of the average man has some truth to it and does indicate real behavioral potential."[54]

There is other evidence, however, that citizen competence and citizen participation reinforce one another.   Herbert McClosky presents data in support of the proposition "that whatever increases the level of political articulateness—education, S.E.S. [socio-economic status], urban residence, intellectuality, political activity, etc.—strengthens consensus and support for American political ideology and institutions."[55] He finds that the politically unsophisticated have difficulty "discriminating political integrity from demagoguery, maturity and balanced judgment from fanaticism, honest causes from counterfeits."[56]   In short, those with the least understanding of American politics subscribe with the least enthusiasm to its principles.   Democratic ideology grows as the articulate class grows.

Relating these observations to the poverty program, it would appear that those deeds of the bureaucracy that constitute merely charitable handouts to people enlarge a sense of alienation rather than of participation, just as voting for a particular candidate because one has been given a bottle of liquor or a five dollar bill to do so denigrates the political process.[57]   Deeds that are the product of participation, on the other hand, instill a commitment to the processes and institutions that engender them.   We must seek through the poverty program and the controls we place over it, therefore, to bolster and multiply the factors that make people articulate and increase their participation.   The poor have been one of the "forgotten groups," or "those who suffer in silence," because, until recently, they have had neither opportunity nor incentive to organize, to establish lobbies, or to take action.[58]   Our objective in increasing participation is not to create a bureaucracy of the poor to countervail the bureaucracy of the poverty program, but rather to fortify the ideology of democracy.   Professor Edelman has pointed out that "our political institutions constitute, among other things, a device for providing symbolic

[53] LESTER W. MILBRATH, POLITICAL PARTICIPATION 147 (1965).
[54] GABRIEL A. ALMOND & SIDNEY VERBA, THE CIVIC CULTURE 487 (1963); MILBRATH, op. cit. supra note 53, at 152.
[55] McClosky, Consensus and Ideology in American Politics, 58 AM. POL. SCI. REV. 361, at 362 (1964).
[56] Id. at 379.
[57] Professor Reich, op. cit. supra note 3, has developed the idea of "entitlement" in evaluating the deeds of government.   He maintains that when an individual lacks sufficient resources to live decently, society has the obligation to provide him with support and the individual has a right to that support.   Reich does not appear worried that entitlement in the absence of leadership or participation in policy formation by the poor themselves would necessarily reduce them to a supine mass.
[58] MANCUR OLSON JR., THE LOGIC OF COLLECTIVE ACTION 165-67 (1965).

reassurance to threatened groups, and the device works admirably for most issues."[59]

How can we provide institutions for the poor that reassure, not only symbolically, but through concrete involvement in institutional processes of innovation and change? Fuller's espousal of a central, indisputable principle of substantive, natural law offers at least a starting point. He says, "open up, maintain, and preserve the integrity of the channels of communication by which men convey to one another what they perceive, feel, and desire."[60] There are no more apt institutions for this purpose than political parties, legislatures, and courts. Traditionally they were designed as devices for access to redress and reform, and no devices superior to these have yet been evolved. That they are themselves often inadequate in performing this role is an argument not for their rejection and replacement but for the continuing drive to improve them. We considered earlier some of the actions taken by Congress to encourage broader access to the policy-making process. Recent developments in law and social work provide additional reasons for optimism over the potentiality of our institutions to raise not only the substantive standards but the commitments to democracy of the poor.[61]

In social work, for example, there has been recent emphasis on the nature of social conditions that provide the context for individual responses. "It is important that the social work profession no longer regard social conditions as immutable and a social reality to be accommodated as service is provided to deprived persons with an ever increasing refinement of technique."[62] Part of the social worker's professional function, according to this view, is to seek solutions to social problems through institutional and organizational change, rather than merely to focus on individual problems in an accepted social setting. Kahn has described this kind of development as a combination of "a policy and a case approach." Examining the relationships between social work and the control of delinquency, Kahn finds, for example, that "social workers have traditionally been concerned more with diagnosis than with legalities, yet the misuse of the authority system when there is no basis for so doing is as much a diagnostic error as an infringement on rights." He admonishes the social work profession to give high priority to the development of coordinated programs and services that can convert such social labels as "delinquency" from a "differential instrument of social control to a social category for special services or help."[63]

For social workers to limit themselves to case measures ignores the degree to

---

[59] MURRAY EDELMAN, THE SYMBOLIC USES OF POLITICS 170 (1964).

[60] LON L. FULLER, THE MORALITY OF LAW 186 (1964).

[61] These standards are conditioned essentially on the assumption that institutionalized social conflict benefits the flexible society. As Coser has said, "In loosely structured groups and open societies, conflict which aims at a resolution between antagonists is likely to have stabilizing and integrative functions for the relationship." LEWIS A. COSER, THE FUNCTIONS OF SOCIAL CONFLICT 154 (1956).

[62] Purcell & Specht, supra note 39, at 75.

[63] Kahn, Social Work and the Control of Delinquency: Theory and Strategy, Social Work, April 1965, p. 3, at 13.

which the client's problem belongs to the community and society as well as to the individual, family, or peer group. No longer need social work be an instrument conducive to resignation, apathy, and adjustment to poverty in perpetuity. It can become in large part an "enabler," to use Grosser's term, by teaching clients that solutions to many of their problems lie in the hands of governmental agencies and that the agencies are sensitive to citizen efforts, especially in election years. This has been the approach of organizations like Mobilization for Youth whose focus has been on achieving social change through community action.[64] Frustration and isolation can thus be channeled into constructive efforts toward redress and reform through these additional dimensions of the social work profession.

If this newer orientation of social work functioned in a vacuum, it would be of limited value. Its special significance lies in its development concomitantly with "the law explosion" of the 1960s. That some roles in any social system receive more rewards than others does not mean that the "differential distribution of sanctions in society"[65] need remain static. Law, through its implementation of access to the rule-enforcing machinery of the society, can make material and explicit what might otherwise remain ineffable aspiration. The law explosion has, in fact, put this issue in the forefront of agenda items for academic groups, civic betterment organizations, and bar associations.

Commenting on the confrontation by the courts of the mid-century law explosion, Harry Jones notes that "new social interests are pressing for recognition in the courts. Groups long inarticulate have found legal spokesmen and are asserting grievances long unheard. Each of these developments has brought its additional grist to the mills of justice."[66]

It would be premature, if not fatuous, to claim that legal facilities are adequate to meet the demands on them, but several developments connote sufficient progress to warrant enthusiasm for the possibility of long-range resolution. The growth of neighborhood law programs in New York, New Haven, Boston, Oakland, Washington and other cities has been the product of new conceptions of legal aid. Persons in need of assistance from legal aid offices can find them not only closer to home but better financed and more adequately manned than ever before.[67] The

---

[64] Grosser, *Community Development Programs Serving the Urban Poor*, Social Work, July 1965, p. 15. In similar vein, Robert L. Kahn and Daniel Katz in a paper delivered at the 1965 Forum of the National Conference on Social Welfare urged social workers to acknowledge the importance of and attempt to utilize "direct systematic change—changes which involve altering formal procedures, policies, and structural arrangements." Kahn & Katz, *Social Work and Organization Change*, in PROCEEDINGS OF THE NATIONAL CONFERENCE ON SOCIAL WELFARE 162, 181 (1965). The January 1966 issue of *Social Work* contains three other significant articles related to this theme: Waterman, *Local Issues in the Urban War on Poverty*, p. 57; Shostak, *Promoting Participation of the Poor: Philadelphia's Antipoverty Program*, p. 64; and Piven, *Participation of Residents in Neighborhood Community Action Programs*, p. 73. Rien and Riessman propose a "third party stance aimed at increasing the demand for services by the poor" in *A Strategy for Antipoverty Community Action Programs*, Social Work, April 1966, p. 3.
[65] NEIL J. SMELSER, THE SOCIOLOGY OF ECONOMIC LIFE 39 (1963).
[66] HARRY W. JONES, THE COURTS, THE PUBLIC, AND THE LAW EXPLOSION 2 (1965).
[67] Patricia Wald's chapter on "Broadening Legal Assistance to the Poor" in her working paper, LAW AND POVERTY, 1965, REPORT TO THE NATIONAL CONFERENCE ON LAW AND POVERTY (1965).

development of group legal services, which are less likely than legal aid to bear the stigma of charity, facilitates collective action to ease the transition from poverty to self-sufficiency.[68] That these programs often call for integration of the skills of lawyers and social workers both in making people aware of their legal rights and in providing access to legal services is another positive factor, since it cultivates social perspectives in lawyers and helps make social workers aware of the nature and function of the legal system.[69] The growth of legal services within existing institutions avoids labeling the poor as such and enhances the belief in one system of justice for all.[70]

To the growth of facilities and the integration of professional services should be added the increase in numbers of students being trained in the law and the revision in law school curricula so as to attune students to community needs beyond those of commerce and business.[71]

Involvement of representatives of bar associations in examining the work of the bureaucracy is another salient development. Too often in the past even the best-intentioned professional associations could do little to check the bureaucracy because of inevitable time lapses between the initiation of government action and the occasion to review it. Recent action by the Board of Governors of the American Bar Association authorizing its Section on Administrative Law to participate in matters affecting agency rules of practice and procedure is a small but significant step in narrowing the time gap. Visibility to unfair or improvident procedures can now be obtained in sufficient time to keep interests from vesting and backs from arching when criticism is voiced.[72] In essence, then, we are witnessing progress in the implementation of Fuller's admonition to enlarge the channels of communication through which men convey their perceptions, feelings, and desires.

---

[68] Id. at 82-85. See also Doverman, Legal Services for the Poor, in PROCEEDINGS OF THE 1965 NATIONAL CONFERENCE ON SOCIAL WELFARE 96 (1965).

[69] See The Lawyer and the Social Worker, in PROCEEDINGS OF THE CONFERENCE ON THE EXTENSION OF LEGAL SERVICES TO THE POOR 133 (1965). See also Isaac, Law and Social Welfare, in PROCEEDINGS OF THE 1965 NATIONAL CONFERENCE ON SOCIAL WELFARE 3, 13-15; Katz, The Lawyer and the Caseworker: Some Observations, 42 SOCIAL CASEWORK 10-15 (1961); Mueller & Murphy, Communication Problems: Social Workers and Lawyers, Social Work, April 1965, p. 2; McRae & Linde, Lawyers and Social Workers: An Emerging Joint Venture, 48 J. AM. JUD. SOC'Y 231 (1965).

[70] Pincus, The Law and Family Relationships, in PROCEEDINGS OF THE NATIONAL CONFERENCE ON SOCIAL WELFARE 78-79 (1965).

[71] The ferment in legal education is in good measure the work of the Association of American Law Schools. See The Role of Law Schools in the Extension of Legal Services, in PROCEEDINGS OF THE NATIONAL CONFERENCE ON THE EXTENSION OF LEGAL SERVICES TO THE POOR 165 (1965); WALD, op. cit. supra note 67, at 89-94. Ferment in legal education, encouraged by the Association of American Law Schools, by innovations in the curricula of leading law schools, and by research grants from such foundations as Russell Sage, Walter E. Meyer, and Ford is adding new dimensions of interest and concern to legal publications. The Yale Law Journal staff's comment, Participation of the Poor, 75 YALE L.J. 599 (1966), and the Columbia Law Review staff's comment, Citizen Participation in Urban Renewal, 66 COLUM. L. REV. 485 (1966) are prototypes of the trend.

[72] 18 AD. L. REV. 5-6 (1965).

Conclusion

Underlying this evaluation of devices to supervise the bureaucracy of the poverty program has been the assumption that control should be consistent with efficacy. Maximization of control without regard to efficacy would make the program a parody. The concern with efficacy has a dual aspect, too: it requires substantive achievement in helping to raise the living standards of the poor; but it also requires enlargement of opportunity for meaningful participation in the processes of government.

Holt has pointed out that "there is a certain minimal level of consensus that is required by any society. If the increase in dissensus exceeds this limit, the society will cease to function."[73] Mere handouts may raise living standards but still contribute to dissensus. Programs that demonstrate the responsiveness of government to citizens' actions, on the other hand, reinforce the institutions and processes of democracy and thereby reduce the servility and alienation that are handmaidens of dissensus.

We have seen that judicial review and congressional supervision can be instrumental in presenting opportunities and outlets for citizen expression. In establishing priorities for action, we should place our emphasis on improving these indigenous mechanisms, rather than on importing devices that place more of a premium on charity than on stimuli to participation. The Ombudsman would be a useful addition to our politico-legal system of control, but the positives of its office would become negatives if it were to become a substitute rather than a supplement. The argument applies as well to specialized administrative courts. Gradual infusion of our legal system with specialized bodies modeled on the Conseil d'État could be beneficial, but not if they were to divert us from the current focus on bringing "equal justice under law" within the range of every man through reforms in judicial administration and accessibility of counsel.

Judge Harold Leventhal reminded us recently that the growth of law in the administrative process has been characterized by imposition of the restraints of checks and balances, curbs against excesses of government power, and evolution of fair procedures for decision-making. "Administrative law represents the effort of a democratic society to preserve liberty while new instruments of government evolve to deal with new problems and needs created by the industrial revolution."[74] Efficacy and fairness, substantive reform and regard for due process are inseparable in societies that aspire to democratic achievement and continuity.[75]

---

[73] Holt, *A Proposed Structural-Functional Framework for Political Science*, in Don Martindale, Functionalism in the Social Sciences 104 (American Academy of Political and Social Science Monograph No. 5, 1965).

[74] Leventhal, *Public Contracts and Administrative Law*, 52 A.B.A.J. 35 (1966).

[75] This, perhaps, is what Lindblom means when he says in his discussion of the values of partisan mutual adjustment: "A democratic political system is one in which values are in some sense democratic and is not simply one in which values are democratically reconciled." Charles E. Lindblom, The Intelligence of Democracy 315 (1965).

The key aspect of the poverty program is its manifold opportunities. It offers to the poor the economic opportunity to rise from the debilitating morass of deprivation and dependency. It offers to the legal profession the opportunity to demonstrate the capacity of law to satisfy "the claims and demands and expectations involved in the existence of civilized society."[76] And it offers to the nation the opportunity to demonstrate to the world that the problems of all men are relevant in framing the policies of the democratic state and that the participation of all men—however time-consuming, contentious, and abrasive—is not only welcome but indispensable in confronting the problems of our time.

---

[76] POUND, *op. cit. supra* note 1, at 47.

THE ROLE OF LEGAL SERVICES IN THE ANTIPOVERTY PROGRAM

A. Kenneth Pye*

It is a truism that law plays a vital role in social change. Likewise, there can be little doubt that lawyers individually and as a profession are frequently the architects of the law and are among the most significant contributors to the reformation of the social order. While it is clear that "lawyers maintain no monopoly on the arts of criticism, protest, scrutiny, and representation," it is equally certain that "lawyers are particularly well equipped to deal with the intricacies of social organization."[1] The attorney's special aptitude may well result from what Riesman has called the "keen sense of relevance"[2] which frequently distinguishes the lawyer's approach to social problems.

Lawyers, as a profession, have appreciated their obligation to utilize these talents for the common good. In 1958 the first Arden House Conference attempted to formulate a definition of the lawyer's professional responsibility. Representatives of the American Bar Association and the Association of American Law Schools undertook to redefine the role of the lawyer in American life, in a report which recognized not only the obligation of an attorney to provide fidelity and expertise to a client who could pay, but also "the lawyer's responsibility as a guardian of due process of law, his responsibility to make legal service available to all, his responsibility for representation of the unpopular cause, his responsibility for leadership in legal reform, and his responsibility to retain independence of thought and action as a citizen."[3]

The newly declared "war on poverty" provides both an opportunity and an obligation for the profession to implement these statements of principle.

The Past

Long before the war was declared, the profession and individual lawyers had taken important steps towards the realization of a legal system in which inequalities in economic status would not preclude the attainment of equal justice for the poor

---

* B.A. 1951, University of Buffalo; LL.B. 1953, LL.M. 1955, Georgetown University; Associate Dean and Professor of Law, Georgetown University Law Center; Chairman, Board of Directors, District of Columbia Neighborhood Legal Services Project. The views expressed are not necessarily those of the author's co-directors. The author expresses his appreciation to Peter D. Manahan, of the class of 1966, Georgetown University Law Center, for his assistance in the preparation of this paper.
[1] Cahn & Cahn, *The War on Poverty: A Civilian Perspective*, 73 Yale L.J. 1317, 1334 (1964).
[2] David Riesman, *Toward an Anthropological View of the Law and the Legal Profession*, in Individualism Reconsidered 440 (1954).
[3] Countryman, *The Scope of the Lawyer's Professional Responsibility*, 26 Ohio St. L.J. 66 (1965). The report may be found in 44 A.B.A.J. 1159 (1958).

as well as the rich. The profession had long recognized that the monopoly to practice the law entrusted to it by the people carried with it a correlative duty to provide "the services that only licensed lawyers can lawfully render to all those in need of such services."[4] It had generally appreciated that it "must bear the responsibility for permitting the growth and continuance of two systems of law—one for the rich, one for the poor."[5]

Before the turn of the century the legal aid movement began. The central idea was to supply legal advice and representation for the poor through a community law office manned by lawyers who were employed by the organization or by volunteers.[6] By the end of the First World War 50,000 persons were served by legal aid, but less than $90,000 was spent in providing the service.[7] In the early twenties the organized bar, stirred by Reginald Heber Smith's classic, *Justice and the Poor*, began to take an active interest in the problem. The movement was benefited by prestigious leadership from men such as Charles Evans Hughes, William Howard Taft, and Elihu Root. However, their expectations were not easily realized and no substantial progress occurred until after the Second World War. Thus in 1951, Emery A. Brownell, at that time Executive Director of the National Legal Aid and Defender Association, concluded that until 1947 the proportion of the need being met over the country had remained virtually static and that "like the Red Queen of *Alice in Wonderland*, the Legal Aid forces have been obliged to run as fast as they could to stay where they were."[8]

Beginning in the late forties, organized legal aid began to move at the national level. Distinguished leadership was provided by Harrison Tweed, Whitney North Seymour, Orison S. Marden, William T. Gossett, Howard C. Westwood, Theodore Voorhees, and others. Able administration was provided by Emery A. Brownell and Junius L. Allison and continued inspiration was supplied by Reginald Heber Smith. Funds became available as a result of the generosity of the bar, industry and labor, and the Ford Foundation.[9]

By April of 1965 there were 247 legal aid offices providing legal services to indigents in civil matters, an increase of over 300 per cent since 1949.[10] Paid staffs

---

[4] Marden, *Equal Access to Justice: The Challenge and the Opportunity*, 19 WASH. & LEE L. REV. 153, 154 (1962).

[5] Kennedy, *Law Day*, May 1, 1964, University of Chicago Law School Address by Robert F. Kennedy, quoted in Cahn & Cahn, *supra* note 1, at 1337 n.27.

[6] Marden, *supra* note 4, at 155. The classic work outlining the history of legal aid in America is EMERY A. BROWNELL, LEGAL AID IN THE UNITED STATES (1951).

[7] Marden, *supra* note 4, at 158.

[8] BROWNELL, LEGAL AID IN THE UNITED STATES 31 (1951), quoted in Carlin & Howard, *Legal Representation and Class Justice*, 12 U.C.L.A.L. REV. 381, 408 (1965).

[9] Marden, *supra* note 4, at 159.

[10] STATISTICS OF LEGAL AID AND DEFENDER WORK IN THE UNITED STATES AND CANADA at 3 (1964) [hereinafter cited as STATISTICS OF LEGAL AID]; Address by Howard C. Westwood, Annual Meeting of the National Legal Aid and Defender Association, Scottsdale, Ariz., Nov. 18, 1965 [hereinafter cited as Westwood Address].

existed in 157 of these offices.[11] Assistance was provided to indigents in 414,000 cases, an increase of almost fifty per cent since 1954.[12] The gross cost of operations of civil legal aid was four and a third million dollars.[13] Legal services in over 206,000 criminal cases were provided by 162 defender organizations at a cost of approximately five million dollars.[14] Thus, by the beginning of 1965, exclusive of volunteer services, organized legal aid was providing representation in over 600,000 civil and criminal cases at a cost of nine and a third million dollars.[15]

Nevertheless there were no legal aid facilities meeting the minimum standards of the National Legal Aid and Defender Association in 130 cities.[16] In thirty-three offices the average caseload per full time attorney was 1678 new cases each year.[17] Twelve other offices had average caseloads of 1090 cases.[18] Only twenty-five of seventy offices reporting had caseloads of less than 1000 cases each year.[19] The average salaries for professional personnel were well below the levels of government, business or private practice.[20] Less than 2/10 of one per cent of the total expenditures for legal services in the country went to finance the operation of all legal aid organizations in the United States handling civil cases.[21] Some authorities estimated that only about ten per cent of the persons needing legal aid were being served by existing legal aid organizations.[22]

The extent to which the legal needs of the poor were being met by organized legal aid and the capacity of the legal aid movement to expand to meet these needs had posed troublesome questions to thoughtful observers for some time. The importance of seeking answers to these questions became paramount with the passage of the Economic Opportunity Act of 1964.[23] Title two of the act authorized the grant of federal funds to cover ninety per cent of the costs for approved community action programs.[24] Shortly after its inception the Office of Economic Opportunity (OEO) determined that projects designed to provide legal services were

---

[11] STATISTICS OF LEGAL AID 2.

[12] Id. at 3; Westwood Address.

[13] Ibid.

[14] Ibid.

[15] Ibid.

[16] NATIONAL LEGAL AID AND DEFENDER ASS'N, PRESIDENT'S ANNUAL REPORT FOR 1965 [hereinafter cited as PRESIDENT'S ANN. REP.].

[17] NATIONAL LEGAL AID AND DEFENDER ASS'N, SUMMARY OF DATA ON LEGAL AID OFFICES IN COMMUNITIES OF 100,000 AND OVER FOR THE YEAR OF 1964, at 1 (1965).

[18] Ibid.

[19] Ibid.

[20] Id. at 2-3. The average salaries for professional personnel range from $3900 (attorneys) and $7332 (executive attorneys) in cities between 100,000 and 250,000 to $7504 (attorneys) and $11,162 (executive attorneys) in cities of over 750,000. Only 33 of 87 reporting offices provided retirement benefits and less than one-third provided hospital or medical benefits such as Blue Cross or Blue Shield.

[21] Carlin & Howard, supra note 8, at 410 (estimated for year 1963).

[22] Ibid. (estimated for year 1964).

[23] 78 Stat. 508, 42 U.S.C. §§ 2701-981 (1964).

[24] Ibid.

among the types of community programs for which federal funding was available under the act.[25]

In February of 1965 the House of Delegates of the American Bar Association pledged itself "to cooperate with the Office of Economic Opportunity and other appropriate groups in the development and implementation of programs for expanding availability of legal services to indigents and persons of low income, such programs to utilize to the maximum extent deemed feasible the expertise and facilities of the organized bar, such as legal aid, legal defender and lawyer referral and such legal services to be performed by lawyers in accordance with ethical standards of the legal profession."[26]

A sound national program necessarily required decisions as to how many people needed legal services, what kinds of programs should be subsidized by federal funds, what were the best ways to provide these services, how much would they cost, to what extent grants of federal funds would be accompanied by the assertion of federal control over local community policy making, to what extent federal policies would require lay participation in deciding matters traditionally determined by the profession and similar matters. Of even greater importance was the determination of the principal objectives of the national program and the establishment of priorities among them. Matters of general concern became matters of urgency. As OEO enters its second year, we still do not know enough about these essential questions.

THE EXTENT OF THE NEED

How many people are in need of legal services and are unable to afford them? The number of variables precludes the development of an equation which can be used as a unit of accurate measurement. It is obvious that we must have some notion of what kind of legal services poor people need and some concept of when a person is to be regarded as poor. The relationship between the kind of legal service sought, the income of the person seeking the service, and his other financial responsibilities may constitute a reasonable test for whether services should be provided to a given individual without charge. But such a standard makes it

---

[25] The 1965 amendments make it clear that legal service programs may be funded. Economic Opportunity Amendments of 1965, § 12, 79 Stat. 973: "The last sentence of section 205(a) of the Economic Opportunity Act of 1964, 42 U.S.C.A. § 2785(a) is amended by inserting after 'including' the following: ', but not limited to,'." The Senate Report clarifies the reason for the change: "The listing of activities in section 205(a), of course is not intended to exclude other types of activities related to the purpose of community action programs, such as legal services for the poor, family counseling, or community organization activities. In order to make this absolutely clear, the committee has also included an amendment to this section which would indicate that programs are to be conducted in fields, including 'but not limited to' those which are specifically enumerated." 14 U.S. CODE CONG. & AD. NEWS 4835 (1965).

[26] Quoted in PATRICIA WALD, LAW AND POVERTY: 1965, REPORT TO THE NATIONAL CONFERENCE ON LAW AND POVERTY 68 (1965) [hereinafter cited LAW AND POVERTY]. See McCalpin, *The Bar Faces Forward*, 51 A.B.A.J. 548 (1965).

difficult to estimate how many others experience a like need, or even the capacity of this individual to afford other legal services of a different nature.

Perhaps the problem can be seen most clearly in the administration of criminal justice. Even in this narrow field there are clear distinctions in the nature and costs of different types of legal services, and inherent limitations upon the manner in which they may be provided, arising out of factors such as the volumes of cases involved, the times at which the services must be made available if they are to be significant, and the degrees and types of expertise required for adequate representation. There can be little doubt that legal services are necessary, and indeed required by the Constitution in felony cases,[27] when a defendant is brought before the court for arraignment or trial. However, legal services are also needed by the defendant who wishes to appeal, to attack his conviction collaterally, to obtain his release from a mental hospital to which he has been committed, to seek parole, and in probation revocation proceedings.[28] Likewise before trial the defendant has need of legal services at a preliminary hearing and may need the assistance of a lawyer in negotiations with the prosecutor before the decision of whether to charge has been made. He may also need a lawyer's advice during a police interrogation.[29] To these examples must be added the cases in which legal advice is needed by persons contemplating conduct the legality of which is unclear, witnesses whose cooperation is sought by the police or defendants, and similar counseling.

The volume of cases involved varies significantly with the stage of the proceeding at which the assistance is needed. It has been estimated that there are approximately 300,000 felony cases and 4,500,000 misdemeanor cases in the state courts each year.[30] To this must be added 33,000 cases in the federal courts.[31] In 1964 there were thirty-five arrests for all criminal acts for each 1,000 persons in the country.[32]

At least half of the defendants charged with felonies cannot afford a lawyer.[33] Presumably a higher percentage could afford an attorney in the less serious misdemeanor case. A small percentage of defendants charged with crime can afford counsel for an appeal, and fewer still will have funds when a hearing is scheduled before a parole board after years of imprisonment. The costs of services of a lawyer at a preliminary hearing or at a station house interrogation may be within the means of more people, but few private practitioners are available at the times when

---

[27] Gideon v. Wainwright, 372 U.S. 335 (1963); cf. Harvey v. Mississippi, 346 F.2d 263 (5th Cir. 1965).

[28] LAW AND POVERTY 35-39.

[29] See Silverstein, *The Continuing Impact of Gideon v. Wainwright on the States*, 51 A.B.A.J. 1023 (1965).

[30] LEE SILVERSTEIN, DEFENSE OF THE POOR IN CRIMINAL CASES IN AMERICAN STATE COURTS: A PRELIMINARY SURVEY 35, 36 (1964).

[31] REPORT OF THE ATT'Y GENERAL'S COMM. ON POVERTY AND THE ADMINISTRATION OF FEDERAL CRIMINAL JUSTICE 16 (1963).

[32] UNIFORM CRIME REPORTS FOR THE UNITED STATES—1964, at 24 (1965).

[33] SILVERSTEIN, *op. cit. supra* note 30, at 1.

these services are needed. The expertise required of the lawyer to try the criminal case is of a different nature than the skills involved in briefing and arguing an appeal or in advising a client whether to cooperate at a police interrogation.

Collateral factors such as the possibility of release on personal recognizance with no necessity of paying a bond premium, whether pretrial release can be obtained soon enough to avoid loss of employment, and the flexibility of court rules permitting alternatives to expensive printed briefs, affect the capacity of the defendant to pay the fee required by the private practitioner.

Perhaps most important are fundamental notions of when free services should be provided. Should we require a defendant to spend the small amount of cash in his possession for an attorney when the funds would otherwise have been used for food, housing and clothing for those who look to him for their support? Should we provide free legal services to a defendant who has an equity in a car, owns a television set, is able to post bond, and has intermittent employment? Such a person may be unable to pay the fee required by established members of the profession but can pay an amount acceptable to the "moonlighter," the occupier of the "mourner's bench," or the newly admitted practitioner who is prepared to take any case for "experience."

Local factors such as the unemployment rate, wage scales, the number of lawyers available, the structure of the bar, its experience with legal aid, the academic, economic, and social backgrounds of its members and its attitudes towards social responsibility also play a significant role.

The variables are even more complex in the civil arena. Here the need for counseling and representation in negotiations, in administrative proceedings, and in court, run the gamut of landlord tenant problems, consumer credit, the administration of public welfare laws, domestic relations cases, proceedings involving juveniles, and countless other problems.

Many of the same legal problems which face the middle class citizen confront the poor man. In addition he may need help in areas in which the more affluent are not involved such as the determination of eligibility of public assistance or the assertion of the right to a partial refund for the payments made on furniture purchased on credit.[34] The poor man because of his lack of education and social status, may need representation in matters such as a dispute with a high school principal over the dismissal of a child,[35] or the assertion of a complaint for a violation of the health or building code by a landlord[36] under circumstances where the

---

[34] The range of legal problems facing the poor is outlined in LAW AND POVERTY 6-35; HEW, CONFERENCE PROCEEDINGS, THE EXTENSION OF LEGAL SERVICES TO THE POOR 17-70 (1964) [hereinafter cited as HEW CONFERENCE PROCEEDINGS].

[35] In May of 1966 the Neighborhood Legal Services Project (NLSP) in Washington, D.C., obtained the reinstatement of a married senior high school student who was expelled from school three weeks before graduation solely on the ground that she had become pregnant.

[36] In another case, NLSP provided representation to a client who claimed that her eviction resulted

better educated citizen could speak for himself. Former Attorney General Robert F. Kennedy has pointed out that lawyers are needed to "make law less complex and more workable," "to assert rights which the poor have always had in theory but which they have never been able to assert on their own behalf"; to practice "preventive law" by counseling "about leases, purchases, a variety of common arrangements whereby he [the poor man] can be victimized and exploited," and "to begin to develop new kinds of legal rights in situations that are not now perceived as involving legal issues."[37]

It is not surprising that estimates of the numbers of persons who need services of these diverse kinds vary widely. Some authorities have indicated a national average of at least seven[38] to ten[39] per thousand of the population as a measure of those needing legal aid services. This would mean a total of 1,400,000 to 2,000,000 persons. In 1958 the Legal Aid Commission of the Bar Association of the District of Columbia estimated the number at eighteen per thousand for the District.[40] Another authority has estimated that one-third of the thirty-five million poor have legal problems.[41] In December, the Director of the Office of Legal Services of the Office of Economic Opportunity stated that the object of its program was to "better the lot of over thirty million people in our nation by providing competent lawyers for them."[42] In January the Office of Economic Opportunity referred to the necessity of providing lawyers for the nation's poor—"some 35,000,000 persons in families with annual incomes under $3,000."[43] This estimate, which seems to have intended to include all of the poor, is probably the most accurate. It is difficult to see how any poor person can attain maturity and at no time have need for legal advice. The fact that many do not know that they have legal problems, or do not seek the assistance of a lawyer to advise them when problems are perceived, does not mean that they have no need for legal assistance. The percentage seeking the advice of a lawyer is only a fraction of those who could and should benefit from such advice. Furthermore, the demand for legal services increases directly in proportion to their availability and the publicity accorded to them. Only after legal services are provided and the poor are informed of their availability and importance will the true dimensions of the problem be known.

Even if it is assumed that all of the poor will need legal services at some time,

---

solely because she gave information of unsafe and uninhabitable conditions of her apartment to the Department of Licenses and Inspections in the District of Columbia. Litigation in the matter is pending.

[37] Kennedy Address, *supra* note 5, at 1337 n.27.

[38] Marden, *supra* note 4, at 54, relying upon BROWNELL, *op. cit. supra* note 6, at 79.

[39] Carlin & Howard, *supra* note 8, at 409, paraphrasing BROWNELL, *op. cit. supra* note 6, at 108.

[40] REPORT OF THE COMM'N ON LEGAL AID OF THE BAR ASS'N OF THE DISTRICT OF COLUMBIA 138-40 (1958).

[41] LAW AND POVERTY 47, relying on BROWNELL, *op. cit. supra* note 6, at 57.

[42] Address by E. Clinton Bamberger, before the Bar Association of Baltimore City, December 15, 1965 [hereinafter cited as Bamberger Baltimore Address].

[43] OFFICE OF ECONOMIC OPPORTUNITY, GUIDELINES FOR LEGAL SERVICES PROGRAM (preliminary copy, 1966) [hereinafter cited as JANUARY GUIDELINES].

the determination of the Plimsoll line of poverty remains. When is a man "poor" in the sense that he should be provided legal services in civil matters without charge? Little light has been cast upon the issue of the standard for eligibility. There has been a broader understanding that the standard must vary in different localities. Attempts to formulate a national standard would be more misleading than helpful.[44] Furthermore, there has been a growing appreciation that what may be poverty for the purpose of entitling an applicant to public welfare assistance may be a totally inadequate standard for determining eligibility for legal services. The problem is complicated by the fact that not only the poor are being deprived of legal services because of an inability to afford them; a substantial portion of our middle class finds that the profession's traditional methods of making legal services available result in a price beyond their capacity to pay.[45] Even if we are able to succeed in "elevating" all of the poor to the middle class, a "services gap" will continue unless the profession alters some of its approaches towards the permissible methods of making legal services available.[46]

Even the most sanguine do not prophesy the end of poverty in the near future. The national assault on poverty and the anticipated increase in national prosperity may reduce the percentage of our population which is classified as "poor," but the absolute numbers will still probably increase. In 1950 our population was just over 150,000,000. By 1965 it had grown to 194,000,000. In five years it will be 209,000,000 and in fifteen years, 245,000,000.[47]

Furthermore, the availability of legal services to individuals is determined in part by the competitive factors of supply and demand. Increases in the size of the profession have thus far kept pace with population growth.[48] However, the expansion in the demand for lawyers by industry and government is increasing at an even greater rate than the demand by private individuals.[49]

---

[44] "The standard should realistically separate those who can afford to pay for legal services from those who cannot. Such a standard may take into consideration the size of the family, the health of its members, recent unemployment, debts and the like. Discretion may be given in order to avoid inflexible rules which cannot cover every particular situation . . . ." *Tentative Guidelines for Legal Service Proposals to the Office of Economic Opportunity, Appendix A,* in LAW AND POVERTY, *op. cit. supra* note 26, at 112, 114-15, [hereinafter cited as SPRING GUIDELINES].

[45] Cheatham, *A Lawyer When Needed: Legal Services for the Middle Classes,* 63 COLUM. L. REV. 973 (1963).

[46] *Ibid.* See also Cheatham, *Availability of Legal Services: The Responsibility of the Individual Lawyer and of the Organized Bar,* 12 U.C.L.A.L. REV. 438 (1965). In this article I attempt to deal only with the problem of providing legal services to the poor—whoever they may be determined to be. For that reason, I have generally ignored the significant contribution of lawyer referral systems, which, while in theory providing an attorney for those who can pay a modest fee, in fact, have been providing legal services to many who could not afford to pay the fee normally charged for the services rendered. The larger problem of making legal services generally available is now under study by the A.B.A. Special Committee on Availability of Legal Services.

[47] Westwood Address. Mr. Westwood's statistics were obtained from U.S. DEP'T OF COMMERCE, BUREAU OF THE CENSUS, CURRENT POPULATION REPORTS 10 (Series p-25, No. 304, 1965).

[48] FAYE A. HANKIN & DUANE W. KROHNKE, THE AMERICAN LAWYER: 1964 STATISTICAL REPORT 26 (1965).

[49] *Id.* at 22.

THE PROBLEMS FOR OEO

The extent of the need for legal services by the poor is only one of the problems. A finding that the need is far beyond the capacity of existing legal aid organizations does not necessarily require the conclusion that OEO should become involved in financing local programs which are primarily designed to provide more legal services to more needy persons. Its professed commitment to the development of programs designed to attack poverty, rather than to programs designed only to provide services to those who are poor, might result in the conclusion that legal services to poor persons with individual problems should be financed primarily from state or local sources; but that federal funds should be used primarily to fund programs which seek to provide legal components to non-service oriented projects designed to evaluate the causes of poverty, develop devices for increasing mobility into the middle class, and devising new institutions and changing existing institutions to increase the power and improve the status of those who remain in poverty.

Even if it is decided that a principal purpose of OEO's legal service program is to increase and broaden the legal services available to the poor in local communities, it is necessary to determine whether this objective can best be met by OEO funding of expanded programs of existing legal aid organizations, new types of organizations, such as neighborhood law offices, programs designed to subsidize individual members of the bar, programs for providing legal services to groups of the poor who have similar legal problems, or by other alternatives.

Flexibility is clearly desirable. New methods should be the subject of experimentation. Combinations of methods should be utilized in some areas. A premium should be placed on novelty and creativity. But agreement on such platitudes can not obscure the necessity of determining the basic objectives of OEO-financed legal service programs. To a large extent the choice of the programs to be financed must depend on the major objectives sought to be achieved.

THE FIRST YEAR AT THE NATIONAL LEVEL: OEO

The experience of the first year may provide an indication of the directions in which we are proceeding. Initially, organized legal aid seemed to take the position that existing organizations, supplemented by new legal aid societies organized after the traditional model in cities where none now exists, could meet the need if provided with the funds necessary to achieve this purpose. Specifically, the Executive Committee of the National Legal Aid and Defender Association adopted a statement in December of 1964 which advanced the propositions:

L. With ample funds, traditional legal aid and defender organizations can be broadened to meet the full legal needs of indigent people in metropolitan centers.

M. The creation of separate, duplicating agencies to offer legal services under

Economic Opportunity programs will be more costly and less effective than will proper use of existing facilities, and serious ethical questions will be raised where nonlawyers attempt to practice law.[50]

Most informed observers agreed that existing legal aid organizations could come closer to meeting their objectives with additional funding, but several knowledgeable observers questioned whether the federal funds could be used best by providing financial support to them. Even if primary emphasis was to be placed on providing services, there was concern that legal aid should not have the monopoly. In November of 1964, Attorney General Katzenbach made the point:

> There has been long and devoted service to the legal problems of the poor by legal aid societies and public defenders in many cities. But without disrespect to this important work, we cannot translate our new concern into successful action simply by providing more of the same. There must be new techniques, new services, and new forms of inter-professional cooperation to match our new interest.[51]

Professor Marvin E. Frankel suggested that there were deficiencies within existing legal aid organizations which prevented them from accomplishing the objectives by themselves. He argued that the mere fact that they were old and established raised the specter of the "negative impact of habit, of routine" and "settled bureaucratization"; that there was a tradition of welfare colonialism in legal aid in which the business community and the bar provided services to a passive poor without any attempt to enlist their participation in a program for their own betterment; that the traditional structure of legal aid followed the model of providing a centralized legal office frequently inaccessible to many of the poor; and that existing legal aid organizations had failed to educate the poor concerning the circumstances in which they needed legal advice or the availability of counsel to assist them.[52] In his opinion legal aid should not be excluded, but new experimental possibilities should be explored.

His Columbia colleague, Monrad G. Paulsen, reached similar conclusions and argued that the participation of existing legal aid organizations should be limited to "the strongest and most adventurous societies."[53] In his opinion if new agencies were not established the full extent of the opportunity to benefit the poor by legal services might not be realized:

> In part, legal services for the poor must aim at constructive social changes. Part of the law work must be undertaken to attack established institutions, practices and rules, in order that social progress may be made. The focus of much of the work will be general reform rather than the special aim of assisting a given

---

[50] Quoted in Frankel, *Experiments in Serving the Indigent,* 51 A.B.A.J. 460 (1965). The text may be found in 51 A.B.A.J. 275 (1965).

[51] HEW CONFERENCE PROCEEDINGS 11.

[52] Frankel, *supra* note 50, at 460-62.

[53] Paulsen, *The Expanding Horizons of Legal Services,* 67 W. VA. L. REV. 179, 190 (1965).

person with his particular legal difficulty. Few legal aid societies are geared to such work.

If the right kind of legal assistance is to be provided, it will often take the form of a new agency, the character of which we ought to see clearly in advance and which we ought to set up in full recognition of its controversial character. . . .[54]

Messrs. Carlin and Howard were even less charitable. They considered that existing legal aid was derelict in excluding many who were unable to pay a fee. Such policies, in their opinion, resulted in no legal services being provided to many applicants, the penalizing of the thrifty, the alienation of the poor, and the de-personalizing of the lawyer-client relationship.[55] They found fault with policies of many legal aid organizations in refusing to take divorce and bankruptcy cases[56] and criticized the standard case loads approved by the National Legal Aid and Defender Association as being grossly excessive.[57]

Spokesmen for organized legal aid were quick to admit that many of the objections had merit but pointed out that the criticisms were not new. The National Legal Aid and Defender Association had called attention repeatedly to the fact that rules governing types of cases handled were too limited; the general eligibility policies of some organizations were too restrictive; that more of the services should be decentralized; that governing bodies were not sufficiently representative of the communities served; and that staff salaries were shockingly low. In the opinion of organized legal aid, however, in most communities there were few deficiencies which could not be cured by an adequate budget.[58] On this premise the National Legal Aid and Defender Association on behalf of its members sought the assistance and funding of the Office of Economic Opportunity.

The decision to seek federal funds was not unanimous. Spokesmen for some legal aid organizations preferred to continue as private charitable organizations without federal funding.[59]

[54] *Id.* at 189. See also Terris, *Legal Representation of the Poor*, in CONFERENCE ON CONSUMER CREDIT AND THE POOR (1965).

[55] Carlin & Howard, *supra* note 8, at 411-12.

[56] *Id.* at 413-16. But in 1964 59 legal aid societies handled 6296 divorce cases, secured decrees for 3652 clients, and defended 1701 actions. Divorce cases constituted approximately one-third of the court cases for these offices. NLDA DIVORCE STATISTICS: 1964 (1965). Other societies declined to represent plaintiffs or applied a standard of "social desirability."

[57] Carlin & Howard, *supra* note 8, at 416. When Carlin and Howard wrote, the standard was that set in 1960 of one full time attorney for the first 750-1000 cases per year and an additional full time attorney for each additional 1200 cases (or equivalent part time attorneys) for cities of more than 100,000 population. In 1965 NLDA amended its standards to provide that in urban communities of at least 75,000 population per 100 square miles of land area, there should be at least one full time lawyer if the society's caseload is 400 or more matters per year. The caseload of a full time lawyer should not exceed 900 matters each year. NLDA STANDARDS AND PRACTICES FOR CIVIL LEGAL AID (1965). It should be remembered that reference is made to minimum standards. Furthermore, there is no clear definition of a "case" or a "matter." Usually any direct contact between a legal aid staff attorney and a client is considered to be a "case" or "matter" for reporting purposes.

[58] PRESIDENT'S ANN. REP. 5.

[59] Schein, *Legal Aid Utopia*, 33 D.C.B.J. 16 (1966); Fisher, *The Role of the Legal Aid Society*, 32 D.C.B.J. 375 (1965); see Bradway, Two's COMPANY, 1966 DUKE L.J. No. 2.

In November of 1964 the Department of Health, Education and Welfare conducted a Conference on the Extension of Legal Services to the Poor. The Conference coordinator, John G. Murphy, Jr., assembled spokesmen with diverse viewpoints from throughout the country to discuss the legal needs of the poor, new models for legal service programs, the relationship between lawyers and social workers, and the role of law schools in the forthcoming war.[60]

Some observers viewed the problem as a choice between two distinct approaches. The first approach would place principal emphasis upon existing legal aid organizations with close relationships with the organized bar; legal aid societies managed by old time legal aiders with higher salaries and with larger staffs, under policies negotiated between OEO and the organized bar and with the major objective of providing more and better representation for individuals who could not afford a lawyer.

A second approach would place the emphasis on federal funding of new organizations staffed by lawyers unconnected previously with the legal aid movement; organizations which sought to effect social change for the poor through a more sophisticated use of the legal process than the representation of masses of individuals with personal legal problems; programs which were prepared to decline legal assistance to eligible applicants if providing representation to such persons would overburden their staffs with caseloads which would hinder them in achieving their major objective of social, economic and legal reform through the litigation of test cases, the drafting of ordinances, rules and statutes and lobbying for their passage, and the participation with other professionals or subprofessionals in the organization of neighborhood groups which would bring economic and political pressure to bear on business, the police, the courts, school boards, administrative agencies, mayors and city councils to obtain redress for real or imagined grievances and the assurance of equal or preferred treatment in the future; projects which would welcome bar support, but which were willing to regard the bar as an adversary if ageement could not be reached on issues such as indigency standards, involvement with groups engaging in civil disobedience, programs advertising the availability of legal services and encouraging the assertion of legal rights, or the representation of groups and members thereof. Others argued that the approaches were not inconsistent. A compromise should be reached.

This was the setting in which the Office of Economic Opportunity began to determine the policies which it would follow. Fortunately, there were capable people available to make the decisions.

Edgar S. Cahn, a brilliant and incisive innovator, left the Department of Justice to join OEO. In July of 1964, the month before the act was passed, Cahn and his wife, Jean, had published the landmark article, *The War on Poverty: A Civilian Perspective*,[61] in which they had advocated as "one kind of institution" the establish-

---

[60] HEW CONFERENCE PROCEEDINGS.

[61] 73 YALE L.J. 1317 (1964).

ment of a university-affiliated neighborhood law firm which "would represent persons and interests in the community with an eye towards making public officials, private service agencies, and local business interests more responsive to the needs and grievances of the neighborhood."[62] For a few winter months Jean C. Cahn also served in the Office with the responsibility of developing a legal services program within the Community Action Program (CAP). Differences of opinion with reference to the status, importance and independence of the legal services program developed and Mrs. Cahn resigned. During the spring of 1965 the organizational status of the legal services program of OEO was unclear. Within the Community Action Program, B. Michael Rauh served as a special assistant for legal services. In the Office of General Counsel, Bruce J. Terris and John G. Murphy, Jr., were also involved in the development of the policies relating to the program. The lines of authority between the Office of the General Counsel and the Director of Community Action Program were not always clear.

A document, *Tentative Guidelines for Legal Services Proposals to the Office of Economic Opportunity,*[63] was prepared in the early spring. It adopted a flexible attitude towards the question of whether existing legal aid organizations should be subsidized:

> . . . Whether the legal services program is run by legal aid, a bar association, an independent organization or by a combination of organizations is a matter for local determination. The only question for OEO is whether the organization, however established, can provide the best possible legal services for the poor.
> The proposal may extend and improve already existing services, such as legal aid, add new legal services through a new institution to those already existing, or provide a full range of services, as where no legal services are provided in the neighborhood. In any event, the new programs should avoid duplication and be conducted in cooperation with other legal programs for the poor in the locality.[64]

The *Guidelines* required that programs be a part of a coordinated community action program wherever possible,[65] but that it nevertheless be organized in such a manner that it was independent of the organizations, including the local community action program, with which it might have a conflict of interest.[66] The memorandum provided that any proposals submitted for funding should attempt to deal with the full scope of legal problems of the poor and at each stage, from advice and counseling through appeal.[67] In addition, emphasis was placed upon providing representation for organizations of the poor.[68] Applicant organizations were cautioned that any pro-

[62] *Id.* at 1334. For a discussion of the development of the neighborhood law offices, see *infra,* pp. 231-43.
[63] SPRING GUIDELINES.
[64] *Id.* at 113, 115.
[65] *Id.* at 113.
[66] *Id.* at 114.
[67] *Id.* at 115.
[68] *Id.* at 116.

posal should give consideration to the role of the legal services program in defining or changing the law where it was unclear or detrimental to the interests of the poor,[69] and that it should contain provisions for the education of the poor.[70] Applicants for funding were warned against "artificial limitations which would prevent comprehensive services," and any limitations or priorities were required to be justified.[71] It was made clear that offices should be decentralized[72] and that proposals should set forth the method of referral of persons who did not meet the standards of eligibility.[73] Notice was given that it was the policy of the act that legal services be "developed, conducted, and administered with the maximum feasible participation of residents of the areas and members of the groups served."[74] Specifically, the *Guidelines* provided: "This participation should be ensured, whenever possible, by having the residents represented on the board of directors and advisory committees to the project. . . ."[75]

Most legal aid organizations were required to change their structure, decentralize their offices, and expand the scope of their services in order to adhere to the *Guidelines* and qualify for federal funds.

Throughout the spring, efforts were made by leaders of the bar and of legal aid (often the same persons) to narrow what originally had seemed to be a substantial breach between OEO and organized legal aid. An important element in the equation was a growing realization by OEO of the importance of continued support from the leaders of the bar. The endorsement of the American Bar Association, obtained in February, needed to be reiterated as charges of the "socialization of the bar" began to be heard.[76]

The chief vehicle of the bar for providing legal services to the poor traditionally had been legal aid. Lack of confidence in legal aid often involved implicit criticism of the profession's past contributions. Those concerned with legal service programs in OEO had well-grounded fears that the bar might oppose the use of federal funds even by existing legal aid organizations if conditioned upon such a broad scope of activities and the necessity of the participation of the poor in policy decisions which would include indigency standards and other matters regarded traditionally as within the prerogatives of the profession. To set up a new organization in competition with an existing legal aid society posed serious problems of lack of bar support in many communities. On the other hand, some of the more militant reformers thought that bar control of legal service programs would preclude any aggressive program aimed at institutional changes.

---

[69] *Id.* at 117-18.
[70] *Id.* at 118.
[71] *Id.* at 116.
[72] *Id.* at 117.
[73] *Id.* at 115.
[74] *Id.* at 114.
[75] *Ibid.*
[76] Bethel & Walker, *Et Tu, Brute!*, Tenn. Bar Ass'n Journal, Aug. 1965, p. 11.

Continued efforts to bring OEO, the bar and legal aid together were made by the American Bar Association, led by its President Lewis F. Powell, Jr., and with almost daily contact by Lowell R. Beck of its Washington staff. OEO obtained independent advice from consultants, most of whom were law professors who had participated in the November 1964 HEW Conference, and from a steering committee selected to plan a National Conference on Law and Poverty, to which leaders of the bar would be invited.

In June, Theodore M. Berry, Director of the Community Action Program, addressed the Conference on the subject of OEO policies:

> I would now like to answer as explicitly and directly as I can the question which has been asked repeatedly by leaders of the bar. What is the role of Legal Aid Societies in OEO's plans? My response is simply that this determination is not OEO's at all; instead, the local community must decide what organization or organizations can best handle legal services for the poor. Indeed, in many places several different groups may well provide services in different kinds of cases or in different geographic areas. Such programs may be run by a Legal Aid Society, a foundation, a university, or by a new nonprofit corporation. The sole standard—which I have stated before—is what group or groups is most dedicated and most competent to provide legal services for the poor and will receive the confidence and use of the poor.
>
> While the determinations will be made in local communities, we in OEO hope and expect that many proposals will come from Legal Aid Societies. Many of these societies are strong organizations which can take on new vitality with additional funds. On the other hand, we also hope that other groups will make proposals to try out different ideas and methods. The resulting competition of ideas and services should benefit everyone.
>
> I think the grants which OEO has already made and the proposals which have come to it indicate the pattern. They demonstrate that Legal Aid Societies far from being excluded will either themselves receive substantial funds or will at least participate with other organizations which will receive funds.[77]

At the same time, however, the policy on "poor on the board" hardened. No longer were the "residents" to be "represented whenever possible." Now it was to be required, and the percentage of representation set forth:

> . . . Normally, this means that approximately one-third of the governing board of the legal service program should be, in the words of the statute, "residents of the areas and members of the groups served." This is a suggested yardstick. Advisory committees of neighborhood residents should be established around each neighborhood office. But this alone is not sufficient. These committees should be permitted to choose representatives on the board of directors of the entire program. . . .[78]

[77] Address by Theodore M. Berry, Director, Community Action Program, Office of Economic Opportunity, to the National Conference on Law and Poverty, June 25, 1965 [hereinafter cited as Berry Address], reprinted in LAW AND POVERTY 127-28. See Cohen, *Law, Lawyers and Poverty*, 43 TEXAS L. REV. 271 (1965).

[78] Berry Address, reprinted in LAW AND POVERTY 124.

Another factor was added by the new requirement that "lawyers from minority groups must also participate in formulating the legal service program and be represented on its governing board."[79]   Again it was emphasized that while it was not an "absolute requirement" that legal service proposals be approved by community action agencies, it was "desirable that the community action agency be used" unless it "can be shown that it is not possible, after reasonable effort has been made to coordinate activities with the agency."[80]   At the same time Mr. Berry stressed that the program must be "independent in its control and operation so that it will remain free to litigate cases" involving its parent organization or organizations represented on its board of directors.[81]   It was again suggested that a legal program should provide a full range of services to individuals,[82] provide representation for organizations,[83] and engage in community education.[84]   Unlike the *Guidelines*, no emphasis was placed on the role of legal service programs in law reform, except to encourage law schools to engage in research into areas of law affecting the poor.[85]   Specific mention was made of the need for a lawyer referral mechanism which "should be fair to all members of the bar including neighborhood lawyers and those in minority groups."[86]

During the summer Theodore Voorhees, NLDA President, Howard C. Westwood, NLDA Washington representative, and Junius L. Allison, NLDA Executive Director, labored to inform legal aid organizations of the opportunity for federal funding and the changes necessary to obtain OEO approval while working simultaneously to persuade OEO that drastic changes in structure, orientation, personnel, and locations of legal aid organizations could not be accomplished overnight.   Flexibility was sought and in August there was good reason to think it had been achieved when Sargent Shriver assured the American Bar Association that "we do not intend to bypass the organized Bar or to exclude legal aid and public defender agencies from our deliberations or financial assistance."[87]   Mr. Shriver went on to attempt to allay fears that the original guidelines would be applied literally:

> Our statute requires maximum feasible participation of the poor in all aspects of anti-poverty programs. We intend to carry out the mandate of Congress on this. But to do so does not require the imposition of inflexible and arbitrary quotas. We have already financed legal service programs approaching this requirement in a variety of ways. We believe in flexibility. But flexibility cannot become a euphemism for evasion of our statutory duty.[88]

[79] *Id.* at 123.
[80] *Id.* at 121.
[81] *Id.* at 123.
[82] *Id.* at 125.
[83] *Id.* at 126.
[84] *Ibid.*
[85] *Id.* at 127.
[86] *Id.* at 125.
[87] Shriver, *The OEO and Legal Services*, 51 A.B.A.J. 1064, 1065 (1965).
[88] Address of Sargent Shriver, before the Assembly, American Bar Association, Miami, Fla., Aug. 11,

In the same address he announced the establishment of a National Advisory Committee on Law and Poverty. Included in its membership were the President, immediate past President, and President-elect of the American Bar Association, the Chairman of the ABA's Standing Committee on Legal Aid and Indigent Defendants, the Chairman of the ABA Special Committee on Availability of Legal Services, the President of the National Legal Aid and Defender Association, and the President of the National Bar Association.

In September of 1965, E. Clinton Bamberger, a Baltimore attorney with a background of distinguished service in bar association work, was named Director of a newly created Office of Legal Services within OEO. Although the funds for legal service programs were to be obtained from the CAP budget, a greater degree of independence was provided with assurances of a direct channel of communication to the Director of OEO, when needed. The Office of Legal Services was promised $15,000,000 to $20,000,000 with which to fund local programs during the present fiscal year. Mr. Bamberger chose as his Deputy Director, Earl Johnson, Jr., who brought with him experience gained from ten months of outstanding service in the Washington Neighborhood Legal Services Project.

In November a new policy memorandum, *An Introduction to the Development of Legal Services Programs*, was prepared. The function of the national program was described as five-fold: to assist community efforts to provide legal advice and representation for people too poor to employ counsel, to encourage and support experimentation and innovation to determine the best methods of providing legal services to the poor, to sponsor education, research and publications in areas of the law that affect the problems of poverty, to acquaint the practicing bar with their essential role to combat poverty, and to provide the means for the involvement of lawyers in the "war on poverty," and to educate the poor to know and recognize the aid of the law.[89] No mention was made of law reform or community involvement in the goals sought to be achieved.

The ordinary role of a legal services program as a component part of a community action program was noted, but it was now made clear that "if there is no community action agency *or if the existing community action agency does not wish to consider a legal services component*,"[90] direct application could be made to the Office of Economic Opportunity. The necessity for the maximum feasible participa-

---

1965. The abridgment of Mr. Shriver's speech in the *American Bar Association Journal* does not contain this language. It does contain this paragraph: ". . . Eighth, we are not trying to dictate to local legal aid organizations and to the public defender agencies the precise composition of the boards of directors of those agencies. Our basic statute passed by Congress requires maximum feasible participation of the poor in all aspects of the antipoverty programs. We intend to carry out that mandate of Congress, but to do so does not require imposition of inflexible and arbitrary quotas." Shriver, *supra* note 87, at 1065.

[89] AN INTRODUCTION TO THE DEVELOPMENT OF LEGAL SERVICES PROGRAMS (preliminary draft, Nov. 1965) 2 [hereinafter cited as NOVEMBER GUIDELINES].

[90] *Id.* at 4. (Emphasis added.)

tion of the poor was stressed but it was also indicated that "there is no national standard for compliance with the provision that the poor must be represented."[91]

The necessity of independence from the local community action program was emphasized. In the spring, the *Guidelines* had stated cautiously that "consideration should be given" to the problem of the insulation of legal services from the local community action program with the admonition that "it will require careful planning to assure independent administrative control of the program."[92] In June it was stressed that the legal services program "must be independent in its control and operation."[93] In November, it was stated that avoidance of the danger of conflict of interest "requires a clear separation between the community action agency and the legal services program."[94]

The new memorandum, like its predecessor, made it clear that "there should be no limit to the scope or type of legal services provided to eligible clients" and that "all areas of the law traditionally dealt with by attorneys should be included and a full spectrum of legal work should be provided."[95] It was suggested that where there was a question of whether the fee generated by the case was sufficient to retain a private attorney, a procedure might be established whereby two or three private attorneys would be given the "right of first refusal" before counsel was provided by the local program. In the spring the *Guidelines* had stressed the desirability of providing representation for "organizations of the poor such as credit unions, cooperatives, and block clubs" both in organizing and litigating.[96] No mention was made of this function in the November memorandum.[97]

The November memorandum, like the spring *Guidelines*, recognized the importance of an educational program to apprise the poor of their rights and obligations. The methodology suggested was different. In the spring it had been stated in these terms:

> Consideration should be given to the form the legal education will take. For example this education may include personal contact with small groups, such as churches and block clubs, by lawyers, whether working for the program or as volunteers, by *consumer education experts, and by others* to discuss legal rights and the legal service program, distribution of model legal forms to help residents with installment contracts, leases, etc., and attempts to persuade businessmen to use them; *dissemination of legal information by social workers and other workers in the neighborhood as part of their regular work* and notification by public agencies to the people with whom they deal that legal counsel is available to represent them before the agencies.[98]

[91] *Id.* at 5.
[92] SPRING GUIDELINES 114.
[93] Berry Address, in LAW AND POVERTY 123.
[94] NOVEMBER GUIDELINES 6.
[95] *Id.* at 10.
[96] SPRING GUIDELINES 116.
[97] NOVEMBER GUIDELINES 10.
[98] SPRING GUIDELINES 118-19. (Emphasis added.)

In November the approach was somewhat different:

> . . . Law schools, *the organized bar and individual attorneys should be involved in this phase of the program.* A strong "preventive" law approach should be established, educating potential clients to become aware of their legal rights and protect them so that legal remedy to be sought after involvement will be the exception rather than the rule. The application should state the method of preventive law. For example this education may include discussions with church groups, block clubs and other groups of poor people to inform them of their legal rights and the availability of the legal services program; *a bar association* may prepare and distribute model forms of installment contracts and leases; and public agencies should be encouraged to inform poor people that legal counsel is available.[99]

There can be little doubt that the November formulation looked towards education of the poor by lawyers. The social worker and the subprofessional should be assigned to different tasks.

The November memorandum made it clear, however, that programs would be evaluated on the basis of answers to two questions: (1) What was the quantity and quality of legal work for clients, and (2) what contributions did the program make to eliminate the cause and effects of poverty.[100]

In January a new *Guidelines for Legal Services Programs* was drafted with the admonition that it, like its predecessors, was a preliminary copy and that a booklet containing definitive guidelines would be published shortly. Few changes had been made since the November memorandum.

Again it was asserted that ordinarily a legal services program would be a component of a local community action program, but exceptions were outlined where the applicant was able to provide "reasonable evidence to justify direct funding" and "evidence that it has made every reasonable effort to coordinate its activities with those of the broadly-based agency."[101] The June speech was echoed in the requirement that the board include representatives of minority groups.[102] In this memorandum it was suggested that in order to achieve coordination with social services, the legal services program might work closely "with a trained person on the staff of a community action agency or social work delegate agency or that the staff may include a person trained in the field of social work."[103] No mention was made of law reform or group representation. While it was again made clear that one of the criteria for evaluating the program would be the contribution that it has made to eliminate the causes and effects of poverty,[104] it was not suggested how any long range effect could be accompanied without substantial involvement in law reform or group organization and representation.

---

[99] NOVEMBER GUIDELINES at 11-12. (Emphasis added.)
[100] *Id.* at 12.
[101] JANUARY GUIDELINES 5.
[102] *Id.* at 9.
[103] *Id.* at 20.
[104] *Id.* at 17.

It would be unfair to conclude that OEO consciously has determined to ignore law reform and lawyer participation in group organization and representation solely on the basis of the failure to mention these functions in the later internal policy memoranda. In at least one case OEO has required a local organization to promise that groups would be represented as a condition for federal funding.[105] Undoubtedly there will be language speaking of the importance of law reform in future permanent guidelines.[105a]

However, there certainly has been no emphasis placed upon achieving institutional change through group organization and representation and efforts aimed at law reform. It seems to have been assumed that these objectives can be achieved by a program in which principal emphasis is placed upon providing lawyers to those in need. The result may be an unintended de-emphasis upon action aimed at the elimination of the causes and effects of poverty.

At the end of 1965 OEO had funded twenty-seven projects in twenty-three local communities and two national projects. A total of $3,127,217 had been expended. There were eighteen formal proposals under consideration. Over one hunded other communities had corresponded with OEO in documents ranging from inquiries to informal drafts of proposals. Some of the grants were very small. Other projects had been funded before many OEO policies had been determined. Many of the funded projects were not yet in operation.

Substantial grants had been made to Buffalo, N.Y. ($106,162) to start four neighborhood offices under the Legal Aid Bureau; Clarksdale, Mississippi ($82,725) to establish one central office with one full-time attorney and five part-time attorneys; Little Rock, Arkansas ($32,582) for the establishment of a full-time Legal Aid Society with a staff of three attorneys; Los Angeles, California ($333,129) for the establishment of Los Angeles Neighborhood Legal Services, Inc., which will operate three neighborhood offices with a staff of ten attorneys; New Bedford,

---

[105] New Bedford, Mass.

[105a] The *Guidelines for Legal Services Programs*, published in February 1966, contain the following provisions:

"Free legal services should be available to organizations composed primarily of residents of the areas and members of the groups served. However, the services should not be provided if the organization is able to retain an attorney for the type of representation it seeks. By pooling their resources, a group of individuals may be able to afford counsel in cases where an individual could not. At the same time, the combined resources of the members of an organization may be insufficient to retain an attorney to handle the particular legal problem in which the organization requires representation. A flexible standard should be applied. The factors to be considered include the size of the organization, the relative poverty of the members of the organization, and the cost of the legal assistance which the organization desires."

1966 GUIDELINES at 21.

"Advocacy of appropriate reforms in statutes, regulations, and administrative practices is a part of the traditional role of the lawyer and should be among the services afforded by the program. This may include judicial challenge to particular practices and regulations, research into conflicting or discriminating applications of laws or administrative rules, and proposals for administrative and legislative changes."

1966 GUIDELINES at 23.

Massachusetts ($46,409) for the establishment of four offices to be operated by a committee of the local community action program using the part-time services of six lawyers; Newark, New Jersey ($279,269) for the Newark Legal Services Project, a new organization, to operate six neighborhood offices and one central office with thirteen attorneys; Oakland, California ($74,593) for the establishment of two neighborhood offices with four lawyers to be run by the Alameda County Legal Aid Society; Omaha, Nebraska ($69,106) to Legal Aid Society of Omaha for the operation of four offices with four attorneys; Pittsburgh, Pennsylvania ($222,516) for the staffing of eight neighborhood offices with eight lawyers under the Legal Aid Society; Portland, Oregon ($11,852) to add one attorney to the Legal Aid staff; St. Louis, Missouri ($267,185) for the establishment of Civil Legal Aid Services, a new organization which plans to staff twelve offices with six full-time attorneys; and Washington, D.C. ($136,874 in 1965; $537,706 for eight months of 1966) for the Neighborhood Legal Services Project, a new organization, established by the local community action program. In addition a major research, demonstration and training grant ($242,579) was made to the University of Detroit for a program by which it undertook to reorient its law school curriculum to emphasize urban problems, undertake research into the legal problems of the poor, operate a clinic, and engage in a program of education of the poor concerning their legal rights. Additional grants were made to two Indian Tribal Councils, to the National Legal Aid and Defender Association and the American Bar Foundation.[106]

THE FIRST YEAR AT THE LOCAL LEVEL: NEIGHBORHOOD LEGAL SERVICES PROJECT (NLSP)

The Washington, D.C., program was the largest OEO-financed project in operation in 1965. An analysis of its performance may provide insights into directions in which OEO programs may go at the local level.

Before the beginning of the national "war on poverty," the Ford Foundation had undertaken to make funds available to several cities to finance programs designed to restore vitality to the blighted "grey areas." Washington was one of the cities selected and the United Planning Organization (UPO), a non-profit corporation, was created to receive the funds and coordinate local efforts. Prior to the organization of UPO, a pilot study of poverty in the Cardozo area of central Washington had been initiated by the Washington Action for Youth (WAY), and a substantial grant had been received from the President's Committee on Juvenile De-

[106] The prestigious American Bar Foundation has undertaken a study of many of the most important questions underlying the problem of providing legal services to the poor. Under the direction of Professor Geoffrey C. Hazard, grants by the Foundation to Professors Robert S. Schoshinski, Bernie R. Burrus, and John R. Schmertz, Jr., of the faculty of Georgetown University Law Center, have permitted research by these gentlemen which has been of great assistance to the author in formulating the views expressed in this article.

linquency for funding projects in that neighborhood. UPO ultimately assumed the programs and grants of WAY.

In 1964 Washington had a private Legal Aid Society which had been in operation for thirty-two years. On a budget of approximately $100,000, provided by the Bar and the United Giving Fund, it was providing representation for the poor in civil cases at one office located in downtown Washington, a branch office at Howard University, and an office in the District of Columbia Court of General Sessions. In 1960, Congress had created the Legal Aid Agency for the District of Columbia which provided representation to a substantial number of defendants in criminal cases and representation in mental health proceedings. During the early months of 1964, James G. Banks, the Executive Director of UPO, and William J. Grinker, his assistant, held conversations with a number of Washington lawyers concerning the desirability of establishing neighborhood law offices as a component of UPO's general program. In the specific formulation of the proposal, they were assisted in great measure by Gary G. Bellow, then Deputy Director of the Legal Aid Agency.

The idea of neighborhood law offices was not new. Such offices had been operating in Philadelphia since the late thirties.[107] However, the Philadelphia offices were primarily aimed only at providing services to individuals who could pay a small fee to an attorney. Different types of neighborhood programs were in operation in New Haven and New York.

Several years previously, William Pincus of the Ford Foundation had reached the conclusion that new approaches were necessary to improve the quality and availability of legal services to the poor. After consultation with local leaders, New Haven, Connecticut, was selected as a city in which an experimental program would be launched.

In 1962 Community Progress, Inc. (CPI), a non-profit corporation, was created in New Haven. CPI, with grants from the Ford Foundation, the federal government, and other sources, set out to provide a "broad roster" of "effectively coordinated" community services as a method of staging a comprehensive attack on the social problems of some neighborhoods in that city.[108] Initially each neighborhood staff was to consist of a neighborhood worker and representatives of public and private health, welfare and recreation agencies under a social worker who had the responsibility for coordinating activities.[109] A neighborhood lawyer was placed on the staff of each of these teams. During the first year of operation the neighborhood lawyers encountered substantial problems. In 1964 the New Haven Legal Assis-

---

[107] Abrahams, *Twenty-Five Years of Service: Philadelphia Neighborhood Law Office Plan*, 50 A.B.A.J. 728 (1964).

[108] Address by Charles J. Parker, President, New Haven Legal Assistance Association, before the National Conference on Law and Poverty, Washington, D.C., June 25, 1965 [hereinafter cited as Parker Address]. See also Parker, *The New Haven Model*, in HEW CONFERENCE PROCEEDINGS 87-93; Cahn & Cahn, *The War on Poverty: A Civilian Perspective*, 73 YALE L.J. 1317 (1964); LAW AND POVERTY 76.

[109] Parker Address at 5.

tance Association, Inc. was organized to operate the legal services program.[110] Independent neighborhood law offices were established. During the months in which UPO was preparing its proposal, Legal Assistance Association, Inc. was being investigated by a special committee of the local bar association which ultimately resulted in local bar association opposition to the program.[111]

In 1964 Mobilization for Youth opened a neighborhood office in New York City's lower East Side.[112] It attempted to integrate its operations with those of neighborhood social workers. No attempt was made to handle all cases coming to it. Routine cases were referred to the New York Legal Aid Society or others. Cases were retained which involved a principle with "pervasive impact" upon a substantial segment of the community or where other representation was not available.[113] It concentrated on direct education of the poor, undertook a number of test cases, and participated in the organization of tenant and consumer groups.[114] To a large extent it provided the model for the UPO proposal.

In May 1964 a proposal by UPO to the Defender Project of the National Legal Aid and Defender Association sought funds for improvement of the Legal Aid Agency and local law school programs in criminal law. This proposal referred to the possibility of the establishment of neighborhood law offices. During the summer Chief Judge David L. Bazelon of the United States Court of Appeals for the District of Columbia Circuit appointed a special committee under the chairmanship of Circuit Judge J. Skelly Wright to study the desirability of neighborhood law offices. After several meetings and discussions of drafts, the Committee approved a September 1964 proposal submitted by the United Planning Organization. This proposal constituted the basis for the organization of the Neighborhood Legal Services Project (NLSP).

The proposal accepted the conclusions of the 1958 Commission on Legal Aid of the District of Columbia Bar Association that the legal aid organizations in the District of Columbia fell short of meeting the need; that the services were inaccessible to many; that others were unaware of the existence of the services; and that the contributions of the present programs were limited by the partial isolation of legal assistance from other agencies in the community.[115] A clear need was seen for a program which would re-examine the legal rules and procedures affecting the poor, as well as to provide services. The main elements of the proposal included the establishment of neighborhood law offices "in coordination" with the Legal Aid

---

[110] *Id.* at 3.

[111] *Id.* at 7, 8.

[112] LAW AND POVERTY 69-74; Grosser, *The Need for a Neighborhood Legal Service and the New York Experience*, in HEW CONFERENCE PROCEEDINGS at 73-80. See also Sparer, *The Role of the Welfare Client's Lawyer*, 12 U.C.L.A.L. REV. 336 (1965).

[113] LAW AND POVERTY 70.

[114] *Id.* at 70-71.

[115] UNITED PLANNING ORGANIZATION, PROPOSAL FOR NEIGHBORHOOD LEGAL SERVICES FOR THE INDIGENT 1-3 (1964) [hereinafter cited as UPO PROPOSAL].

Society of the District of Columbia; development of an effective system of screening and referral of non-indigent cases; coordination of legal services with agencies providing non-legal services to lower economic groups; development of educational and clinical training programs for lawyers, law students and graduate students in other disciplines concerned with the problems of the poor; and the initiation of non-technical educational programs on legal rights, obligations and remedies for the residents of the community.[116]

Heavy emphasis was placed on the role of research directed at the long-range impact of the program and to short-range research projects directed at the re-evaluation of standards of indigency, the mechanism of lawyer referral, and similar matters.[117]

The new offices were to function in "close coordination with the offices of the Legal Aid Society" but independently.[118] There was to be consultation on standards of eligibility and maintenance of records, and cooperation in the utilization of non-legal services. If feasible, one full-time or part-time Legal Aid Society attorney should be in each neighborhood office.[119] The basic nature of the neighborhood offices was made clear:

> It is recognized that the neighborhood law offices will not be able to handle a large proportion of the cases coming from the community. Allocation between the Legal Aid Society offices and the neighborhood law offices will be made on a case-by-case basis in accordance with standards developed after discussion with the Legal Aid Society based on experience in the neighborhood. The Legal Service Program is conceived as supplementing rather than competing with existing legal aid organizations. Attempts will therefore be made to concentrate on types of cases which place burdens of time and resources on existing legal aid organizations beyond their present capacities. Consideration will also be given to accepting cases involving individuals who have had contact with the staff of the Neighborhood Development Program. Such cases will afford a basis for further experience in the effective coordination of legal and nonlegal services.[120]

The program was "conceived as an adjunct to existing legal aid, entering areas and exploring methods not heretofore fully explored by legal aid organizations."[121]

Provision was also made for close cooperation with the Legal Aid Agency in criminal matters. Clear emphasis was placed on the coordination of legal services with agencies providing non-legal services.[122] It was anticipated that there would be consultation on individual cases between staff attorneys and social workers supplemented by an informal continuing relation for the purpose of clarifying the

[116] UPO PROPOSAL 4-5.
[117] Id. at 14-15.
[118] Id. at 5-7.
[119] Id. at 6.
[120] Ibid.
[121] Id. at 19.
[122] Id. at 8-10.

problems of the client, developing solutions to avoid anticipated future problems, and the exploration of new interviewing and consultative techniques.[123]

The new program was to be a component of the UPO but supervision and control over it was to be vested in an uncompensated board of directors made up of members of the bar and the judiciary.[124] Specific provision was made that UPO "will exert no control over the operation of the project after initial consideration of the proposal and the budget."[125] Neighborhood offices were to be established in areas included in UPO's Neighborhood Development Program.[126] Each office would have full time lawyers, an investigative staff, and clerical personnel.[127] Volunteer attorneys and interns pursuing graduate programs in legal problems of the poor would supplement the staff.[128]

In November of 1964 NLSP was created by action of the UPO Board of Trustees. It has no separate legal existence. The President of the Board of UPO chose eleven private practitioners, one government attorney, the Deputy Director of the Legal Aid Agency, and two law school professors to serve on the board. The author was selected as chairman.

The board met for the first time on December 7, 1964. Included in the membership of the board was the President of the Washington Bar Association, a former President of the D.C. Bar Association, three members of the Board of Directors of the D.C. Bar Association, the current Vice-President and immediate past Vice-President of the Legal Aid Society Board of Directors, two members of the Legal Aid Agency's Board of Trustees and the Deputy Director of the Agency, two members of the Ethics Committee of the D.C. Bar Association, and a member of the District Court's Committee on Admissions and Grievances.[129] During the year there were to be four resignations; one member was appointed to the federal bench, a second to the position of United States Attorney for the District of Columbia, and a third as Deputy Executive Director of the United Planning Organization.

The immediate problems involved staffing, determination of job descriptions and salary scales, the formulation of basic policies, and the establishment of neighborhood offices. The board met weekly during the first two months. Committees dealing with policy, personnel, relations with the bar, and relations with UPO met regularly between meetings. The top level staff was appointed, the initial policy determinations made, and the first office opened by the beginning of January.

[123] *Id.* at 8, 9.
[124] *Id.* at 15.
[125] *Id.* at 16.
[126] *Ibid.*
[127] *Id.* at 16-17.
[128] *Id.* at 16, 12.
[129] UNITED PLANNING ORGANIZATION, FIRST SEMI-ANNUAL REPORT OF THE NEIGHBORHOOD LEGAL SERVICES PROJECT (Jan. 1, 1965-June 30, 1965) 2-3 [hereinafter cited as SEMI-ANNUAL REPORT]. This report was prepared by the Director Julian Riley Dugas and the Deputy Director Earl Johnson, Jr., with the assistance of Marna Tucker. Data in this article has been brought up to date as of January 1, 1966, but citations will be made to the Semi-Annual Report.

Julian R. Dugas, an attorney in private practice with substantial government experience in the Office of the Corporation Counsel, was selected as Director. Earl Johnson, Jr., an attorney with the Criminal Division of the Department of Justice, accepted an appointment as Deputy Director. The functions of the project were outlined as follows:

1. To advise residents of low-income neighborhoods concerning their legal problems;
2. Where appropriate, to represent them before Courts, administrative agencies and boards;
3. Where otherwise appropriate, to refer them to other agencies providing legal services to the poor, such as the Legal Aid Society and Legal Aid Agency;
4. To enhance the ability of residents of low-income neighborhoods to foresee common legal pitfalls and avoid them;
5. To identify non-legal problems in our clients' situations and guide them to resources within the United Planning Organization or in the rest of the community which can minister to their needs;
6. To promote legal education and research concerning the law most relevant to the problems of the poor.[130]

It was determined that no member of the staff would be permitted to engage in the private practice of law. Initially no registration fee would be charged until a study of the effect of the traditional practice of minimal registration fees upon relationships with clients could be conducted.[131] The eligibility standards followed by the Legal Aid Society since 1961 were adopted, pending future study.[132] The Lawyer Referral Service of the D.C. Bar Association was selected as the device for referral of ineligible applicants, until a system of referrals to neighborhood lawyers could be developed.[133]

It was agreed that NLSP would accept for direct handling cases involving legal problems in the fields of housing, consumer credit, public assistance and veterans' benefits; juvenile problems; adult felony cases before the initial appearance in court; and adult misdemeanor cases where counsel could not be provided by the Legal Aid Agency.[134] Domestic relations cases would be referred automatically to the Legal Aid Society, but in custody or non-support actions where both parties were indigent, and the Legal Aid Society was representing one party, NLSP would

[130] SEMI-ANNUAL REPORT at 1.
[131] Id. at 4.
[132] Id. at 5: The standard is: "A base minimum income which would not permit the payment of legal fees would be for a single person $55.00 per week take-home pay, for a married couple $70.00 per week take-home pay, and for families with dependent children and aged family member $70.00 per week take-home pay, plus $15.00 per week for each such dependent."
Account must be taken of special circumstances, including outstanding debts, illness, recent unemployment and the probable extent of equity in any property which is owed. "In addition representation is not provided to an applicant who has a claim which a private attorney would be willing to handle on a contingent fee basis."
[133] Id. at 5, 6.
[134] Id. at 6.

undertake to represent the other.[135] Permission was granted to undertake other types of cases, but priority was to be accorded to the designated categories.[136] The board attempted to prevent the overburdening of the staff by granting discretion to staff attorneys to decline representation of eligible applicants and to refer such cases to the Legal Aid Society. It provided that before deciding whether a given case should be accepted or referred, the staff attorney should consider the extent to which the legal problem was related to the non-legal program of UPO, the extent to which the legal program was not being handled adequately by other agencies because of a shortage of staff or financial resources, and the extent to which the problem involved legal issues of general significance to the poor of the area being served.[137]

It was recognized that groups might seek representation and that no specific rules could be formulated which would be adequate to cover groups of different composition, resources and objectives. The board agreed that requests for representation by groups should be referred to the Director who would then submit a recommendation to the Executive Committee of the board. In determining whether to undertake representation of a particular group, consideration would be given to the size of the group, the relative poverty of its individual members, the probable expense of representation in addition to attorney's fees, the time and effort required to provide adequate representation, and the recovery anticipated, if any.[138] Authority was also granted for staff attorneys to provide advice to other components of UPO in emergency situations, with the understanding that the UPO component and not its clients would be the NLSP client.[139] The staff was specifically instructed to formulate a broad program designed to educate the neighborhoods being served concerning basic legal rights and obligations and the availability of legal services.[140]

The first neighborhood law office was opened on January 7, 1965, in the Cardozo area. Application was made to OEO for funds to open additional offices outside of the Cardozo area shortly after its opening. During February 1965, two offices were opened in the southeast section of the city. In April, a second office was opened in the Cardozo area. The last of the three Cardozo area offices was placed in operation and a sixth office opened in central Washington during June. By the end of 1965 two additional offices were in operation in northeast Washington. Two new offices were planned for 1966. Several of the offices were located in storefronts, several in the same building as other UPO components, others in the only rentable space which could be obtained.

At the end of 1965 the staff consisted of a secretariat composed of the Director, Deputy Director, Administrative Assistant (non-lawyer), Staff Assistant (lawyer),

[135] Ibid.
[136] Ibid.
[137] Id. at 7.
[138] Id. at 7, 8.
[139] Resolution of Board of Directors, May 10, 1965.
[140] SEMI-ANNUAL REPORT 8.

and an Executive Secretary; and eight offices manned by twenty-one staff attorneys, eight legal secretaries, four clerk-typists, and twelve investigators. It had an operating budget of approximately $700,000.[141] Funds for 1966, with the exception of the local contributions, were made available by OEO. By the end of 1966 a staff of ninety-three, including thirty-five lawyers, was planned.[142]

The staff attorneys have diverse backgrounds. The age range is between twenty-four and sixty, the average age is thirty-nine. The staff includes graduates of the law schools of American University, Boston College, Catholic University, University of Chicago, Cornell University, Georgetown University, George Washington University, Harvard University, Howard University, University of Iowa, University of Virginia, and Yale University. Nine staff members were on law reviews; nine were in the upper quarter of their law school graduating class; five ranked in the top ten per cent. The level of legal experience of staff members ranges from less than one to over seventeen years; the average is five. Approximately one-half had prior experience in private practice. Ten had government experience in the Departments of Justice or Labor and the Office of the Corporation Counsel. Two had previously served with the Peace Corps.[143]

Few staff attorneys had expertise in the legal problems of the poor when they joined NLSP. An emergency training program was initiated immediately with the assistance of professors from local law schools, volunteers from the bar, and staff members of other UPO components.[144] A legal secretary with considerable experience in the operation of legal aid was retained to develop a directory of the social resources available in the community to which non-legal problems could be referred.[145] She also provided valuable assistance in the beginning of an NLSP manual which includes forms, guidelines, procedures and other materials to assist a lawyer joining the staff. A formal training program was conducted at Howard University as a result of an OEO training grant. This program was designed to provide more detailed instruction in the special problems involved in the representation of the poor.[146] Considerable materials were accumulated but the intensive systemized training program sought by the board failed to develop, in large measure because of administrative difficulties encountered in dealing with Howard University.

An effort was made to develop a community education program. Speeches were made to over one hundred groups by staff attorneys.[147] A pamphlet was prepared outlining rights and obligations in consumer credit and landlord-tenant relationships and the availability of Legal Aid Society and NLSP to provide advice to those

---

[141] On December 30, 1965, OEO approved a budget of $537,360 for eight months of the fiscal year. GR. NO. DC CAP 66-380.
[142] Ibid.
[143] Semi-Annual Report 15, 16.
[144] Id. at 16.
[145] Id. at 36-39. Invaluable assistance was provided by Miss Blossom Athey.
[146] Id. at 16.
[147] Id. at 35.

in need of assistance.[148] A manual was also developed for non-professional neighborhood workers to enable them to recognize when a member of the community needed legal assistance.[149] At the close of the year a referral manual was prepared for UPO and other social agencies in order to facilitate the referral of cases involving legal problems to NLSP and Legal Aid Society.[150] At the end of the year NLSP was considering other programs seeking to utilize radio and television for educational purposes.

Staff attorneys and law students undertook research memoranda in several areas and cooperated with local law schools in providing problems for faculty and student research. Test cases involving a retaliatory eviction and the right to bail in the juvenile court were litigated. One became moot and the other was pending at the end of the year. The Director provided advice to an individual congressman concerning proposed legislation amending the housing code and responded to a questionnaire from the District of Columbia Crime Commission. The board undertook to study and to endorse in principle housing legislation proposed by another organization. No formal proposals for changes in existing law were initated by NLSP.

There were frequent consultations between the top level staff and officials of UPO, attorneys in the neighborhoods attended neighborhood center meetings with counterparts from other UPO components, and a high level of mutual referrals developed, resulting in almost fifty per cent of NLSP applicants receiving advice both from a lawyer and from some other component of UPO.[151] Joint consultations were the exception rather than the normal routine. NLSP staff complained of a lack of understanding by UPO staff of the role of the lawyer, and UPO neighborhood center heads complained that staff attorneys were not serving as members of the UPO team.

During the first year no groups were represented either in organizing or in litigating, although staff attorneys did provide advice to individuals seeking to organize on several occasions.

During the year 4,937 persons applied for services at neighborhood offices.[152] There was an average caseload of fifty cases per attorney with approximately forty new cases each month in the five offices which had been open six months or more. Slightly less than one half of the applicants came directly to the offices; almost one half were referred by a component of UPO or by some other social agency. NLSP attorneys retained approximately two-thirds of the cases for direct handling. Approximately nine per cent were referred to the Legal Aid Society. Over three per cent were sent to lawyer referral, approximately seventeen per cent were referred to other

[148] *Id.* at 36.
[149] *Id.* at 37; NEIGHBORHOOD LEGAL SERVICES PROJECT, WHEN PEOPLE NEED A LAWYER (1965).
[150] *Id.* at 37.
[151] *Id.* at 34.
[152] NLSP Monthly Progress Report, Jan. 1966.

UPO components for non-legal services, and slightly over seven per cent were sent to other social agencies. Ten per cent were rejected without referral.[153]

Over thirty per cent of the cases involved housing problems. Consumer rights problems accounted for approximately eleven per cent. Eight per cent involved welfare problems. Slightly over seven per cent involved adult criminal matters, while juvenile problems constituted over five per cent of the total. The remaining cases covered a wide spectrum.[154]

Results were generally good. In a high percentage of cases evictions were prevented or postponed, criminal charges dismissed, or favorable settlements negotiated.[155] Flagrant miscarriages of justice were avoided in a number of cases.[156]

Despite the large number of cases undertaken by NLSP, no reduction in the caseload of Legal Aid Society (LAS) resulted. In fact LAS reported the largest caseload in its history for 1965.[157] There could be no doubt that the services existing before 1965 did not meet the real needs of the city.

At the close of 1965 many observers questioned whether the bar would continue to provide the funds necessary for LAS in view of the federal appropriations available to NLSP. Furthermore, the existence of two organizations with concurrent jurisdiction over civil legal aid and with referrals from one to the other seemed unnecessarily complex and contrary to the best interests of the poor of the city. The decision of NLSP to refer domestic relations cases to LAS and the refusal of LAS to undertake the representation of clients seeking a divorce unless it was "socially desirable" created a gap in services that could not be tolerated on a permanent basis. In December of 1965 the Judicial Conference Committee on Civil Legal Aid requested the views of LAS, NLSP, and the Bar Association of the District of Columbia concerning the desirability of merger.

The difference in structure of the two organizations posed formidable problems. During 1965 the Board of Directors of NLSP twice declined to accept proposals that representatives of the poor sit upon the board. The board thought it essential that an opportunity be provided the residents of the neighborhoods being served to be heard, to criticize and to propose changes. However, it thought that this could be accomplished in a more meaningful way by the formation of neighborhood advisory committees which would be invited to appear before the board at regular intervals. The board questioned the expertise of the representatives of the poor to select the

[153] SEMI-ANNUAL REPORT 29. Included in this category were applicants who financially were ineligible for NLSP services, but who selected an attorney without NLSP referral.
[154] Id. at 27, 28.
[155] Id. at 29-33.
[156] See notes 35, 36 supra. In other cases, NLSP obtained favorable settlements for a client who had paid $395 plus $108 in carrying charges for a television set with a suggested retail price of $199; obtained the release of a six-year-old child who had been detained by juvenile authorities for over five months without authority; obtained the return of a down payment after a merchant refused to deliver merchandise purchased on credit and insisted that the down payment be applied towards the purchase of other merchandise.
[157] See Schein, Legal Aid Utopia, 33 D.C.B.J. 16, 20 (1966); Bamberger Baltimore Address.

best qualified attorneys for the staff, fix salary scales, negotiate a system of lawyer referral, coordinate activities with the Legal Aid Society, maintain good relations with the bar, work out the relationship with the United Planning Organization, oversee the conduct of litigation seeking to restrain it from providing services, determine the appropriate books for office libraries, and dispose of similar matters with which the board was concerned. In the long run other members were troubled by the necessity of filling future vacancies on the board with board members selected in part for their fund-raising potential if additional local funds were to be raised to expand the program. There was genuine fear that the board might grow too large to be effective.

Pressure from UPO and OEO developed, as criticism of the poverty program for its failure to "involve the poor" was voiced in the Congress and the press. Under pressure the board agreed that three of its fifteen members would be selected by the poor in the neighborhoods being served. OEO served notice that the number must be increased to five at the end of 1966. LAS continued with its board unchanged.

At the end of its first year NLSP could look with pride at its representation of persons who otherwise would have been unable to obtain counsel. The UPO neighborhood advisory councils praised its performance.[158] Indeed, some measure of its success may be indicated by the fact that three lawyers filed suit against it and the Legal Aid Society seeking treble damages and injunctive relief for a claimed violation of the antitrust laws.[159] In addition a few attorneys who practice primarily in the landlord and tenant and small claims divisions of the District of Columbia Court of General Sessions voiced complaints over too aggressive representation and too frequent assertion of procedural rights by NLSP attorneys.

The community education program, although still in its infancy, was off the ground and seemed capable of imaginative expansion during the second year. NLSP could take some satisfaction in the fact that its policies had been used as a model for the development of OEO guidelines in many particulars.

However, a price had been paid for the valuable services rendered to the residents of the neighborhoods. NLSP gradually became service-oriented without any decision by its board to proceed in that direction.

During its first year it failed to realize the objectives of an experimental program which would re-examine systematically the legal rules and procedures affecting the poor, which would investigate new areas and utilize new methods in the representation of the poor, which would coordinate effectively legal and social services for a joint approach to the problems of the poor. It did not develop into a program in which attorneys, relieved of heavy caseloads, could concentrate on a limited number of cases of significance to the community, could develop drafts of

---

[158] The Washington Post, Nov. 19, 1965, p. B-1.
[159] Harrison v. United Planning Organization, Civil No. 2282-65, D.D.C.

new rules, regulations and statutes, and could provide leadership in the formation and representation of neighborhood organizations.

The reasons for its failures were complex. The board, the staff, and UPO shared the responsibility. The board spent the year dealing with major problems of policy but had little opportunity to evaluate the extent to which its policies were being implemented. Much of its time was devoted to trying to find out what was happening in the neighborhood offices, determining whether there should be poor on the board, explaining its purposes and operations to the bar, establishing a system of neighborhood lawyer referrals, and attempting to work out its anomalous relationship with UPO. In theory it had the responsibility to administer and control the legal services program but UPO approval was needed for its budgets, UPO contracted for its office space, provided its supplies and paid its staff, and distributed its educational material (under the name of UPO). UPO regarded NLSP as part of its team and NLSP staff attorneys as its employees.

The staff attorneys performed their tasks with an attitude of dedication and provided aggressive representation for individual clients. But many demonstrated an approach of cautious conservatism towards the subjects of group representation, participation in attempts to organize groups, and relationships with social workers and UPO organizers. Some of the senior staff members demonstrated a rigid attitude towards indigency standards, an interpretation of the canons of ethics which was, perhaps, unduly strict, and a literal approach to board policies. A self-imposed restraint developed on activities other than individual representation and community education. Some assumed that they should not act unless the board had ordered action, rather than acting with prudence if the board had not denied authority.

The board and the staff shared responsibility for failing to formulate and articulate a clear statement of the lawyer's role in community protest and organization. The situation was complicated by disagreements within the board concerning what kind of a showing a neighborhood group should make with reference to its inability to obtain private counsel and the relative merits of providing an NLSP lawyer or a volunteer attorney to neighborhood groups.

UPO was a small organization when NLSP began operations. It expanded quickly but with the consequence of administrative chaos during the first six months of NLSP's existence. NLSP developed at a faster rate than did many of the other UPO components. Many of these programs were not service-oriented and hence had no services to offer a client who had a non-legal problem. Many of the personnel were neighborhood workers without professional training. UPO neighborhood development center leaders differed concerning the objectives and methodology to be employed by the legal and non-legal programs. Some encountered difficulties in understanding what the lawyers were seeking to accomplish and the restrictions placed on their permissible activity by professional standards.

The pressure on neighborhood law offices to accept cases was great. The original concept of referring cases to the Legal Aid Society had serious shortcomings. The Legal Aid Society already had more cases than it could handle. It had an overworked and underpaid staff. It simply was incapable of providing quality representation for several thousand new clients. The neighborhood lawyer was placed in the situation where he was not sure that a client would be represented adequately if the case was referred. In such circumstances he frequently decided that justice required that he retain the case for direct handling. Furthermore, the citizens of the areas being served wanted lawyers to help them. The maintenance of community support required that they be given representation and NLSP was the only organization capable of providing it.

Whatever its causes, the results were clear. An atmosphere did not develop in which the neighborhoods could look to staff attorneys for leadership in community affairs. NLSP staff attorneys were outsiders who came into the neighborhoods to represent those needing legal services and who left when the task was done. There was a growing lack of confidence between UPO and NLSP personnel. The concept of a joint interdisciplinary approach to social problems disintegrated into a relationship of mutual referrals in which each discipline dealt separately with the particular problems within its expertise. The staff failed to develop a plan which could utilize the services of volunteer lawyers, with a loss of creativity and resources which could have resulted from a greater involvement of the bar.

By the end of 1965 NLSP seemed to be heading towards a status of a first-rate legal aid society of the traditional type. In January of 1966 the board undertook to compare its performance with its objectives, with a realization that clearer priorities must be established if something more than individual representation and community education were to be accomplished. It appreciated that it must decide what part of NLSP's energies should be devoted to providing services to individuals and what part should be allocated for different purposes. It must decide whether it should assign attorneys exclusively concerned with law reform, the litigation of test cases, and community education to its central staff or whether these functions could better be performed by individual staff attorneys in neighborhood offices. It must stop the drifting and steer a new course if the opportunities presented were to be used to the fullest.

THE FUTURE

The experience of NLSP would seem to indicate that the choice of a new organization or an established legal aid society will not determine necessarily the nature of a local program. An established society can alter its functions and goals to devote substantial resources toward community education, law reform, group organization and representation; it may formulate programs with local social organizations in order to encourage a joint interdisciplinary approach to the problems of its

244 LAW AND CONTEMPORARY PROBLEMS

clients; it can decentralize its operation to provide greater accessibility. At the same time a new organization can undertake so many cases for private litigants that it has no remaining resources to devote to any other purpose. It may be true that some existing legal aid organizations may have replaced creativity and imagination with settled routine. However, there is no reason why new people added to their staffs cannot inject vigor into the operation. Likewise, there is no reason to believe that new organizations will not fall prey to bureaucratization as time passes and youthful optimism is blunted by a realization of the dimensions of the problems.

Whatever the kind of organization, new or old, there must be a recognition that the shortage of funds and the plentitude of cases require that priorities be established and resources allocated to enable them to be met. It is doubtful if any organization can represent all eligible applicants and still devote any substantial portion of its efforts towards changing the institutions associated with poverty. Action must be taken by local organizations and OEO to insure that the efforts of old and new organizations do not sink into the abyss of mass low-quality services. Little has been done in this direction.

Thus far OEO has not attempted to establish priorities. Its guidelines seek a commitment from applicants that they will undertake all kinds of legal services to all of the poor at all stages, and simultaneously undertake group representation, research, law reform, bar involvement, community education, and allied activities. Local programs like NLSP will move inevitably towards meeting the demands of the community for services with the sacrifice of emphasis upon other objectives unless there is firm leadership exerted at the national level.

It should be recognized that the consensus which forms the basis for bar support may be jeopardized if OEO requires local communities to allocate resources to activities aimed at institutional reform. Many lawyers will give steadfast support to organizations designed primarily to provide services to individual poor persons with middle-class legal problems but are either apathetic or opposed to organizations with substantial commitments to providing representation to groups contemplating civil rights demonstrations, economic boycotts, or rent strikes. Many lawyers who have no objection to providing legal services to persons who cannot pay a reasonable fee will balk at the idea of an organization which plans to devote a substantial part of its energies to the representation of groups some of the members of which can afford legal fees acceptable to lawyers practicing in the community. Yet representation of such groups may be an essential ingredient of effective community organization and action.

The loss of some support must be accepted. Groups whose support is sought are entitled to candor regarding the objectives sought to be achieved. Hostility is certain to result in the future if the support of the bar is achieved under the guise of giving a poor man a right to counsel when the real objective is providing the legal leadership for institutional reform.

Furthermore we must determine our objectives in order to evaluate our progress. We cannot know whether we are succeeding unless we know what we are trying to accomplish.

It is too early to predict with certainty what will be the long term result of OEO's legal service programs. Certain directions seem likely, unless firm policies are developed in the near future.

It seems probable that most of the funds available for legal services will be channeled through existing legal aid organizations, which have altered their structure to accept representatives of the poor on their boards, have decentralized their offices, have broadened their scope to provide representation in all civil matters, and have in theory undertaken new functions such as community education, the organization of groups, and law reform.

The decision of choice of organization will be made initially at the local level but leaders of the bar who devote their time to helping the indigent will generally have close ties with the local legal aid organization and will have confidence that with funds it can produce the novelty, creativity and imaginative new ideas sought by Washington. OEO may not agree and if it does not it will decline to fund the proposal. Only on rare occasions will OEO fund a new organization against the opposition of the local bar. In a few cities where the bar has become disenchanted with existing legal aid societies, new organizations may gain bar approval. Likewise new organizations will develop in cities with no history of legal aid and new programs, perhaps involving the subsidization of private practitioners, will develop for rural areas. These new organizations will soon fall under the umbrella of organized legal aid and will seek and gain admittance to its councils.[160]

The NLDA will change its standards as more money permits improved legal aid operations.[161] With the passage of time there will be little difference in the personnel, attitudes, objectives or accomplishments of the old and the new.

The principal objective will be to provide legal services to individuals who cannot afford them. Community education programs will be expanded. More and better lawyers attracted by higher salary levels will inject new ideas into the process in a few test cases which will effect some changes in the law. Caseloads will be much lower than in the older legal aid operations, but much greater than the caseloads of private practitioners. There will be more full time lawyers, and young

---

[160] The National Legal Aid and Defender Association has manifested a willingness to accept the new organizations as members. The Director of NLSP has been elected to its Board of Directors.

[161] Amended Standards for Defender Services and Standards and Practices for Civil Legal Aid were promulgated in 1965. It is interesting to note that in the amended standards, it is provided that "to the extent feasible and for the purpose of establishing community participation, representation of the areas covered and people served should be included on the agency's governing body or on a separate community arbitrary group."

lawyers with better academic qualifications will be involved. After the first few years many of the best will leave to undertake more lucrative positions in private practice, governments, or business because salary scales will be competitive only at the beginning and lower middle ranges. Those who remain may not compare favorably with their colleagues who represent the major private and public institutions with whom the poor come in conflict. The separate institutionalized system for legal services may provide effective representation in disputes among the poor but may achieve less success in disputes between the poor and the establishment.[162]

Representation will be provided to small groups where the general level of poverty is clear; but the pressure of caseloads, the fear of unfavorable reaction from the bar, and ethical problems will discourage the representation of mixed groups of neighborhood residents in which many are poor but some are middle class. The lawyers will be located *in* the neighborhoods, but will not be *of* them. There will be more mutual referrals between lawyers and social workers but little joint action towards dealing with the underlying problems of the neighorhood being served.

The poor will sit on boards of directors, but the basic policies governing matters such as standards of indigency and permissible professional conduct will be determined by the bar. Lawyers will listen, they may even be influenced, but they will decide themselves. In some areas the marginal poor man may be sacrificed in order to protect the marginal lawyer. The quid pro quo for "poor on the board" may be retreat from the battle for the reform of the institutions which contribute to the perpetuation of poverty. In some communities opposition from the local bar will prevent the initiation of any program, no matter how limited in scope.

There will be no national offensive against existing legal economic institutions, because the funds will have been expended to provide emergency relief to the victims of the present system. A decade hence we will need more funds for more lawyers to provide the same services to more people with the same kinds of problems.

In the future the chief problems will be whether OEO shall fund legal service programs directly or require the legal service program to obtain the funds from the local community action program; to what extent regional offices of OEO will be able to block or modify legal service programs which a local bar wants and which the Office of Legal Services of OEO has approved; what share of the national and CAP budgets will legal service programs receive, and to what extent will the policies of the Office of Legal Services be controlled by the Community Action Program within OEO. In short, the issue will be the extent to which a bar-managed program of legal services can be isolated from community action programs and still obtain federal financing.

These are dire predictions. There is still time to avoid such consequences.

---

[162] See Address by William Pincus before the National Conference on Social Welfare, Atlantic City, N.J., May 1965.

We are still fighting the preliminary skirmishes in the war against poverty. Only a small percentage of our strength has been committed. Thus far we have been largely occupied with the task of tooling the war machine. There have been local actions which have resulted in good reports from the front. But tactical successes cannot substitute for strategic victory. Strategy requires a clear determination of objectives and the assignment of priorities to them if all cannot be accomplished simultaneously. Only when the strategy has been determined can we decide what tactics will be most effective.

Perhaps our objective should be more and better legal aid in its traditional form supplemented by community education. Perhaps we will determine that there is a moral obligation to represent all who need help and that this must take precedence over other considerations. Perhaps we will reach the conclusion that the objectives of group organizations and protest and law reform through the litigation of test cases and legislation are more important in the long run. Even then we may disagree how this can best be accomplished.

There are those who say that there is no way to determine the best test cases in advance; that they simply emerge unexpectedly out of a mass of routine matters. There are those who think that reform can be accomplished more quickly through pressure placed on the system by a large volume of cases in which new rights are asserted or attempts made to implement older rights. Such people think that the representation of all needing assistance without segregating efforts directed at community organization or law reform will have the best chance of changing the institutions of society.

Others fear that the representation of all will mean caseloads that will preclude the concentration of effort upon a few cases which may have the greatest impact upon the system. From the many cases involving the poor, a few each year might be chosen with a concentration of effort that would not be possible if an effort is made to undertake all cases.

Many question whether the litigation process is the best device to achieve the reforms sought. The laws which bear heavily on the poor have developed over a long history. Achieving change by decisions in individual cases is of course the genius of the common law. However, few appellate courts, and even fewer trial courts, have demonstrated the crusading spirit of the early common law judges in discarding traditional precedents because of new social attitudes or changed social conditions. In many cases the provisions of law most onerous to the poor are found in statutes or rules incapable of equitable interpretation. Many trial judges in urban areas, faced with the massive problem of court congestion, and conditioned to the summary disposition of small claims and landlord and tenant matters, will shy away from the use of their courts as the laboratories for social experimentation. The political power of the poor can be brought to bear upon legislatures and mayors in a way which is impossible, or improper, with courts. For these reasons some have reached the conclusion that many of the changes sought must be accomplished by new statutes, rules, and regulations. Lawyers specially assigned to these tasks may be essential for the drafting and the lobbying necessary to transform grievances into changes.

We may choose to abandon the concept of the lawyer as a catalyst for community organization. We can play down the contribution that can be made through group protest or minimize the importance of the lawyer in helping groups to organize and choose the alternatives most likely to accomplish their goals. During the last century the corporate lawyers played a significant role in the development of our economic institutions. We must now decide if lawyers for the poor will make contributions of equal significance in changing our social institutions.[163]

Many of the decisions facing us must be made at the national level. The pressures in many local communities will result in demands for services now rather than new institutions in the future. OEO has not hesitated to require local communities to adopt its ideas concerning the range of services to be provided or the structure of organizations which will be funded. It should not hesitate to require assurances concerning the number of attorneys, the percentage of resources, and the methodology to be employed in the representation of groups and in law reform. OEO should examine the feasibility of making grants to local neighborhood councils to enable them to retain their own attorney if a community legal services program

---

[163] It is clear that the Director of Legal Services is aware of the problem. In his Baltimore Address, *supra* note 42, Mr. Bamberger stated:

"We want lawyers to be not only advocates for individuals trapped by poverty, but to be the articulate spokesmen for the fifth of our population who suffer from being poor—invisible, inarticulate, unrepresented, depressed and despairing—living the contradiction of poverty in an affluent society. . . . Lawyers committed to the finest traditions of the bar can speak for the inarticulate, can challenge the systems that generate the cycle of poverty, can arouse the persons of power and affluence."

In an Address to the Pennsylvania Bar Association on January 20, 1966, he stated:

"Our pose is not just to stimulate and implement community efforts to provide a lawyer for a poor person in a particular case. We want lawyers to be advocates for a class of people who are inarticulate and unsophisticated—and who do not have advocates. Lawyers will be a voice of the poor in the community. . . ."

In his Address to the National Legal Aid and Defender Association's Annual Meeting in Scottsdale, Arizona, on November 18, 1965, he stated the issue clearly:

"I ask myself each day—how will lawyers representing poor people defeat the cycle of poverty? This is the purpose of the Office of Economic Opportunity, and unless we can justify our contribution to that purpose, the program I direct is not properly a part of the War on Poverty. . . . Our concern is more broad than a compilation of statistics of the numbers of clients, the kinds of cases and even the results. We must address ourselves to the much more difficult task of assessing the impact on the community, its rules, its regulations, and the concern for its disadvantaged citizens."

In his Address to the National Conference of Bar Presidents on February 19, 1966, he stated:

"It is fallacious to think of lawyers as guardians of tradition—rather we are the guardians and watchdogs of orderly change. It is perhaps the greatest genius of the Anglo-American system that we have always, except when confronted with the terrible agony of the Civil War, been able to change the deepest and most fundamental characteristics of our society peacefully, with a stability of government and laws that is the awe and envy of other nations."

either encounters a conflict of interest or chooses to devote its energies primarily to the representation of private individuals. It should consider funding law school legal internship programs as the instruments of law reform to supplement local services-oriented legal programs.

Our alternatives are many, once the strategy is determined. The time is now. The profession and the nation cannot afford to miss the opportunity. If we do not determine our strategy soon we can reasonably anticipate a war of attrition in which a decisive victory is impossible. The legal front of the war against poverty must not be permitted to grind to a halt in the mud of a Passchendaele.

Anti-Poverty Programs
  309.20973
  An 8

5966